DO YOU HAVE WHAT IT TAKES?

In The Envelope, Please *you'll find countless quizzes and hundreds of fascinating facts on every aspect of the Oscars. For example:*

- What director, known for his Westerns, won the most Oscars for directing—none for a Western?

- What was the first remake to win Best Picture?

- Who was the first person to reject his Oscar in protest?

- Who is the only Nobel laureate to win an Academy Award?

- What four musicals won the Best Picture Oscar in the 1960s?

- What Best Song winner was the best-selling popular song of the 1970s?

- And who the hell is Jack Valenti?

Read on for the answers, and enjoy!

THE ENVELOPE, PLEASE

The Ultimate Academy Awards® Trivia Book

Arnold Wayne Jones

AVON BOOKS ◆ NEW YORK

AVON BOOKS, INC.
1350 Avenue of the Americas
New York, New York 10019

Copyright © 1999 by Arnold W. Jones
Published by arrangement with the author
Library of Congress Catalog Card Number: 98-93545
ISBN: 0-380-79944-8
www.avonbooks.com

First Avon Books Printing: March 1999

AVON TRADEMARK REG. U.S. PAT. OFF. AND IN OTHER COUNTRIES, MARCA REGISTRADA, HECHO EN U.S.A.

Printed in the U.S.A.

WCD   10 9 8 7 6 5 4 3 2 1

To the best writer I know, my grandfather,
John K. O'Doherty;
to Hunter Joe Benedict, just a swell guy,
and the only person who loves to talk about
the Oscars as much as I do.

And to Toby.

Acknowledgments

A lot of people helped me write this book, some without even knowing it. They encouraged me to write, or to see movies, or both; they set examples or gave me a break or kept me going with their ideas and enthusiasm. So special thanks go out to my mom and dad, Patty and Arnold Jones, who indulged my habit (Mom also helped with the typing, and Dad came up with one of the best categories in the book); Bruce Fretts, to whom I gave his first break as a writer, and who has since repaid me in kind; Bryant Snapp and Carol Guiles, who, ridiculous as it seemed at the time, always thought I would make a mark with my knowledge of movies and Oscar trivia; and to my editor at Avon, Stephen S. Power, whose commonsensical suggestions kept my excesses in check, and who is better than I am at guessing Oscar winners. Others who helped out with their time, ideas, comments, and encouragement are: Jay Mallar, Benny Holliday, Lettie Flores, Gavin Shearer, Ron Pogue, Barbara Roberts, and no doubt others who showed interest and contributed ideas who I will regret omitting later but whose contributions did not go unnoticed.

Contents

Part IV: Trivia by Category

Introduction

A MOVIE MEMORY:
HOW I LOST IT TO THE OSCARS

Two days before my twelfth birthday, my mother drove from our home in suburban Virginia to the Uptown Theatre in Washington, D.C., to buy a present for me: two tickets to a movie, opening the next day, and about which she had read some good reviews. I had seen some ads for the film on television, and I was only mildly interested in it, but my dad loved to go "all out" at the movies—buying popcorn and candy and Cokes—so I was never one to turn down an opportunity. Also, we didn't go into the city very often, so this really was a treat—a field trip that merely culminated in a movie. Although my mom thought the movie *was* the present, for me it was just the reason for spending the day with my dad.

The Uptown is one of those grand old movie palaces that multiplexes have, regrettably, completely succeeded but never replaced. As I remember it, it had just one gigantic screen and a large, ornately decorated auditorium—much more like going to live theater than the movies. When we arrived at the Uptown, I was surprised to see that the line stretched around the block; I was glad we already had tickets. I never liked crowded theaters (still don't), and as it turned out we had to sit in the back row of the upper balcony—hardly ideal moviegoing circumstances, but it was no reason to complain: I had a bag of popcorn in my lap, a large Coke in one hand, and some Jordan almonds in the other. The trip was already a success.

The reason I remember the trip so vividly now has less to do with the munchies than the movie we saw. It was the opening night of *Star Wars*, which was only released on a handful of screens in 1977. As its legend grew, so did its distribution (although on its initial release it never hit anything like the 2,000 screens most films debut on nowadays), and it eventually went on to become one of the highest-grossing films of all time.

Star Wars changed my life. I had seen films I liked before, but nothing that captured my imagination quite so forcefully and energetically. For the first time, I became aware of the movies as providing something more than an opportunity to keep cool in the heat of summer; they could shape your outlook on life, and you appreciated the artistry and craftsmanship of people who knew how to entertain you. The following March was the first year I recall watching the Academy Awards. I had no idea who most of the other nominees were, although at the time I recall thinking how wonderful it would be if my fellow preteen, Quinn Cummings, won for best supporting actress in *The Goodbye Girl*. (The award went instead to Vanessa Redgrave. ''Who's that?'' I remember thinking. We all have our lapses in good judgment.) What I really wanted to see, though, was *Star Wars* take the cake. It was eligible in most categories, and I felt it was a shoo-in for best picture, and for Alec Guinness (Obi-Wan Kenobi) as best supporting actor. (I didn't even know who the director was.) When Jason Robards defeated Guinness, I was incredulous; when *Annie Hall* won for best picture, I was simply puzzled; the guy who directed *Sleeper* made a film I'd never even heard of, and beat out *the greatest movie I'd ever seen?!?!?!?* *Star Wars* did go on to win eight awards—more than any other film that year—but even at a tender age I knew the difference between the "biggies" and the technical categories: "like kissing your sister," someone once said. (I might have been appalled by the judgment of the shadowy "Academy," but the numerical success of *Star Wars* showed they must know *something;* although I had no idea what "cinematography" was, I had seen *Jaws* and I knew who John Williams was—everyone was whistling that battle cry in 1977 just as they had hummed the sharks' dirge in 1975.) I was angry at this "Academy," whatever that was ("How do I join so I can set them straight?" I remember thinking), but I knew what I had to do: I watched again the next year to see what all the hoopla was. (Winner: *The Deer Hunter*, which was rated R and so I had not seen it, and which beat *Heaven Can Wait*—what were these people *thinking?*) I gritted my teeth for *one more year*, just to see if they finally got it right. (They did, at least at the time I thought so, when *Kramer vs. Kramer* won; in retrospect, *Apocalypse Now* was robbed.) In 1980, when the best *serious* movie I ever saw won the best picture award (*Ordinary People*; I didn't see *Raging Bull* until years later), I was officially an Oscar junkie. I rewarded the Academy for their appropriate course correction by tuning in every year thereafter; I haven't missed a ceremony since, and I doubt I ever will again.

I suspect many people have similar memories. After all, there was *one year* in which we all *first* saw the Oscars, and we more or less decided, from then on, whether we would watch again. But do I always agree with who wins? Rarely. Among my friends, I went on record in 1989, picking who I would vote for every major category, and *not one person* I would have picked won the award that year. Not that I can fault the Academy for rewarding Daniel Day-Lewis, or even softening up to Jessica Tandy; it was just that, for me, the Oscars have rarely been about excellence; rather, they have been about *celebrating Hollywood*—industry insiders patting themselves on the back for a job well done, if they must say so themselves.

This book, then, is my opportunity to celebrate everything that I love—and hate—about that giant wet, sloppy French kiss that actors, directors, producers, designers, and studios give themselves in front of one of the largest television audiences worldwide every year. The Oscars can be high camp and high drama; a great American tradition and a bald expression of kitsch. You can dismiss them for being corrupt and fickle, but you have to acknowledge that, like it or not, the Oscars make careers, sculpt popular culture, and sometimes even endow a patina of shiny gold on an otherwise overlooked film and transform it into what really matters to the industry: money.

Inside this book is what I hope proves to be the single most authoritative collection of trivia, tidbits, quizzes, and commentaries you're likely to find on the Academy Awards, dealing with everything from memorable speeches to the record holders to the most jaw-dropping statistics of winners and losers you'll find anywhere. Enjoy.

A NOTE ON THE ORGANIZATION AND NOTATION

Just as the Academy distinguishes between nominees and winners, so does this book. Not every statistic is about a winner—sometimes more interesting is who did *not* win and why; and occasionally, knowing who was not even nominated is the most fascinating statistic of all. So keep an eye out for information that specifies the differences between candidacy and victory.

In a similar vein, trivia about any topic—perhaps even particularly the Oscars—would be of dubious value if it did not appeal to the reader. As much as everyone who wins an Oscar is happy to be on stage, it is a simple if sad fact that most people are not as interested in short films and art direction as they are the major categories. When the term "majors" is used in the book, it primarily will refer to what are generally considered to be the top categories: picture, director, actor and actress, supporting actor and supporting actress, and the writing awards (usually original and adapted screenplay). A reference to the "craft" categories will normally entail those such as cinematography, film editing, art direction, costume design, sound, etc. A reference to a "performer" will most often mean an actor or actress (leading or supporting) known primarily for on-screen work, especially when recognized by the Academy as such. Thus, although Sydney Pollack has frequently acted in films, his two Oscars—for producing and directing *Out of Africa*—are not considered to be awarded to a "performer," whereas people like Clint Eastwood and Warren Beatty, although well-regarded for their directing (both won Oscars for it), are primarily known for their acting.

Occasionally, the name of a nominee will be followed by either an [n] or a [w]. The [n] signifies that the person whom the notation accompanies was nominated for the film mentioned; the [w] denotes a win. If accompanied by a plus sign—[w+]—the named person received multiple nominations beyond the one listed. Also, unless the word starts a sentence, the name of the category is not capitalized; so you will not find many references to "Supporting Actress Winner," but rather "supporting actress winner."

Because awards are usually given after the end of a calendar year, a reference to the "1996 awards ceremony," or a statement that someone "won his Oscar in 1942," generally refers not to the year that it was bestowed, but the competition year in which it was earned. Thus, the "1978 Oscar ceremony" actually occurred on April 9, 1979. References to hours of the day, unless otherwise specified, apply to Eastern Standard Time.

Part I
General Trivia

Chapter One

The Nominees Are . . . :
Oscar's Inner Workings

THE NOMINATING PROCEDURE: POTHOLES IN A BUMPY ROAD

Before we jump headlong into the hardcore trivia, let's answer an important question: How exactly do you get *nominated* for an Oscar? As a rule, you are voted upon by other members of the Academy within your own branch of membership. Thus, every Academy member in the actors' branch gets to write down his five nominees for actor, actress, supporting actor, and supporting actress; members of the writing branch cast their votes for original and adapted screenplay; directors nominate directors, etc. Everyone in the Academy gets to nominate best picture choices—keep that in mind the next time someone grouses that "I don't know how *The Prince of Tides* could be nominated for best picture in 1991, and Barbra Streisand could not be nominated for best director." I've always felt that the reverse was true: How could Ridley Scott have been one of the (deservedly) best director nominees for *Thelma & Louise*, but the film not nominated for best picture? (The reason: Sappy, sentimental voters selected the treacly *Prince of Tides* over the more daring feminist road movie.)

🎞 Nomination requirements

Although the rules have changed a lot over the years, the general process is as follows:

• **Eligibility period**. The calendar year in which the film is released.

• **Venue requirements**. The film must play during the calendar year at an Academy-approved theater in the New York or Los Angeles area. This accounts for why many films that do not enter wide release until January are eligible for the preceding year.

• **Academy membership**. The Academy does not release a formal list of its members, but the people who are eligible and who vote every year has varied substantially over its history. There are now a few thousand Academy members in all fields of film production, each with its own "branch" within the Academy based upon its role in the industry. Multitalented hyphenates—director-editor, actor-writer, etc.—can only belong to one branch. You have to pay dues to be an Academy member, and membership is not automatically available to anyone with a Screen Actors Guild card—the Academy is more selective. First-time nominees are extended an Academy membership, the rationale apparently being that you should have the right to vote for yourself.

• **Nominators**. Although generally members of each branch nominate from within their own branch, some categories have special nominating committees.

• **Voters**. Unlike the pigeonholing of the nominating procedure, the entire membership of the Academy can vote in virtually every category, ir-

respective of branches. There's not even a requirement that you have seen all (or any) of the
nominated films you vote for, except in the specialized categories (shorts, documentaries).

• **Balloting**. Nominating ballots are mailed out
usually the first week of January; by the first week
of February, nominations are closed. The second
week of February, the Academy publishes its final
list of nominees. Since 1986, they have read the
nominees live over the morning network news
shows. The voting ballots are distributed soon
thereafter, and voting closes in late March. The
awards ceremony usually occurs in late March or
early April.

• **Counting**. As almost everyone knows by now,
the accounting firm of Price Waterhouse has, for
many years, tabulated the ballots. Since 1940, the
names of the winners have been placed in sealed
envelopes

• **Presenting the awards**. The trophies themselves are unmarked when they are presented to
the winners. The Academy takes them back and
engraves the winners' names on them. The Oscars
themselves have been numbered since 1949, beginning, somewhat mysteriously, with number
501.

Not all the categories are as subject to the same kind of
arbitrariness as best picture seems to be, but they often
undergo a different form of discrimination: elitism, club-
biness, and simple politics, especially those selected by
committees.

Foreign language film

One of the most controversial areas of the Oscar nominating procedure arises in this category. Facts that create

this questionable reputation include that: (1) each country is permitted only one submission to be considered for the Oscar; (2) if a film is not "wholly" of that country, it is not eligible for the foreign language film award; and (3) the countries themselves—not a peer review committee—get to select the submissions. The process has often led to perplexing results. *Il Postino (The Postman)*, although made in Italy, spoken mostly in Italian, and starring an Italian, was written and directed by an Englishman, and thus considered ineligible for best foreign language film (so it was nominated for best picture). At the same time that *Das Boot* was marching toward a record six nominations for a foreign language film, it was not in the running for foreign language film, *Fitzcarraldo* having been instead submitted by the German government. That Germany had to decide between those two masterpieces is one of the great injustices of the procedure.

Documentaries and shorts

The documentary and short film categories are not selected by branches inside the Academy, but rather by committees specially convened for selecting. As with the foreign film competition, nominators must be able to say that they have seen *every eligible submission*—and those who vote for them must say so, too. This policy varies wildly from the requirements of general Academy voting—if a member wants to nominate a friend, even if he hasn't seen her movie, that's perfectly permissible. And as for voting—well, that's obviously not a problem. You might think that this process would ensure that only the best films get nominated for the documentary Oscar, but this has proven to be puzzlingly untrue. Particularly in the 1980s and 1990s, with the rise in film festivals, satellite TV, and cable, access to documentaries and shorts—and a concomitant growth in awareness and respect—people have been surprised to see high-profile, exquisitely made documentaries get snubbed by the committees. There has been speculation about the reasons for such treatment: Because the committees are like clubs, members may tend to form voting blocs, supporting pet causes of their friends; because these films are some of the least commercial, and "big" documentaries like *Hoop Dreams* won't benefit from the boost an Oscar will bring (the makers of successful documentaries will be able to write their own ticket anyway), the committees let the little guys get a break instead. Thus, documentarians such as Fred Wiseman and Errol Morris have never been awarded Oscars.

Controversial or inexplicable omissions from the best documentary category

• *The Titticut Follies* (1967). Frederick Wiseman's controversial, disturbing portrait of a Massachusetts mental institution for the criminally insane; it includes an amateur talent show the inmates stage. Wiseman, one of the most prolific of documentarians, has never been nominated for an Academy Award.

• *Grey Gardens* (1975). An hypnotically creepy view of a mother and daughter, branches of the Kennedy clan, living in spinsterly isolation in their decaying manse.

• *Gizmo* (1976). Howard Smith's loopy but fascinating account of man's inventiveness—and his remarkable capacity for banality. It comically and entertainingly traces the creation of ridiculous and interesting contraptions with outlandish applications.

• *The Thin Blue Line* (1988). Errol Morris's grippingly inventive chronicle of a lesser-known murder mystery in Dallas, a documentary told in the format of a fictional detective story. The film, with its multiple, *Rashomon*-like recreations, use of moody music (by Philip Glass), and tiered narrative, virtually reinvented the entire genre.

• *Roger and Me* (1989). Michael Moore's satirical, political, highly charged social commentary about the economics, and human toll, of plant closings, especially as they affect the town of Flint, Michigan.

• *Hearts of Darkness: A Filmmaker's Journey* (1991). Eleanor Coppola's widely praised account of her husband Francis's making of *Apocalypse Now*.

• *A Brief History of Time* (1992). Morris's explication of the theories and life of acclaimed physicist Stephen Hawking, whose body is seized by Lou Gehrig's disease but whose brilliance as a scientist is unmatched.

• *Hoop Dreams* (1994). The universally heralded, three-hour documentary about the attempts by two inner-city youths to get out of the ghetto by playing basketball, following them over several years in their high school careers, is perhaps the most startling omission in the documentary category to date.

• *Crumb* (1995). Terry Zwigoff's unapologetic look at the life and works of cartoonist R. Crumb (best known for the ''Keep on Truckin' '' logo and odd album covers) crosses over from mere documentary into brilliant psychoanalysis of its complex, exceedingly introspective subject and his pain, neuroses, and family dynamics.

• *Fast, Cheap and Out of Control* (1997). Errol Morris again, making a series of remarkably sophisticated connections between the activities of a

"mole rat" specialist, a wild-animal trainer, a to-
piary gardener, and a robotics scientist. The
quirky, beautifully photographed (and comparatively popular) film was overlooked.

THERE'S NO REASON FOR IT,
IT'S JUST OUR POLICY

Equally as aggravating are the arcane eligibility rules
that have plagued the Oscars almost since their inception. In the first year the awards were presented, the
eligibility period was more than 12 months; it was later
shortened, and finally made to run basically as a calendar
year. But it isn't really as simple as all that. Films technically must play in Academy-approved theaters, usually
released no later than Christmas Day—wait much later,
and you'd better gear up your campaign for the following year.

Once again, if that were the only problem, the rules
might still be easy to follow. But the rules don't end
there. To be eligible, a film needs to be more than just
screened in NYC or L.A.—it also must *not* have been
generally available anywhere else, especially television.
The effort to maintain the sanctity of the "film" industry
(the same industry that made Ali MacGraw a nominee
for *Love Story*) led to the exclusion of television movies
and shows from consideration. There's nothing wrong
with the goal itself, but it tends to overlook legitimate
and inventive film products, and indicates that Hollywood has not kept current with an age of direct TV,
cable, and direct-to-video fare. Especially with the
growth of sophisticated movie channels on TV like
HBO, quality need not suffer. This problem is brought
into even sharper relief when you consider how timing
and carelessness can make a difference in eligibility—
a film released in theaters even days before appearing
on TV may be in contention, but not vice versa.

The Academy's track record in enforcing its own rules—especially prospectively—is checkered as well. On several occasions, the Academy has been put in the awkward position of having to rescind nominations and awards based upon sloppy application of the rules. Moreover, the Academy became a conspirator in the Communist witch-hunts of the 1950s when it altered eligibility rules (mostly for screenwriters) for people who refused to testify before Senator Joseph McCarthy's House Un-American Activities Committee. (For a more detailed discussion of the blacklisting era, see chapter nine, "The '50s: Television Be Damned!") These embarrassments alone might be reason enough to consider revamping the rules process.

Among the additional rules problems are those related to the naming of categories. You might think that coming up with a name like, say, "best music score," would be simple enough, but in fact this deceptively simple undertaking has led to substantial confusion. "Best score," "best dramatic score," "best original score," and "best original dramatic score" are just some of the mind-numbing permutations that category names have gone through. From the addition and subtraction of categories divided into black-and-white and color, to the flip-flop of special effects between an honorary and a competitive award, and to the tortured renaming of the writing categories, what the Academy will decide to call the categories generates almost as much excitement as who is actually nominated.

Oscar's stupid rules: The real victims ... and some winners

- *The Last Seduction* (1994). Linda Fiorentino was widely praised for her dastardly *femme fatale*, and the studio rushed the film into theaters for Oscar consideration ... only to find out later that because the film showed on a cable movie network first, Fiorentino was not eligible for best actress honors.

• *The Snapper* (1993). This delightful, well-received comedy by director Stephen Frears was hailed as a triumph for star Colm Meaney, but because the movie had been made for (and appeared on) British TV, Meaney and company were deemed unlucky losers.

• *Face to Face* (1976) and *Das Boot* (1982). In light of the fiascoes with *The Last Seduction* and *The Snapper*, the Academy was at a loss to explain how *Face to Face*, an Ingmar Bergman film, and *Das Boot*, a German thriller, both walked off with multiple nominations—they had both been made for, and shown on, television in their respective countries before making it to the U.S.

• *Richard III* (1956) and *Testament* (1984). Sometimes, you just have to beat them at their own game. When *Richard III* was made in 1956, it was released *simultaneously* in theaters and on television. It took home several nominations. *Testament*, originally made for PBS's American Playhouse, was released first in theaters to confer Oscar hopes on director Lynn Littman and star Jane Alexander; Alexander was indeed nominated for best actress.

• *The Godfather* (1972). Nino Rota was originally nominated for his score to the film, until it was discovered that the score was very similar to one he had done for an Italian film, *Fortunella*, in the 1950s. The nomination was withdrawn, and the score to *Sleuth* substituted. Ironically, two years later, Rota and Carmine Coppola won the Oscar for the score to *The Godfather Part II* . . . despite the fact that *Part II* employed the same languid theme that made the score to *Part I* so memorable.

• *Limelight* (1952/1972). Charlie Chaplin was one of the true geniuses of the cinema, but his politics made him unpopular in Hollywood for decades. During this period, his 1952 film *Limelight* (Claire Bloom's film debut) was not released in America. It finally made it to the United States in 1972, was nominated for best dramatic score, and actually won (defeating, notably, the *Sleuth* score and now-ineligible score from *The Godfather*). It was Chaplin's only competitive Oscar.

• *'Round Midnight* (1987). After Herbie Hancock won the best score award for this picture, the rules were changed, since Hancock's score was largely a reinterpretation of previously composed jazz tunes. Now, an original score award can only be presented to a film that does not heavily rely on previously produced or tracked music.

• *The Gold Rush* (1925/1942). Charlie Chaplin's silent classic about a prospector in Alaska, originally released in 1925 (before the Academy was even created), was rereleased in 1942 with a soundtrack (containing music and some narration) added. It was deemed eligible for the best sound recording category as a result.

• *Dive Bomber* (1941). This film and its entire team was originally announced as a nominee for best special effects, but within two weeks the nomination was unilaterally replaced (with the same individual technicians intact) by *The Sea Wolf* (also from Warner Brothers) without explanation. Perhaps Warners simply decided they were more proud of their team's work on *The Sea Wolf*, and thought it stood a better chance of winning. It did not.

• *Hellzapoppin'* (1942). Impossibly, the song "Pig Foot Pete" does not appear in *Hellzapoppin'*, the film for which it received a best song nomination. The song was in fact contained in a film released by the same studio in 1941, and was therefore completely ineligible for the 1942 awards. The mistake was attributed to the fact that Academy rules permitted the studios to submit their own selections for consideration as best song.

• *Hondo* (1953). Louis L'Amour's only Oscar nomination, for best motion picture story, was withdrawn after the nominations were announced. L'Amour informed the Academy that his screenplay was actually based on a story he had previously published, and was thus not eligible for an "original screenplay" award (whose predecessor name was "motion picture story").

• *High Society* (1956). MGM's musical remake of *The Philadelphia Story* would seem to have been the intended nominee for best motion picture story; unfortunately, the nomination was actually bestowed upon Edward Bernds and Ellwood Ullman, who did not write that film, but another movie also named *High Society*, also released in 1956—starring the Bowery Boys. Cognizant of the error, the writers rejected the nomination. (Ironically, because it was an adaptation of a prior screenplay, the MGM version of *High Society* was not even eligible for an original screenplay Oscar.)

• *The Longest Day* (1962). Although four cinematographers are listed in the credits for this film, only three were included on the original list of nominees. Mysteriously, the number dropped to two some time later, without any explanation from the Academy for the exclusions.

• *Journey into Self* (1968). The final recipient of the best documentary feature award was this film, even though it finished second in the balloting. The top finisher, *Young Americans*, had its award rescinded when the Academy deemed it ineligible—it had played at one theater in North Carolina the year before.

• *Shoah* (1995). Claude Lanzmann's ambitious nine-hour, two-part Holocaust documentary was not even submitted as best documentary feature, and because part two was not screened in Hollywood during its eligibility year, the film itself could not be considered for other Oscars.

YOU MUST LOVE ME: A NOTE ON THE OSCAR CAMPAIGNS

Campaigning in itself is one of the pink elephants of Oscardom—nobody likes to acknowledge it, and how successful it can be, even though it is as prevalent as the sunrise. In the early days of the Academy, campaigning could be as simple as the studio bosses wielding their influence over contract players: It was not above Louis Mayer of MGM, or Harry Cohn of Columbia, or Jack Warner of Warner Brothers to "suggest" to everyone on the lot whom they should vote for. Walter Brennan, who won three of the first five best supporting actor awards ever presented, was seen as a favorite at a time when "extras" could vote, since they all liked him personally.

With the collapse of the studio system, the onus for campaigning fell on production companies, sometimes the candidates themselves, or their own publicists. Famously, Chill Wills made a plaintive plea in the trade papers after his appearance in *The Alamo* (he lost to Peter Ustinov in *Spartacus*); Miramax's push for *The Crying Game* (buoyed by great reviews and sur-

prisingly strong box office) resulted in multiple nominations for what had not been considered much of a
mainstream movie; and October Films' campaign netted
art-house staple *Secrets & Lies* six nominations, including best picture. It is now not uncommon—in fact, it is
a virtual necessity—for "screeners": videotaped copies
of movies, often of films not yet available on video, to
be mailed directly to Academy voters for screening a
film at home.

Sometimes, stars can do their best to give the appearance of dignity to the Academy while prostituting themselves elsewhere. Sally Kirkland's career was virtually
dead when she acted in a reasonably well-received independent film called *Anna*. She campaigned vigor-
ously—but more with the members of the Hollywood
Foreign Press Association, which hands out the Golden
Globe awards, than with Academy members. The
Golden Globes are often derided for being populist and
arbitrary, and for good reason: The Hollywood Foreign
Press Association isn't much of an organization. Its
membership is fairly small (dozens of members, not
thousands), and the voters are industry reporters, not
filmmaking peers. The positive upshot of this is that it
is far easier to woo each member of the Hollywood Foreign Press than members of the Academy (after all, Sally
Kirkland would be more pleased to sit and chat with a
free-lance entertainment reporter than Meryl Streep
would be). In the case of *Anna*, Kirkland not only managed a nomination, but also a win; it was practically
ordained that a best actress nomination would follow,
although no one thought she ever stood a chance. Whatever the Academy may claim is their "official" policy
on campaigning, there's no denying how important the
Oscars are to the stars and to the bottom line. As Warren
Beatty once observed: "The Golden Globes are fun; the
Oscars are business."

Quiz—Acting Blocs

Q. Despite the studios' constant push for big stars who can "open" movies, some best picture Oscar winners managed to take home the gold without getting a single nomination for acting. Which of the following nine best picture winners didn't receive a single acting nomination?

Wings (1927/28); *All Quiet on the Western Front* (1929/30); *Grand Hotel* (1931/32); *An American in Paris* (1951); *The Greatest Show on Earth* (1952); *Around the World in 80 Days* (1956); *Gigi* (1958); *The Last Emperor* (1987); and *Braveheart* (1995).

A. All of them.

Special mention. The following list of films *nominated* for best picture also received no acting nominations: *The Racket* (its *only* nomination in any category was as best picture); *Hollywood Revue*; *East Lynne*; *Trader Horn*; *Arrowsmith*; *Bad Girl*; *Five Star Final*; *One Hour with You* (its only nomination was for best picture); *The Smiling Lieutenant*; *A Farewell to Arms*; *Forty-Second Street*; *She Done Him Wrong*; *Smilin' Through*; *State Fair*; *Cleopatra*; *Flirtation Walk*; *The Gay Divorcée*; *Here Comes the Navy*; *The House of Rothschild*; *Imitation of Life*; *Viva Villa*; *The White Parade*; *The Broadway Melody of 1936*; *Captain Blood*; *David Copperfield*; *Les Misérables*; *Lives of a Bengal Lancer*; *A Midsummer Night's Dream*; *Naughty Marietta*; *Ruggles of Red Gap*; *Top Hat*; *Libeled Lady* (its only nomination in any category); *A Tale of Two Cities*; *Three Smart Girls*; *One Hundred Men and a Girl*; *The Adventures of Robin Hood*; *Alexander's Ragtime Band*; *Le Grande Illusion*; *Test Pilot*; *Of Mice and Men*; *The Wizard of Oz*; *The Long Voyage Home*; *One Foot in Heaven* (its only nomination was for best picture); *The Invaders; Kings Row; The Talk of the Town; Heaven Can Wait; In Which We Serve; The Ox-Bow Incident* (its only nomination was for best picture, the last such lonely nominee); *The Bishop's Wife; Great Expectations; The Red Shoes; A Letter to Three Wives; King Solomon's Mines; Decision Before Dawn; Ivanhoe; The Robe; Seven Brides for Seven Brothers; Three Coins in the Fountain; The Ten Commandments; Twelve Angry Men; The Guns of Navarone; The Longest Day; The Music Man; America, America; How the West Was Won; Doctor Doolittle; Romeo and Juliet; Butch Cassidy and the Sundance Kid; Hello, Dolly!; Z; A Clockwork Orange; Deliverance; Cries and Whispers; The Conversation; Barry Lyndon; Jaws; Bound for Glory; Tess; Raiders of the Lost Ark; E.T.: The Extra-Terrestrial; The Mission; Hope and Glory; Field of Dreams; Beauty and the Beast* (a unique case: the first all-animated film to be nominated for best picture, and thus, no actors were eligible for a nomination under Academy rules); *Four Weddings and a Funeral; The Full Monty.*

Q. **What was the first year when *every* best picture nominee had at least one nominated performance? What were the films?**
A. 1944; *Double Indemnity, Gaslight, Going My Way, Since You Went Away,* and *Wilson.* After that, generating acting nominations for the best picture contenders became fairly common, occurring also in 1945, 1946, 1955, 1958, 1959, 1960, 1964, 1965, 1966, 1970, 1978, 1979, 1983, 1984, 1985, 1988, 1990, 1992, and 1993.

Q. **What best picture of 1934 was the first film to win both best actor and best actress?**
A. *It Happened One Night.* There were no supporting categories until two years later.

Q. **For what film did Barry Fitzgerald get nominated *both* for best actor and as best supporting actor for *the same role*?**
A. *Going My Way* (1944). Bing Crosby was also nominated for best actor; Fitzgerald won the supporting award; Crosby the leading. Thus, something quite remarkable: The movie gets three *nominations*, only two different *performances* share them.

Q. **What was the first film to garner *three* acting nominations, as well as the first to have three performers compete against each other in the same category (best actor)?**
A. *Mutiny on the Bounty* (1935). It is still the *only* time that three leading performer candidates competed directly against one another, all unsuccessfully. It was the fourth nominee, Victor McLaglen, who took home the trophy, winning for *The Informer*.

Special mention. Three performers were nominated against each other in the same category on four other occasions as well:

• *On the Waterfront* (1954). Five nominations, three for best supporting actor. None of the supporting nominees win, but the leading actor and supporting actress do.

• *Tom Jones* (1963). Five nominations, three for best supporting actress. Its only win is for supporting actor Hugh Griffith.

• *The Godfather* (1972). Four nominations, three for best supporting actor. Only leading actor Marlon Brando is victorious.

• *The Godfather Part II* (1974). Five nominations, three for best supporting actor. Finally, a victory in the three-way race, as Robert De Niro wins against Less Strasberg and Michael V. Gazzo.

Special mention. Other "threefers"—films to generate three acting nominations (though not in direct competition)—include:

- *The Philadelphia Story* (1940)
- *The Song of Bernadette* (1943)
- *Gaslight* (1944)
- *Since You Went Away* (1944)
- *All the King's Men* (1949)
- *Death of a Salesman* (1951)
- *Marty* (1955)
- *The Apartment* (1960)
- *Hud* (1963)
- *My Fair Lady* (1964)
- *Ship of Fools* (1965)
- *A Man for All Seasons* (1966)
- *The Graduate* (1967)
- *Anne of the Thousand Days* (1969)
- *They Shoot Horses, Don't They?* (1969)
- *The Exorcist* (1973)
- *One Flew Over the Cuckoo's Nest* (1975)
- *The Goodbye Girl* (1977)
- *The Deer Hunter* (1978)
- *Raging Bull* (1980)
- *Ordinary People* (1980)
- *Only When I Laugh* (1981)
- *Victor/Victoria* (1982)
- *Places in the Heart* (1984)
- *Prizzi's Honor* (1985)
- *Children of a Lesser God* (1987)
- *Moonstruck* (1987)

- *Driving Miss Daisy* (1989)
- *Dances with Wolves* (1990)
- *In the Name of the Father* (1993)
- *Pulp Fiction* (1994)
- *As Good As It Gets* (1997)
- *Good Will Hunting* (1997)

Q. **What was the first film to be nominated in *each* of the four acting categories (as well as for best director), for a total of *four* acting nominations?**
A. *My Man Godfrey* (1936). It occurred in the first year that supporting categories were offered. Remarkably, none of the nominees won, and it marks the only time that a film has swept the acting and directing nominations and failed to generate a best picture nod as well.

Special mention. Other examples of spreading the wealth evenly across all four acting categories—one nomination in each of the four—are:

- *For Whom the Bell Tolls* (1943)
- *Johnny Belinda* (1948)
- *Sunset Boulevard* (1950)
- *A Streetcar Named Desire* (1951)
- *Who's Afraid of Virginia Woolf?* (1966)[1]
- *Guess Who's Coming to Dinner?* (1966)
- *Coming Home* (1978)
- *Reds* (1981)

Q. **What was the first film to received five acting nominations?**
A. *Mrs. Miniver* (1942).

---

[1]One of only two occasions where virtually the entire cast was nominated in each of the acting categories.

Special mention. Other movies to have each acting category recognized, but with multiple nominees in at least one category, are:

- *From Here to Eternity* (1953)
- *Bonnie and Clyde* (1967)
- *Network* (1976)

Special mention. The habit of performers competing against each other in the same category is one hard to break. The conventional wisdom of the jinx has been that, overall, the nominations tend to cancel each out. Consider these:

- *Gone with the Wind* (1939). Four nominations, two for best supporting actress. Hattie McDaniel wins, as does leading actress Vivien Leigh.

- *Gentlemen's Agreement* (1947). Four nominations, two for best supporting actress. One nominee, Celeste Holm, wins.

- *I Remember Mama* (1948). Four nominations, two for best supporting actress. No wins.

- *Come to the Stable* and *Pinky* (both 1949). Both received three nominations, one for best actress and two each for best supporting actress. The solo best supporting actress nominee, Mercedes McCambridge in *All the King's Men*, won.

- *All About Eve* (1950). Five nominations, two for best actress, two for best supporting actress. Solo best supporting actor nominee George Sanders is the lone acting winner from the film.

- *Quo Vadis* (1951). Two nominations, both for best supporting actor. No wins.

- *From Here to Eternity* (1953). Five nominations; two for best actor. It wins only in the supporting categories.

- *The High and the Mighty* (1954). Two nominations, both for best supporting actress. No wins.

- *Giant* (1956). Three nominations, two for best actor. No wins.

- *The Bad Seed* (1956). Three nominations, two for best supporting actress. No wins.

- *Peyton Place* (1957). Five nominations, two for best supporting actor, two for best supporting actress. No wins.

- *The Defiant Ones* (1958). Four nominations, two for best actor. No wins.

- *Anatomy of a Murder* (1959). Three nominations, two for best supporting actor. No wins.

- *Suddenly Last Summer* (1959). Two nominations, both for best actress. No wins.

- *Imitation of Life* (1959). Two nominations, both for best supporting actress. No wins.

- *Judgment at Nuremberg* (1962). Four nominations, two for best actor. Leading actor nominee Maximilian Schell wins—the first time a performer competing against another performer from the same film has won since Celeste Holm in 1947 for *Gentleman's Agreement*.

- *The Hustler* (1962). Four nominations, two for best supporting actor. No wins.

- *Becket* (1964). Three nominations, two for best actor. No wins.

- *Othello* (1965). Four nominations, two for best supporting actress. No wins.

- *Bonnie and Clyde* (1967). Five nominations, two for best supporting actor. Its only win is for supporting actress.

- *Midnight Cowboy* (1969). Three nominations, two for best actor. No wins.

- *Airport* (1970). Two nominations, both for best supporting actress. Supporting actress nominee Helen Hayes wins.

- *Sleuth* (1972). Two nominations, both for best actor. No wins[2].

- *Paper Moon* (1973). Two nominations, both for best supporting actress. Tatum O'Neal defeats costar Madeline Kahn.

- *Nashville* (1975). Two nominations, both for best supporting actress. No wins.

- *Network* (1976). Five nominations, two for best actor. Three wins, including leading actor nominee Peter Finch defeating William Holden.

- *The Turning Point* (1977). Four nominations, two for best actress. No wins.

- *Julia* (1977). Four nominations, two for best supporting actor. Supporting actor Jason Robards wins.

- *Kramer vs. Kramer* (1979). Four nominations, two for best supporting actress, including a win for Meryl Streep.

- *Tootsie* (1982). Three nominations, two for best supporting actress. Jessica Lange defeats costar Teri Garr.

- *The Dresser* (1983). Two nominations, both for best actor. No wins.

- *Terms of Endearment* (1983). Four nominations, two for best actress, two for best supporting actor. Shirley MacLaine and Jack Nicholson turn up winners, defeating both of their costarring opponents.

- *Amadeus* (1984). Two nominations, both for best actor. F. Murray Abraham wins.

---

[2]Along with *Who's Afraid of Virginia Woolf?*, one of the two times a film's entire cast has been nominated.

- *The Color Purple* (1985). Three nominations, two for best supporting actress. No wins. It was the first and only time that three African-Americans have been nominated from the same film.

- *Platoon* (1986). Two nominations, both for best supporting actor. No wins.

- *Working Girl* (1988). Three nominations, two for best supporting actress. No wins.

- *Enemies, a Love Story* (1989). Two nominations, both for best supporting actress. No wins.

- *Bugsy* (1992). Three nominations, two for best supporting actor. No wins.

- *Thelma & Louise* (1992). Two nominations, both for best actress. No wins.

- *Bullets Over Broadway* (1993). Three nominations, two for best supporting actress. Dianne Wiest wins.

Chapter Two

Do You Have What It Takes?

A PRIMER FOR ENJOYING THE GLORIOUS KITSCH OF OSCAR

I take trivia very seriously. Since that dark day when my mother made the colossal mistake of her life—buying me *The Book of Lists* to keep me occupied on a long train trip (it backfired: I read every list aloud to her)—I have not been able to keep minutiae out of my mind. My rationale has always been simple: Useful facts, by definition, are common enough that you can usually ask a stranger on the street and get all the information you need. Today's weather is a useful fact; all you need to do is look out the window and there it is. But the weather during the Oscar ceremony of 1937 (mudslides; they postponed the ceremony by several days): Now *that's* great trivia!

Knowing trivia has, I have often found, made me more popular. Friends will call me at work long-distance to ask me the name of an actor who appeared in some movie, or the name of a killer, or what Rosebud was. When people find out you know a lot about the movies, especially the Oscars, their ears prick up. It's a terrific icebreaker, assuming you can slip it discreetly into conversation.

Admittedly, though, I am something of a trivia snob. Everyone has his or her favorite style of trivia, and sometimes, it bores me. When my brother-in-law relates to me every score the Detroit Lions have ever made, and against whom, my eyes glaze. My dad can walk me through all 74 shots of each 18 holes he has played; when I've played the course with him, it adds to my enjoyment, but I will never know how he remembers *so many golf shots!* That's the mystery of good trivia, though: The niggling obsession with details can add to your enjoyment, not detract from it.

As far as this book goes, you'll need to have a genuine commitment to film *and* kitsch in order to do well taking the quizzes, answering the questions, or getting caught up in the fun of it. Naturally, I tried to put together a resource that contains everything that has ever interested me about the Oscars. I've also tried to answer questions people have often put to me (even if of no particular interest to me) out of a misplaced sense of duty.

You say you don't *care* who received more Oscar nominations for acting than anyone else? What are you, a theater snob? How about naming every African-American performer ever nominated for an acting award? If you don't know these things, but have always wanted to, this book is for you. Below are 20 questions about the Oscars—some testing basic information about the awards themselves (like the first best picture winner), others seeking a more complete picture of the whole of Oscar silliness. If you can answer at least 14 correctly, you're well on your way toward ''Oscar Genius.'' But be careful! In the longstanding tradition of good trivia, your first thought is not *necessarily* the best—traps abound! And even if you *don't* answer the questions correctly . . . well, if you can get caught up in the campiness of it, if you care what the answers are, I suspect that you will enjoy yourself immensely.

Quiz

Q. What film won the first best picture Oscar?
A. Technically, *Cimarron* (1929/30) was the first film to win ''best picture''; for the first three years

the Oscars were presented, the award was called "best production." (You get extra credit if you knew that.) Whatever label you give it, though, *Wings* was the first film bestowed with the Academy's top honor. (For more information on "firsts," see chapter five, "First and Foremost.")

Q. Name at least one of the three categories that were given in the first year only.
A. The categories were: comedy direction (winner, Lewis Milestone for *Two Arabian Knights*), title writing (Joseph Farnham won for three films, *Laugh, Clown, Laugh; The Fair Co-ed*; and *Telling the World*), and artistic quality of production (also called unique and artistic picture; the award went to Fox's *Sunrise*). Title writing was only required for silent films, which essentially disappeared after 1928. (For more information on the early days of the Oscars, see chapter seven, "The '20s and '30s: Growing Pains.")

Q. Who famously exclaimed, "I can't deny the fact you like me; right now, you *like* me!" in her acceptance speech?
A. Sally Field, effusing about her second best actress award for *Places in the Heart* (1984).

Q. With what Disney character did Rob Lowe sing his infamously awful opening number at the 1988 Oscars?
A. Snow White.

Q. Only three films have won all five of the top awards: picture, actor, actress, director, and screenplay (original or adapted). Name two.
A. The sweeps belong to *It Happened One Night* (1954), *One Flew Over the Cuckoo's Nest* (1975),

and *The Silence of the Lambs* (1991). In each case, the films won no Oscars *other* than the top awards.

Q. **The following Oscar-winning performers were also nominated, at some time in their careers, in a category other than acting. Match the multi-talented actor at left with the "other" category at right.**

a.	Ruth Gordon	i.	adapted screenplay (and won!)
b.	Alec Guinness	ii.	original screenplay
c.	Emma Thompson	iii.	producer
d.	Barbra Streisand	iv.	story and screenplay (three times)
e.	Paul Newman	v.	song (and won!)
f.	John Houseman	vi.	documentary feature (and won!)
g.	Lee Grant	vii.	producer

A. a.-iv.; b.-ii.; c.-i.; d.-v.; e.-iii. or vii.; f.-iii. or vii.; g.-vi. (If you get at least four correct, consider yourself smart.)

Q. **Who is the only person ever to win an Oscar through a write-in vote?**
A. Hal Mohr, for cinematography on *A Midsummer Night's Dream* (1935). The rules no longer permit write-ins.

Q. **What is unique about all three supporting actress nominations Celeste Holm has received?**
A. Holm was always in the running as one of two nominated supporting actresses from the same movie: in 1947 for *Gentleman's Agreement* (Holm and Anne Revere; Holm's only win); in 1949 for *Come to the Stable* (Holm and Ethel Barrymore);

and in 1950 for *All About Eve* (Holm and Thelma Ritter).

Q. Name at least one of the only three best picture winners that were not also nominated for best director.
A. *Wings* (1927/28), *Grand Hotel* (1931/32), and *Driving Miss Daisy* (1989).

Q. Who are the only performers to have been twice-nominated for Oscars while playing the same role in separate films? Who is the only person to have won for playing the same role in a sequel?
A. Bing Crosby was twice-nominated for playing Father O'Malley: in 1944's *Going My Way* (a win) and its sequel, *The Bells of St. Mary's* (a loss in 1945). Al Pacino was nominated twice for playing Michael Corleone (as supporting actor in 1972's *The Godfather*; and as leading actor in 1974's *The Godfather Part II*). Peter O'Toole received two nominations for playing King Henry II in two un-related films: *Becket* in 1964, and *The Lion in Winter* in 1968. (Sigourney Weaver received her first nomination for *Aliens*, a sequel to *Alien* in which she also appeared, but she was not nominated for the original.) Paul Newman is the only actor to win an Oscar for reprising a role in a sequel (*The Color of Money*; 1986) to an Oscar-nominated performance in prior film (*The Hustler*; 1960).

Q. What character has been played to an Oscar most often?
A. The only *character* to have won more than one Oscar—with separate actors playing the same role in different films—is Don Vito Corleone, played by best actor Marlon Brando in *The Godfather* and supporting actor Robert De Niro in *The Godfather Part II*. Several parts, such as Henry VIII (Charles

Laughton in *The Private Life of Henry VIII*, Robert Shaw in *A Man for All Seasons*, Richard Burton in *Anne of the Thousand Days*), Mr. Chips (*Goodbye, Mr. Chips*, once starring Robert Donat, once Peter O'Toole), and Cyrano de Bergerac (played by José Ferrer and then Gerard Depardieu), have won the first actor an award, but not his unlucky followers. An exception that made number two the lucky one: Professor Henry Higgins, played by Leslie Howard in *Pygmalion* (1938) without Oscar success, but who in the person of Rex Harrison sang a few songs in *My Fair Lady* (1965) and walked away the champ. The characters of Esther Blodgett and Norman Main from *A Star Is Born* were nominated the first two times the film was made (by Janet Gaynor and Fredric March; later by Judy Garland and James Mason); in neither instance did the performers win.

Q. **What is the only single film for which two performers were nominated for playing the same character?**
A. In *Titanic* (1997), both Kate Winslet (actress [n]) and Gloria Stuart (supporting actress [n]) were nominated for playing Rose, but at different ages.

Q. **What do Judy Garland, Margaret O'Brien, Peggy Ann Warner, Claude Jarman Jr., Ivan Jandl, Bobby Driscoll, Jon Whiteley, Vincent Winter, and Hayley Mills all have in common?**
A. All were awarded miniature honorary Oscars for "best juvenile performance" in their given years; Whiteley and Winter were corecipients for the same film, *The Little Kidnappers*. The award has not been presented since 1960. Shirley Temple, Deanna Durbin and Mickey Rooney also received mini-statuettes, but the recognition was for a body of work rather than a particular performance. Patty Duke, Tatum O'Neal, Timothy Hutton, and Anna

Paquin all won supporting awards outright for their preteen or teenaged performances.

Q. What host of the 1979 Oscarcast referred to the ceremony as "two hours of sparkling entertainment spread out over a four-hour show"?
A.   Johnny Carson.

Q. Whose acceptance speech for best supporting actor in 1990 was simply: "It's my privilege. Thank you."?
A.   Joe Pesci for *GoodFellas*. Pesci later explained that he expected Al Pacino to win for *Dick Tracy*, and was unprepared.

Q. What was the last all black-and-white film to win the best picture Oscar?
A.   *The Apartment* (1960). *Schindler's List* (1993) was shot mostly in black-and-white, except for a girl in a red cape and the opening and closing sequences

Q. When an unexpected streaker dashed across the stage at the 1973 awards, who wittily ad-libbed: "Just think, the only laugh that man will probably ever get is for stripping and showing off his shortcomings"?
A.   David Niven.

Q. Since the establishment of the award for adapted screenplay in 1956, only once has the Oscar gone to a movie not also nominated for best picture (in 1996). Name it.
A.   Billy Bob Thornton, *Sling Blade*.

Q. Who griped about Elizabeth Taylor's sentimental win for *Butterfield 8*: "I lost to a tracheotomy"?
A.   Shirley MacLaine, who was nominated for *The Apartment*. An even better quote came from Debbie Reynolds, whose husband (Eddie Fisher) divorced

her after he met Taylor. Agreeing that sentiment played a part in Taylor's victory, Reynolds reportedly said, "Hell, even I voted for her."

Q. **What legendary actress received an honorary Oscar (her only one) which contained as its tribute: "for unforgettable screen performances"?**
A.   Greta Garbo.

Scoring your "Oscar Cool"

Correct answers: 18–20+—Oscar Genius (you get to present the best picture award next year); 14–17—Oscar Fanatic (you might not know it all, but you pay attention); 10–13—Oscar Dweeb (you know more than a casual viewer, but not enough to win the Silver Screen edition of Trivial Pursuit); 7–9—Oscar Watcher (you tune in every year, but hey, it's only about *movies*); 0–6—Oscar the Grouch (pay attention from now on!).

Chapter Three

Missed Opportunities

FAILED FAVORITES

Ellen Burstyn, after winning her best actress Oscar for *Alice Doesn't Live Here Anymore*, wondered aloud how important the award was in the scheme of things. She was advised that its significance was that her obituary would begin "Oscar-winning actress Ellen Burstyn died."

But just as many of the celebrities listed earlier—some legendary—failed to win, sometimes the ones that *did* win were considered upsets in their year. In fact, it's a truism of the Academy Awards that, almost as often as not, the favorite winds up empty-handed on Oscar night. It might be hard to believe, now that they have entered the record books, that some winners took home the prize to the shock of all.

Everybody has their favorite complaints about the Oscars: How could *Citizen Kane*, justifiably hailed as the greatest film ever made, escape almost award-free (particularly in the directing and cinematography categories)? The answer to that is: by being ahead of its time, by being blackballed by the Hearst publishing empire, and by upsetting the delicate balance of Hollywood at the time. Everyone knew it was brilliant, but no one expected it to win. What follows is a somewhat arbitrary list of major-category Oscar winners who were not the only ones surprised when they won. Although there's a degree of subjectivity to this (as every) list, most of the ones identified went against the conventional wisdom of the day.

1997

The category: Best actor. **The favorite**: Peter Fonda, *Ulee's Gold*. **The winner**: Jack Nicholson, *As Good As It Gets*. **What happened**: The former *Easy Rider* costars were clearly the two favorites, but Fonda seemed to have the slight edge. Both his sister and his father had Oscars, he was releasing an autobiography, his comeback was well-received, and his film was released early enough in the year that the buzz had been brewing for months that he was "the one to beat." Nicholson was superb as usual, and his film was popular, but having won twice before, a third acting Oscar (putting him in the company of Katharine Hepburn, Ingrid Bergman, and Walter Brennan) was perhaps too much to wish for. Not so.

The category: Best supporting actress. **The favorite**: Gloria Stuart, *Titanic*. **The winner**: Kim Basinger, *L.A. Confidential*. **What happened**: Among critics, Basinger had the obvious advantage, delivering a strong performance as a tragic variation on the *femme fatale*. But Stuart not only had sentiment on her side—a starlet in the '30s, she reemerged to give a human side to the gigantic sinking-ship epic—but also the phenomenal popularity of the film pulling in her favor: Both Stuart and fellow nominee Kate Winslet were the only humans in contention in the special effects–laden spectacle. But as had been proven the year before (see below), New Hollywood's sense of obligation to stars of the past has dimmed significantly.

1996

The category: Best supporting actress. **The favorite**: Lauren Bacall, *The Mirror Has Two Faces*. **The winner**:

Juliette Binoche, *The English Patient*. **What happened**:
Bacall received her first-ever nomination for her haunt-
ingly brittle and funny performance as a faded glamour
queen, the kind of career capstone that Oscar voters used
to reward reflexively. Although she was considered a
sure bet, the evening got off to an astonishing start when
Binoche's name was called out. Binoche's role as a
nurse tending a burn victim during World War II was
tender and deep, but her winning of the Oscar was completely unexpected. Bacall's defeat marked a strong in-
dication that a new generation of Young Turks might
have finally seized control of the Academy.

The category: Best adapted screenplay. **The favorite**:
Anthony Minghella, *The English Patient*. **The winner**:
Billy Bob Thornton, *Sling Blade*. **What happened**: This
award marked the first time since the adaptation category
was implemented in 1958 that the winner was *not* also
a best picture nominee. The hotly fancied Minghella,
who smoothly assayed the task of writing a screenplay
for a book most observers had labeled "unfilmable,"
had to be content with the best director trophy. Thornton's win was one of the delights of the evening, as he
was also nominated for best actor in what was the
sleeper success of the year, a plainspoken, deeply moving rendering of a Southern morality play.

1993

The category: Best supporting actress. **The favorite**:
Winona Ryder, *The Age of Innocence*. **The winner**:
Anna Paquin, *The Piano*. **What happened**: Because two
of the nominees in this category (Holly Hunter and
Emma Thompson) were also nominated the same year
for best actress (Hunter a lock on that award, Thompson
herself the previous year's winner), this was considered
a three-way race, with Rosie Perez in *Fearless* also in
contention. The conventional wisdom was that Ryder

would get it as a consolation prize to her movie overall, and anyway, preteens rarely win. Paquin's chances weren't considered great, although as the talking half of the women in the film, she advanced the narrative beautifully. Her victory was enchanted, especially when she stood at the podium silent and motionless in her beaded snood for more than 20 seconds, taking in her shock.

1992

The category: Best supporting actress. **The favorite**: Judy Davis, *Husbands and Wives*. **The winner**: Marisa Tomei, *My Cousin Vinny*. **What happened**: Tomei was the only American among the nominees, and her broad comic performance from early in the year was considered an aberration—and a long shot, when contrasted against Davis's subtle work as a sophisticated but fragile New York housewife in what was one of Woody Allen's best recent films. It wasn't merely that Tomei defeated Davis, but that she defeated her entire competition, a stellar category that year which also included highly praised performances by Joan Plowright, Vanessa Redgrave, and Miranda Richardson. There has been a persistent rumor, denied by the Academy, that presenter Jack Palance misread the winner as a joke, and the Academy was too embarrassed to correct it retroactively.

1991

The category: Best picture. **The favorite**: None. **The winner**: *The Silence of the Lambs*. **What happened**: The easiest way to walk home an Oscar winner might well be to compete in a divided year. 1991 was one of the most eclectic and impressive years in Oscar history: The first animated film nominated for best picture (*Beauty and the Beast*), two "prestige" pictures (*JFK*, *Bugsy*), and the popular sentimental favorite (*The Prince of Tides*, the only entry that didn't belong) all got trounced by an insidious little thriller released the previous January. *Silence* went on to sweep the major categories, legitimate director Jonathan Demme as a major talent, and revive Anthony Hopkins's sagging career.

The category: Best actor. **The favorite**: Nick Nolte, *The Prince of Tides*. **The winner**: Anthony Hopkins, *The Silence of the Lambs*. **What happened**: If *Silence*'s win for best picture was an upset, Hopkins's win was a coup. His performance as the demented psychiatrist Hannibal Lecter, chilling as it was, was considered by many to be a supporting role which couldn't hold up against the leading-man weight of a larger part. Nolte carried the romantic mantle gracefully, even a much-hyped scene where he cried. The look on Nolte's face when Hopkins's name rang out is best described as dumbstruck.

1990

The category: Best actress. **The favorite**: Joanne Woodward, *Mr. and Mrs. Bridge*. **The winner**: Kathy Bates, *Misery*. **What happened**: I may have been one of the few people *not* surprised by Bates's win. Woodward and Anjelica Huston (*The Grifters*) were both *par excellence* in small art-house films, with Woodward's delicate, frail turn as a mousy Midwestern housewife gaining the slight advantage. (The other nominees, Julia Roberts and Meryl Streep, were considered long shots.) But the lack of consensus about Huston and Woodward—and the fact that Hollywood actresses, who do a lot of the nominating and voting, are often quick to award women who "play their own age" (it's a form of job security)—made Bates the most predictable upset of the 1990s.

The category: Best supporting actor. **The favorites**: Al Pacino, *Dick Tracy*; Bruce Davison, *Longtime Companion*. **The winner**: Joe Pesci, *GoodFellas*. **What happened**: Again, the split in who was the "favorite"—

insiders claimed it was Pacino, who was passed over in the actor category the same year for *The Godfather Part III*; critics figured Davison, for playing the first openly homosexual character in the first film about AIDS to be nominated—caused many to bet that social conscience would win out. They were wrong. So was Pesci, whose entire acceptance speech ("It's my privilege. Thank you") he later attributed to expecting a Pacino victory.

1989

The category: Best supporting actor. **The favorite**: Martin Landau, *Crimes and Misdemeanors*. **The winner**: Denzel Washington, *Glory*. **What happened**: Landau was an old hand who had experienced a minor career surge in the late '80s. He had lost the previous year while also considered a favorite, so Washington's win was something of an upset—especially when you take into account that Washington didn't even give the best performance in *Glory*, his win caught most observers unawares.

1988

The category: Best supporting actor. **The favorite**: Martin Landau, *Tucker: The Man and His Dream*. **The winner**: Kevin Kline, *A Fish Called Wanda*. **What happened**: Kline's riotous performance as the stupid, maniacal Otto was a delight, but his victory against Landau's emotionally wrecked executive still qualifies as an upset. Interestingly, unlike with Marisa Tomei's win several years later, there was never a backlash against Kline.

The category: Best supporting actress. **The favorite**: Sigourney Weaver, *Working Girl*. **The winner**: Geena Davis, *The Accidental Tourist*. **What happened**: Although many believed Davis gave a warm and wonderful performance that "in another year" might win, it was the conventional wisdom of the time that whenever a performer is nominated twice in the same year, he or she usually wins in the supporting category. Weaver was up for best actress in *Gorillas in the Mist* and best supporting actress in *Working Girl*. Her dual defeat broke that tradition. (It also created some additional tension in the best actress category to come later that evening, with speculation that she might have won for the leading role instead; as it turned out, Jodie Foster, who was considered to be in a two-way race with Glenn Close, walked away with the award.) No one faulted Davis for the upset, who by acclamation gave the year's most winsomely entertaining performance. In retrospect, the Academy's decision was justified, paving the way for many of the upsets to come.

1985

The category: Best supporting actor. **The favorite**: Klaus Maria Brandauer, *Out of Africa*. **The winner**: Don Ameche, *Cocoon*. **What happened**: Ameche's nomination—his only one—was considered an aberration; his win, a long-overdue valentine. What seemed to catch people off-guard was the fact that Ameche was only one of several old-timers in *Cocoon*, and thereby failed to distinguish himself. On closer inspection, though, his dignified buffoonery holds as one of the most elegant testimonials imaginable to the gracefulness of old age.

1981

The category: Best picture. **The favorite**: *Reds*. **The winner**: *Chariots of Fire*. **What happened**: With precious few exceptions (only four times since 1957), best picture and director winners usually match up; even more rarely (only thrice during the same period) has there been identity in the nominations, including 1981. When Warren Beatty took the directing Oscar for *Reds*, his epic history (and the top nomination-getter its year) was seen as a lock against less "ambitious" fare. But *Chariots* proved that a groundswell of personal feeling among voters can make the difference between a sure thing and a dark horse upset. As William Goldman noted in his excellent chronicle of Hollywood, *Adventures in the Screen Trade*: "[N]o one has the least idea who'll win. When I was researching this book, I asked everybody whom they were voting for, and truly *everyone* said the same thing: *Chariots of Fire*, but it hasn't got a chance."

The category: Best actress. **The favorite**: Diane Keaton, *Reds*. **The winner**: Katharine Hepburn, *On Golden Pond*. **What happened**: Having already set the record for wins *and* nominations, Hepburn's nod seemed to be upstaged by costar Henry Fonda's delicate irascibility. Her triumph over Keaton, then at the peak of her popularity, was a sentimental favorite.

1977

The category: Best actor. **The favorite**: Richard Burton, *Equus*. **The winner**: Richard Dreyfuss, *The Goodbye Girl*. **What happened**: Perhaps the most out-and-out populist best actor choice in Oscar history, Dreyfuss's victory as an egotistical actor (and, moreover, not a very good one) defeated the winless Burton. It didn't help that they both shared the same first name—you could practically see Burton leaping to the aisles before the name was finished.

1974

The category: Best actor. **The favorites**: Jack Nicholson, *Chinatown*; Al Pacino, *The Godfather Part II*. **The winner**: Art Carney, *Harry and Tonto*. **What happened**: *Chinatown* is still one of the seminal films of the '70s—even then, it was recognized as the best of neo-*noir*—and Pacino posed a considerable challenge reprising his role as Michael Corleone, but 56-year-old Carney blew them away with his touching performance as a pensioner with a cat.

The category: Best actress. **The favorites**: Faye Dunaway, *Chinatown*; Gena Rowlands, *A Woman Under the Influence*. **The winner**: Ellen Burstyn, *Alice Doesn't Live Here Anymore*. **What happened**: Once again, the split decision probably contributed to a dark horse surprise. Dunaway's cold, tragic beauty Evelyn Mulwray competed with the earthy, difficult-to-watch Rowlands, and Burstyn sneaked in as a single mom.

The category: Supporting actress. **The favorite**: Valentina Cortese, *Day for Night*. **The winner**: Ingrid Bergman, *Murder on the Orient Express*. **What happened**: No one could ever quibble successfully with anything Bergman ever did—she remains one of the enduring talents in film history—but there was nothing so special about her performance here that would have suggested an overwhelming desire to recognize her. (She had been ill, and that likely contributed to her win.) Bergman herself made one of the most elegant tributes ever from the acceptance podium: "Last year, when *Day for Night* opened, Valentina Cortese gave the most beautiful performance that all we actresses recognize. Here I am her rival and I don't like it at all. . . . Please forgive me, Valentina; I didn't mean to."

1970

The category: Best actor. **The favorite**: George C. Scott in *Patton*. **The winner**: George C. Scott, *Patton*. **What happened**: This is one of those rare instances where the favorite *winning* was the upset itself. Scott had publicly announced his disdain for the Oscars, rejecting his nomination even from the get-go. Who would have thought that the Academy would defy his wishes and vote him the award anyway? More than anything, it was a slap in the face to all the nominees who *wanted* to be considered.

1969

The category: Best actress. **The favorite**: Jane Fonda, *They Shoot Horses, Don't They?* **The winner**: Maggie Smith, *The Prime of Miss Jean Brodie*. **What happened**: After years as a light comedienne (*Tall Story, Barefoot in the Park*) and sex kitten (*Barbarella*), Fonda surprised her detractors *and* fans with her scorching, cynical portrayal of Gloria. Her politics must have remained a barrier, however, and Smith sneaked in with a smallish film released early in the year—all but forgotten by most until she won the Oscar.

1968

The category: Best director. **The favorite**: Anthony Harvey, *The Lion in Winter*. **The winner**: Carol Reed, *Oliver!* **What happened**: The Directors Guild award is one of the more reliable bellwethers indicating likely Oscar success, and Harvey, with his serious, rousing "prestige" picture took that honor, and looked like a lock. The Academy, though, showed itself a fickle mistress, voting instead for the great Sir Carol, whose best work was behind him but won for a musical, of all things.

The category: Best actor. **The favorite**: Peter O'Toole, *The Lion in Winter*. **The winner**: Cliff Robertson, *Charly*. **What happened**: O'Toole made a gigantic splash his first decade in movies: In ten films over five years, he tallied up three nominations. His swashbuckling, modern interpretation of King Henry II was a high point for acting in the 1960s, but the lightweight Robertson, in a touching portrayal of a mentally retarded man who gains an intellect and loses it, apparently touched a heartstring in the voters, and O'Toole was overlooked—an omission that to this day goes uncorrected.

1967

The category: Best actor. **The favorite**: Spencer Tracy, *Guess Who's Coming to Dinner.* **The winner**: Rod Steiger, *In the Heat of the Night.* **What happened**: All right, maybe Tracy didn't deserve it anyway, but the details of his performance are legendary: his last screen appearance with Hepburn, his half-day schedule, his death within days after shooting ceased. If ever there was a sentimental favorite, he was it—so Steiger's turn as a racist cop must have *really* wowed voters.

1962

The category: Best actress. **The favorite**: Bette Davis, *What Ever Happened to Baby Jane?* **The winner**: Anne Bancroft, *The Miracle Worker.* **What happened**: Davis was one of the first aging screen queens not to go gracefully into that good night. Unlike Garbo and Colbert, who phased out their careers when they couldn't play the romantic leads anymore, Davis clung mercilessly to her star, going so far as to place an ad in a trade paper touting her availability. Her next project turned out to be *Baby Jane*, in which she paired with former Warners rival Joan Crawford. The film did good business, but Davis's nomination was significant in that Crawford went honorless. Davis maintained for years that Crawford campaigned against her, and that she lost by only a handful of votes to Bancroft, who until then was a nonentity and who became one of the biggest stars of the '60s and '70s. (Katharine Hepburn, widely praised for her performance in *Long Day's Journey into Night*, was also favored over Bancroft.) Ironically, Bancroft was in New York on Oscar night, and the statuette was accepted on her behalf by Joan Crawford.

1956

The category: Best supporting actor. **The favorite**: Robert Stack, *Written on the Wind*. **The winner**: Anthony Quinn, *Lust for Life*. **What happened**: Quinn's small part as Paul Gauguin in the van Gogh biography wasn't considered memorable enough to steal Stack's thunder, especially since Quinn had won only four years before. *Written on the Wind* was one of the steamier potboilers of the '50s, a deliciously naughty Douglas Sirk tale of Texas double-dealings and torrid romance. Stack's costar, Dorothy Malone, won as expected, but Stack came up empty, and was never in competition again. The reason for this arbitrary choice is one of the lingering mysteries in Academy lore.

1954

The category: Best actress. **The favorite**: Judy Garland, *A Star Is Born*. **The winner**: Grace Kelly, *The Country Girl*. **What happened**: Garland came into her own as an actress of power and musical ability, and was hopeful for a win, but Kelly's dowdy performance as an apparently domineering stage wife stole the trophy. In some ways, the upset wasn't *so* astonishing—Kelly had appeared in several films in 1954, and was the hot new Hollywood property (and her performance was impressive). Garland probably suffered as well from the studio's re-cut of her film soon after its initial release.

1951

The category: Best picture. **The favorite**: *A Place in the Sun*. **The winner**: *An American in Paris*. **What happened**: Two strong, "serious" contenders that year—*Sun* and *A Streetcar Named Desire*—split most of the big awards, with *Sun* getting director, screenplay, and cinematography, and *Streetcar* sweeping the acting awards. That schizophrenia apparently worked against

each film (both were black-and-white) in the members'
decision to vote for the splashy color musical. *A Place
in the Sun*'s director, George Stevens, became something
of a perpetual spoiler—the two-time best director recipient lost the best picture race each time he personally
won the trophy (the other was for *Giant* in 1956). Each
time, his serious films were defeated by the spectacle of
more approachable Technicolor treats.

1950

The category: Best actress. **The favorites**: Gloria Swanson, *Sunset Boulevard*; Bette Davis, *All About Eve*. **The
winner**: Judy Holliday, *Born Yesterday*. **What happened**: Norma Desmond and Margo Channing stand in
sharp relief as two of the most vivid, striking, and
smashingly performed female roles Hollywood ever
turned out, but it was the ditzy Billie Dawn (Holliday)
who won over the voters. Swanson's omission especially
stands out because her intense, darkly comic character-
ization of ego and theatricality lingers and is perhaps the
most haunting portrait of faded glamour descending into
madness: Swanson is comic, sad, and arresting, while
Holliday is just ditheringly funny.

1947

The category: Best actress. **The favorite**: Rosalind Russell, *Mourning Becomes Electra*. **The winner**: Loretta
Young, *The Farmer's Daughter*. **What happened**:
Young was a light comedienne and romantic B lead
who, over a lengthy career, hadn't demonstrated much
in the way of acting chops when she walked off with a
best actress nomination this year. Russell, one of the
spiciest, most comically sexual actresses of her day, was
considered the better actress, and tried to demonstrate it
in the long, dour, depressing rendering of Eugene
O'Neill's play. When presenter Fredric March began to
read the winner, he started by saying "Rosalind..."

and had to catch himself. Young won, and commentators swore that Russell was already halfway out of her seat before the names were read. An early edition of the *Los Angeles Times* even (wrongly) proclaimed that Russell was the victor in its headline.

1946

The category: Best actress. **The favorite**: Celia Johnson, *Brief Encounter*. **The winner**: Olivia de Havilland, *To Each His Own*. **What happened**: De Havilland's weepy soaper was pretty standard fare even in the '40s, certainly nothing as lasting or archly bittersweet as Johnson as the married woman having a tender but reserved (i.e., very *British*) affair with a married man. (De Havilland also acted in the popular thriller *The Dark Mirror* the same year, and may have been rewarded for having two hits.) Ginger, subtle, emotional acting didn't bring Johnson home the prize.

1943

The category: Best actor. **The favorite**: Humphrey Bogart, *Casablanca*. **The winner**: Paul Lukas, *Watch on the Rhine*. **What happened**: In the pantheon of Oscar's boneheaded moves, neglecting Bogart's Rick stands as one of the boneheadedest—especially considering the uninspired, oddly unmoving performance by Lukas. Hands down, this win qualifies as the most egregious ''What???'' in Oscar history.

1940

The category: Best actor. **The favorite**: Henry Fonda, *The Grapes of Wrath*. **The winner**: James Stewart, *The Philadelphia Story*. **What happened**: Much as I love Jimmy, his win this year was the most transparent consolation prize ever doled out. It's hard to blame the Academy for regretting their mistake the year before (see below), but Fonda's 41-year delay, himself cheated for *Grapes*, shows just how fickle the tit-for-tat process can be.

1939

The category: Best actor. **The favorites**: James Stewart, *Mr. Smith Goes to Washington*; Clark Gable, *Gone with the Wind*. **The winner**: Robert Donat, *Goodbye, Mr. Chips*. **What happened**: *GWTW* was a co-release of Metro-Goldwyn-Mayer and David O. Selznick's upstart independent studio, Selznick International, and MGM head Louis Mayer wasn't about to let his studio go winless on its own (even if Selznick was Mayer's son-in-law). He threw his full support behind Donat, who gave a delightful performance. (In retrospect, while Gable's Rhett Butler has soared into legendary status, Donat's performance is the more finely tuned.) Stewart, who gave one of his two or three best performances ever in *Mr. Smith*, got lost in the crossfire, but made up for it in 1940—this time, causing best friend Henry Fonda to play the bridesmaid.

1937

The category: Best actress. **The favorite**: Greta Garbo, *Camille*. **The winner**: Luise Rainer, *The Good Earth*. **What happened**: Garbo was the great female idol of the silent movies, and her transition into talkies was probably the most anticipated and successful of all the silent stars'. She had decent competition that year, but nothing as lulling and romantic as her own *Camille*. But the Viennese-born Rainer walked off with the trophy in the role of O-Lan, the long-suffering wife of Chinese peasant Paul Muni. The harrowing look perpetually affixed to Rainer's face is a sad remnant of the ham of the silent era, and resulted in what is probably the first official upset in Oscar history, as Rainer became the first person to win back-to-back Oscars. It remains an inexplicable

oddity as well; Rainer's performance, which had its sup-
porters, seems one-dimensional and repetitive by today's
standards, whereas Garbo still seems fresh.

And a special case: 1934

The category: Best actress. **The favorite**: Bette Davis,
Of Human Bondage. **The winner**: Claudette Colbert, *It
Happened One Night*. **What happened**: What makes
this upset unique was that the favorite, Davis in the classic role of Mildred in Somerset Maugham's modern
tragedy, was not even a nominee. The outcry over her
omission was so powerful that Davis became the first
recipient of a write-in campaign, eventually pulling in
more votes that any other actress except the official nominee, Colbert, and Norma Shearer in *The Barretts of
Wimpole Street*. Although she failed in her bid, there
were two notable consequences: First, the Academy allowed write-in votes for a period of time to correct its
still-developing procedures; and second, Davis became
what is arguably the first recipient of the traditional consolation Oscar when she won best actress the following
year for her less impressive work in *Dangerous* (Davis
herself called the script "mawkish," but it was a hit).

Consolation Prizes

Some people seemed to win more for their long
string of losses than for the genuine quality of a
single performance. The following also-rans are
probably the best indications of people who won
more for their continued dignity after losing so
often—or for having to wait so long between
wins—than for having given the most outstanding
performance of that year:

- **Joan Crawford**, *Mildred Pierce*. The size of her ego demanded she win it eventually.

- **Ronald Colman**, *A Double Life*. A belated win after three prior nominations.

- **John Wayne**, *True Grit*. Only one prior loss, but a screen icon who managed to convey a character convincingly, despite bad press to the contrary.

- **Jessica Tandy**, *Driving Miss Daisy*. A stellar performance, but the subtext was a reward for having been passed over for the screen version of *Streetcar*, which she originated on Broadway 38 years before.

- **Jack Palance**, *City Slickers*. Two prior losses in the '50s; he won after getting back in the saddle again.

- **Al Pacino**, *Scent of a Woman*. With seven failed nominations to his credit, he had to win this time—even if it wasn't Pacino at his best.

- **Susan Sarandon**, *Dead Man Walking*. Four prior losses and a reputation for being gutsy and sexy helped validate Sarandon's versatility playing a nun.

Still others are consoled for more political reasons: having lost in a prior year which, in retrospect, the Academy felt guilty for overlooking, or for some "personal" reason that had little to do with the film itself. Such winners include:

- **Bette Davis**, *Dangerous*. For being overlooked for *Of Human Bondage* the previous year.

- **James Stewart**, *The Philadelphia Story*. After losing for *Mr. Smith Goes to Washington*.

- **Humphrey Bogart**, *The African Queen*. Everyone agrees Bogey deserved an Oscar for

Casablanca—or any number of other films—but was he *really* better than Brando in *Streetcar*?

• **Ingrid Bergman**, *Anastasia*. Bergman was always great, but this win owed more to Hollywood forgiving her for having a child out of wedlock than for acting circles around her competition.

• **Elizabeth Taylor**, *Butterfield 8*. Her health problems led many to believe she wouldn't live long enough to accept it, but she pulled through and went on to win a second Oscar.

• **Julie Andrews**, *Mary Poppins*. The best way to embarrass Jack Warner for not letting Andrews reprise her Broadway role in *My Fair Lady* was to give the award to her the same year for *another* movie—one released by Disney.

• **Katharine Hepburn**, *Guess Who's Coming to Dinner*. Her longtime love, Spencer Tracy, died days after filming completed, and rewarding her with an Oscar was the rough approximation of a sympathy card.

• **John Houseman**, *The Paper Chase*. He never won for producing, Welles dumped him as a fellow *wunderkind*, so why not throw the crusty old dog a bone?

• **George Burns**, *The Sunshine Boys*. Clearly no one in 1975 expected the 80-year-old winner to last another 20 years and enjoy the most thriving period of his century-long career.

• **Fay Bainter, Teresa Wright, Barry Fitzgerald**, and **Jessica Lange**. All were nominated as leading performer the same year they won the supporting award; apparently the Academy didn't want them to walk home empty-handed. (Sigourney Weaver and Emma Thompson weren't so lucky—both received two nominations in one year without winning.)

🎞What Were You *Thinking?*

A humble rumination on the 10 craziest inclusions in Oscar history:

1. Luise Rainer, actress, *The Good Earth* (1937).

2. *How Green Was My Valley*, picture winner (1941). Okay, maybe not a *bad* movie, but when up against *Citizen Kane*, you think they couldn't have chosen better? The same could be said for overlooking Orson Welles's direction and Gregg Toland's brilliant photography.

3. Paul Lukas, actor, *Watch on the Rhine* (1943).

4. Barry Fitzgerald, supporting actor, *Going My Way* (1944). A part tailor-made for the curmudgeonly old bear, but hardly a gem. Clifton Webb's stinging, still-modern performance as Waldo Lydecker in *Laura*, by contrast, is as fresh and lively today as it was back then.

5. Judy Holliday, actress, *Born Yesterday* (1950).

6. Anthony Quinn, supporting actor, *Lust for Life* (1956).

7. Lee Marvin, actor, *Cat Ballou* (1965). Maybe I'm missing something, but for playing a drunken cowboy in a lame slapstick comedy Marvin walked home with an Oscar? Maybe the award was meant for his performance in *Ship of Fools* the same year, but handing out honors for comedy performances like these is what gives comedy a bad name. Richard Burton (*The Spy Who Came in From the Cold*) and Oskar Werner (*Ship of Fools*) were far better choices.

8. Sandy Dennis, supporting actress, *Who's Afraid of Virginia Woolf?* (1966). Dennis, a delicate, easily drunken flower of a housewife, and her tic-filled, neurotic whining easily drowns what little sympathy the audience might otherwise be able to generate for her. Virtually any of her competitors (admittedly not a strong category that year) would have been a better choice.

9. *Oliver!*, picture (1968). Admittedly an ebullient musical, skillfully directed by Carol Reed—and the last one to win a best picture Oscar—but against a challenging, popular, literate, and fresh film such as *The Lion in Winter* this selection seems somehow defiantly ordinary.

10. Marisa Tomei, supporting actress, *My Cousin Vinny* (1993).

Part II
Some Noteworthy Achievements

Chapter
Four

For the Record Book:
Some of Oscar's Most Notable
Statistical Achievements

The Academy Awards purport to celebrate the "best" and the "greatest" and the "most outstanding," but is that always—or *ever*—the case? Certainly a random poll of film critics and historians would suggest that the greatest American film ever made was *Citizen Kane*, and while it *was* nominated for nine Oscars, it took home only the screenplay trophy. Winning isn't even necessarily a question of popularity; although *Star Wars, E.T.*, and *Raiders of the Lost Ark* were all nominated for best picture, their creators had to be satisfied with craft recognition only.

The best illustration of Academy capriciousness is not really its failure to reward individual films; often, that's more a result of distribution, marketing, and timing. What *is* true is that many of the great veterans of Hollywood have walked home empty-handed year after year—or never been nominated at all—while other talents seem to rack up nominations and awards like so many billiard balls.

In this chapter, the superlatives of Oscarcana will be explored—the best, the least, the most, the longest, the shortest, the worst, the youngest, the oldest, the newest, the first, the last, and more—disputing what you've always been told: It isn't necessarily quality that counts, it's quantity.

Quiz—The Mosts and Longests, Leasts and Shortests of Oscar Lore

Q. **Who has won the most total Oscars in any category?**

A. Conventional wisdom says it is Walt Disney, with 22. Close behind him are Cedric Gibbons and Alfred Newman. To be fair, though, you should discount at least some of these wins—after all, Walt got the awards as the studio chief (he wasn't drawing those cartoons himself, and his competition in the animation category was virtually nonexistent for years); and Gibbons and Newman, as heads of their departments, often got final credit for the work done by subordinates. With that in mind, Edith Head (eight for costuming) and Edwin Willis (eight for set decoration) top the list for individual achievement. Alan Menken (six for song and score) and Billy Wilder (six for writing, producing, and directing) have won the most in multiple categories.

Q. **Who has received the most nominations in any one category?**

A. Again, Gibbons received a record-setting 40 nominations for design work. Edith Head, nominated 33 times for costuming (which, like art direction, was for a while divided into color and black-and-white films), is the best example of a legitimate champion.

Q. **What *actress* has received the most acting nominations? The most acting wins?**

A. Katharine Hepburn wins handily (male or female) with 12 nominations and four wins: *Morning Glory* (1932/33; win); *Alice Adams* (1935); *The*

Philadelphia Story (1940); *Woman of the Year* (1942); *The African Queen* (1951); *Summertime* (1955); *The Rainmaker* (1956); *Suddenly, Last Summer* (1959); *Long Day's Journey into Night* (1962); *Guess Who's Coming to Dinner* (1967; win); *The Lion in Winter* (1968; win); *On Golden Pond* (1981; win). All of her nominations were in the best actress category. Bette Davis was formally nominated 10 times for best actress, although Academy records now credit her with 11, owing to a write-in campaign for *Of Human Bondage* (1934), which placed her third in overall balloting. Meryl Streep has been nominated 10 times, twice for supporting actress. Both Davis and Streep won twice. Ingrid Bergman won three times, once for supporting actress.

Q. What *actor* has received the most acting nominations? The most acting wins?

A. The actor with the most nominations is Jack Nicholson, with 11, followed by Laurence Olivier with 10. One of Olivier's nominations was for supporting actor, and four of Nicholson's were, so the nominee with the most nominations wholly in the best actor category is, ironically enough, Hepburn's frequent on-screen partner, Spencer Tracy, with nine. Remarkably, despite nine on-screen collaborations, the only film for which Tracy and Hepburn were both nominated was Tracy's last film, *Guess Who's Coming to Dinner*, although Tracy had died before the nominations were announced. Paul Newman has been nominated for acting eight times, and also received a best picture nomination, an honorary award, and the Jean Hersholt Humanitarian award. In 1997, Nicholson tied Walter Brennan for the most wins by a male performer, taking home three trophies.

Q. Who is the most nominated performer, irrespective of category?

A. That champion is probably Woody Allen, who received one best actor nomination, but has been nominated 19 other times for writing and directing.

Q. What performers have received the most nominations without tallying up a single win?

A. Peter O'Toole [*Lawrence of Arabia* (1962); *Becket* (1964); *The Lion in Winter* (1968); *Goodbye, Mr. Chips* (1969); *The Ruling Class* (1972); *The Stunt Man* (1980); *My Favorite Year* (1984)] and Richard Burton [*My Cousin Rachel* (1952); *The Robe* (1953); *Becket* (1964); *The Spy Who Came in From the Cold* (1965); *Who's Afraid of Virginia Woolf?* (1966); *Anne of the Thousand Days* (1969); *Equus* (1977)] have each been nominated seven times without a win, or without receiving even honorary recognition. As Burton's first nomination was in the supporting category and all of O'Toole's are leading nominations, O'Toole's slight seems the greater embarrassment—not to him, but to the Academy. Deborah Kerr received six leading actress nominations without winning, but was awarded an honorary Oscar in 1993. In the supporting category, Thelma Ritter received six nominations and Agnes Moorehead five, without either taking the statuette home with them. All of Claude Rains's four unsuccessful bids for the Oscar were in the supporting actor category; Arthur Kennedy was nominated four times for best supporting actor as well as once for best actor (*Bright Victory*, 1951) without winning.

Q. What performer has received the most Oscars—without receiving a single nomination?

A. Bob Hope has received *five* honorary awards or other citations from the Academy (ranging from a lifetime Academy membership to the statuette itself).

Q. Who is the *youngest* performer ever to be nominated for a competitive Oscar? To win?
A. The youngest-ever winner is Tatum O'Neal, 10 years old when winning best supporting actress for *Paper Moon* (1973). Justin Henry, nine, was the youngest-ever nominee for *Kramer vs. Kramer* (1979). (For more information on young nominees and winners, see the sidebar on page 72.)

Q. Who is the *oldest* performer ever to be nominated for an Oscar? To win?
A. The oldest-ever winner is 81-year-old Jessica Tandy, best actress for *Driving Miss Daisy* (1989). The oldest nominee is Gloria Stuart, who was 87 years old when nominated for her performance in *Titanic* (1997). (For more statistics on older nominees and winners, see the sidebar on page 73.)

Q. What film received the most Oscar wins? What film has received the most nominations? What is the "magic number" in each case?
A. The records held for a long time: *Ben-Hur* won 11 Oscars out of 12 nominations in 1959, losing in only one category: adapted screenplay. *All About Eve* (1950) received 14 nominations, owing in large part to its five acting nominations—two for best actress, two for best supporting actress, one for best supporting actor. It won six, including best picture and best direction. In 1997, *Titanic* tied both *All About Eve* in record nominations and *Ben-Hur* in record wins.

Q. Always a bridesmaid: What films have received the most nominations without a single win?
A. This dubious distinction is shared by *The Turning Point* (1977) and *The Color Purple* (1985), both of which received 11 nominations and walked

home empty-handed. For 46 years, the record had been held by *The Little Foxes* (1941), with nine. The film with the most nominations without winning any *and* without receiving a single nomination in *any* of the six major categories—picture, leading and supporting actor and actress, direction, or writing—is *Pepe* (1960), which received an impressive seven nominations (color cinematography, color costumes, color art direction, film editing, scoring, song, and sound) and walked home empty-handed. *Ragtime* (1981) received eight nominations, but not for best picture; it also won *bupkis*.

Q. True sweeps: Only two best picture winners have won every award they were nominated for (in each case, they went nine for nine). Name one.

A.   *Gigi* (1958) and *The Last Emperor* (1987).

Q. Who have received the most nominations for a single film? The most wins for a single film?

A.   Orson Welles received four nominations for *Citizen Kane* (1941)—for producer, director, actor, and screenplay; Warren Beatty did the same, twice: for *Heaven Can Wait* in 1978, and for *Reds* in 1981. Each won only one trophy: Welles for his original screenplay, and Beatty for directing *Reds*. Billy Wilder won three awards (producing, directing, and writing) for *The Apartment* (1960), Francis Ford Coppola repeated that with *The Godfather Part II* (1974), followed by James L. Brooks in 1983's *Terms of Endearment*. James Cameron also took home three for *Titanic* (1997), only he was not even nominated for his screenplay—he won for directing, producing, and editing. Marvin Hamlisch won three awards in 1973, but for two films: original score and song for *The Way We Were*, and adapted score for *The Sting*.

Q. **What performers waited the longest between a first nomination and a first win?**

A. For men, and overall, the winner is Henry Fonda, who won for *On Golden Pond* (1981) 39 years after his first (and only other) acting nomination, *The Grapes of Wrath* (1940). (He was also nominated for producing best picture nominee *Twelve Angry Men* in 1957.) If you take into account Fonda's producing nomination, then Jack Palance holds the record, going 38 years between *Sudden Fear* (1953) and *City Slickers* (1991). Peter O'Toole's first nomination for best actor came in 1962; despite six subsequent nominations, he has yet to win. If he ever wins, he'd undoubtedly hold the record. For women, Helen Hayes holds the record, the same as Palance's: 38 years between *The Sin of Madelon Claudet* (1931/32) and *Airport* (1970).

Q. **What multiple Oscar winner has had to wait the longest time to take home the first and last Oscar?**

A. Katharine Hepburn currently holds the record for the greatest span of wins: 48 years lapsed between her first and her fourth award.

Q. **Winning streak: Who received the most nominations in consecutive years, and in what category?**

A. Edith Head, who received at least one costume design nomination for the first 19 years that the category was in existence. Her final tally was eight wins.

Q. **Who has received the most nominations for best director?**

A. William Wyler, with 12: *Dodsworth* (1936), *Wuthering Heights* (1939), *The Letter* (1940), *The*

Little Foxes (1941), *Mrs. Miniver* (1942), *The Best Years of Our Lives* (1946), *The Heiress* (1949), *Detective Story* (1951), *Roman Holiday* (1953), *Friendly Persuasion* (1956), *Ben-Hur* (1959), and *The Collector* (1965). He won three (*Miniver, Best Years,* and *Ben-Hur*).

Q. **What director, known for his Westerns, won the most Oscars for directing—none for a Western?**
A. John Ford, with four [*The Informer* (1935), *The Grapes of Wrath* (1940), *How Green Was My Valley* (1941) and *The Quiet Man* (1952)]. He received only one other directing nomination, for a Western, *Stagecoach* (1939), giving him one of the best betting averages in Oscar history. William Wyler (above) and Frank Capra [*It Happened One Night* (1934), *Mr. Deeds Goes to Town* (1936), *You Can't Take It with You* (1938)] have each won three.

Q. **Who are the only four multiple-winning performers to have a "perfect record"—two nominations, two awards? (Hint: they are all women.)**
A. Helen Hayes, Luise Rainer, Vivien Leigh, and Sally Field.

Q. **Who are the only five performers to have won acting Oscars in consecutive years?**
A. Luise Rainer (best actress for *The Great Ziegfeld* and *The Good Earth*, 1936/37), Spencer Tracy (best actor for *Captains Courageous* and *Boys Town*, 1937/38), Katharine Hepburn (best actress for *Guess Who's Coming to Dinner* and *The Lion in Winter*, 1967/68), Jason Robards (best supporting actor for *All the President's Men* and *Julia*, 1976/77), and Tom Hanks (best actor for *Philadelphia* and *Forrest Gump*, 1993/94).

Q. **What performers were the first prior winners in a leading category to be nominated in a supporting category?**

A. The first, Jennifer Jones, best actress in 1943 for *The Song of Bernadette*, was nominated the following year for her supporting role in *Since You Went Away*. Victor McLaglen, best actor for *The Informer* (1935), received his only other nomination, as best supporting actor, for another John Ford picture, *The Quiet Man* (1952).

Q. **Who was the first performer to win a leading Oscar, followed by a supporting Oscar win?**

A. Helen Hayes, who won leading actress for *The Sin of Madelon Claudet* (1931/32) and supporting actress for *Airport* (1970). Since Hayes, four more performers have crossed over categories, working their way from leading status to character parts: Ingrid Bergman (best actress, *Gaslight*, 1944, and *Anastasia*, 1956; best supporting actress, *Murder on the Orient Express*, 1974), Jack Nicholson (best actor, *One Flew Over the Cuckoo's Nest*, 1975; best supporting actor, *Terms of Endearment*, 1983), Maggie Smith (best actress, *The Prime of Miss Jean Brodie*, 1969; best supporting actress, *California Suite*, 1978) and Gene Hackman (best actor, *The French Connection*, 1971; best supporting actor, *Unforgiven*, 1992).

Q. **What performers have won a supporting Oscar, followed by a leading acting award?**

A. Jack Lemmon won best supporting actor in 1955 for *Mister Roberts*, and later followed it with a best actor trophy for *Save the Tiger* (1973). Others include: Robert De Niro (best supporting actor, *The Godfather Part II*, 1974; best actor, *Raging Bull*, 1980), Meryl Streep (best supporting actress, *Kramer vs. Kramer*, 1979; best actress, *Sophie's Choice*) and Jessica Lange (best supporting actress,

Tootsie, 1981; best actress, *Blue Sky*, 1994). Jack Nicholson managed a remarkable feat in following a supporting win with *another* leading win for best actor in *As Good As It Gets* (1997), the only performer to switch categories twice.

Q. Who were the first performers to receive statuettes in supporting categories?

A. If you said Walter Brennan and Gale Sondergaard, technically you're wrong. From 1936–1942, supporting performers were given plaques. Katina Paxinou and Charles Coburn, the winners in 1943, were the first to receive ol' Oscar himself.

Q. What is the best picture winner with the longest running time?

A. Various sources report the running times of movies differently, but neck-and-neck for the top spot are *Gone with the Wind* (1939), *Ben-Hur* (1959), and *Lawrence of Arabia* (1962), all of which clock in at more than three and a half hours (about 220 minutes, according to most sources).

Q. What Oscar-winning film has the longest running time?

A. In this more general category, *Lawrence of Arabia*, *Ben-Hur*, and *Gone with the Wind* are not even close. The record is handily held by *War and Peace*, the 1968 foreign language film winner from the Soviet Union. It originally clocked in at about eight hours (and a price tag of $100 million *in 1968 dollars!*); the version released in the United States, though, ran a mere six and a quarter hours.

Q. What is the shortest film to win the best picture award?

A. Again, accounting for some variations in how length is calculated, it appears that the shortest best picture winner is *Marty* (1955), at 91 minutes. A close second is *Annie Hall* (1977), at 94 minutes.

Longer pictures normally do better in competition: only 23 films less than two hours have won best picture; since 1966, only nine have won.

Q. When was the longest Oscar ceremony, and how long did it run?
A. In 1997, the award ceremony lasted three hours, 47 minutes, besting the 1983 ceremony by about four minutes.

Q. What best picture nominee had the longest title?
A. *Dr. Strangelove: Or, How I Learned to Stop Worrying and Love the Bomb* (1964).

Q. What best picture winner had the longest title?
A. Depending on how you define "longest," *All Quiet on the Western Front* has 25 letters in its title; while *One Flew Over the Cuckoo's Nest* has 25 letters and one punctuation mark. The number "80" in *Around the World in 80 Days* is usually written as a numeral, but if spelled out would result in 26 letters without any punctuation marks, making it the longest-named best picture winner.

Q. What nominated film overall had the longest title?
A. *Those Magnificent Men in Their Flying Machines; Or, How I Flew from Paris to London in 25 Hours and 11 Minutes* (1965, story and screenplay).

Q. What best picture nominee had the shortest title?
A. *Z* (1969).

Q. What best picture winner had the shortest title?
A. *Gigi* (1958).

Q. What nominated film overall had the shortest title?
A. *Z* (1969).

Q. What category and what year had the most nominees?

A. A remarkable 25 films were nominated as best documentary in 1942, only the second year of the category. There were four winners. Most dealt with some aspect of World War II.

🎞 "Wasted on the Young": The Youngest Performing and Directing Nominees and Winners

Can you name the youngest nominee and the youngest winner in each of the five major categories?

• **Actor**. Youngest nominee: Jackie Cooper, *Skippy* (1931; age 10). Youngest winner: Richard Dreyfuss, *The Goodbye Girl* (1977; age 30).

• **Actress**. Youngest nominee: Isabelle Adjani, *The Story of Adele H.* (1975; age 19). Youngest winner: Marlee Matlin, *Children of a Lesser God* (1986; age 21).

• **Supporting actor**. Youngest nominee: Justin Henry, *Kramer vs. Kramer* (1979; age 9). Youngest winner: Timothy Hutton, *Ordinary People* (1980; age 19).

• **Supporting actress** Youngest nominee: Mary Badham, *To Kill a Mockingbird* (1962; age 9). Youngest winner: Tatum O'Neal, *Paper Moon* (1973; age 10).

• **Director**. Youngest nominee: John Singleton, *Boyz N the Hood* (1991; age 24). Youngest winner: William Friedkin, *The French Connection* (1971; age 32). (Norman Taurog, who won an

Oscar for directing *Skippy* in 1931, was also 32 at the time he received the Oscar, but Friedkin was younger by several days on the day the award was presented.)

Extra credit. Who was the overall youngest Oscar recipient? Shirley Temple was a tender six years old when she received an honorary award in 1934.

***

"Of a Certain Age": The Oldest Performing and Directing Nominees and Winners

The same, in reverse: Can you name the oldest nominee and oldest winner in each of the five major categories?

• **Actor**. Oldest nominee: Henry Fonda, *On Golden Pond* (1982, age 76). Oldest winner: Fonda.

• **Actress**. Oldest nominee: Jessica Tandy, *Driving Miss Daisy* (1989, age 81). Oldest winner: Tandy.

• **Supporting actor**. Oldest nominee: George Burns, *The Sunshine Boys* (1975; age 80). Oldest winner: Burns.

• **Supporting Actress**. Oldest nominee: Gloria Stuart, *Titanic* (1997; age 87). Oldest winner: Peggy Ashcroft, *A Passage to India* (1984; age 77).

• **Director**. Oldest nominee: John Huston, *Prizzi's Honor* (1985; age 79). Oldest winner: George Cukor, *My Fair Lady* (1965; age 65).

Extra credit. Who was the overall oldest Oscar recipient? The oldest person to ever receive an Oscar is probably Hal Roach, creator of the Little Rascals, who was over 90 when he was presented with an honorary award.

Chapter
Five

First and Foremost

THE TENSION FOR RECOGNITION

When you consider that the Academy was founded originally as a public relations device, its receptiveness to
social concerns and its tendency to reward people for
the wrong reasons seem fairly predictable: After all, they
need to give the audience what it wants. But especially
in the days of the big moguls, issues ranging from race
to poverty, drug addiction to single motherhood were
staples of entertainment.

The industry was somewhat slower to allow women
to come into their own, however. Only two women have
ever received best director nominations, and only three
have ever directed best picture nominees; none has ever
won. There has *never* been a female winner of the cinematography award, either, and even today the most
powerful of female movie stars still complain that the
strong, independent roles are hard to come by.

The following questions test your knowledge of
"firsts" in Oscar history, most dealing with sex, race,
and similar taboos. At least as interesting as the names
that answer the questions are the dates that accompany
them. The social education that is reflected in our culture
is nowhere sharper than in a review of these Oscar "records." Many of the other questions and answers merely
give some insight into important "firsts" within the in-

dustry itself—the superlatives of Oscar that get bandied about like the statistics baseball fanatics can quote.

Quiz: Who (Or What) Was the First . . .

Sex and Sexuality

Q. ... woman to be nominated for an Oscar in a category other than acting?

A. There were two: Josephine Lovett, *Our Dancing Daughters*; Bess Meredyth, *A Woman of Affairs* and *Wonder of Women* (both for best writing, 1928/ 29).

Q. ... woman to *win* an Academy Award in a category other than best actress?

A. Frances Marion, best writing, *The Big House* (1930).

Q. ... woman to be nominated for best director?

A. Lina Wertmuller, *Seven Beauties* (1976). No woman has ever won.

Q. ... film to be nominated for best picture which was directed by a woman?

A. *Children of a Lesser God* (1986; directed by Randa Haines). Subsequent nominated pictures from female directors include: *Awakenings* (1990, directed by Penny Marshall); *The Prince of Tides* (1991, directed by Barbra Streisand), and *The Piano* (1993, directed by Jane Campion). Campion remains the only woman to have directed a best picture nominee *and* to have received a best director nomination herself. None of the best picture nominees directed by women has ever won. (Something some male actor-producers should take note of, though: every nominated female director or female who directed a best picture nominee has also garnered best acting nominations for her leading performers.)

Q. ... woman to win a best picture Oscar (as producer)?

A. Julia Phillips, *The Sting* (1973). Phillips was nominated again for *Taxi Driver* (1976). Subsequent women nominated for producing include: Tamara Asseyev, *Norma Rae* (1979); Kathleen Kennedy, *E.T.—The Extra-Terrestrial* (1982) and *The Color Purple* (1985); Mildred Lewis, *Missing* (1982); Arlene Donovan, *Places in the Heart* (1984; the first solo woman to be nominated for producing); Sherry Lansing, *Fatal Attraction* (1987); Norma Heyman, *Dangerous Liaisons* (1988); Lili Fini Zanuck, *Driving Miss Daisy* (1989; aside from Phillips, the only woman to win for producing); Lisa Weinstein, *Ghost* (1990); Barbra Streisand, *The Prince of Tides* (1991); and Jan Chapman, *The Piano* (1993).

Q. ... woman to win the best score Oscar as a solo?

A. Remarkably, it was not until 1996, when Rachel Portman won, for *Emma*. In the past, women had won scoring and song awards, but always as part of music writing teams, usually for music for musicals, or for songs, which included men.

Q. ... person playing an openly homosexual character to be nominated for an Oscar?

A. This is a more complicated question than it implies. Laurence Olivier received a nomination for playing Richard III in 1956—an historical figure known to be gay, but whose sexual orientation is not mentioned explicitly in the movie. A frank depiction of gay characters was not permitted in the days of the Hays Codes—the censorship arm of the industry until the 1950s—so many implicitly homosexual characters, such as Professor Henry Higgins (played by Leslie Howard in *Pygmalion*, 1938), probably don't count. Lots of times, code words were used to convey the same thing, so "spinsterly aunts" like Agnes Moorehead in *The Magnificent Ambersons* (1942), "confirmed bachelors" like Clifton Webb in *The Razor's Edge* (1946), and androgynous people like the MC played by Joel Grey in *Cabaret* (1972) really don't qualify. Two of the earliest film performances to suggest the homosexuality of a major character are those of Peter O'Toole in *Lawrence of Arabia* (1962), with its images of male-on-male sadomasochism, and Warren Beatty as Clyde Barrow in *Bonnie and Clyde* (1967), which contains several references to him not being much of a lover boy, as well as an abortive attempt at lovemaking. One of the first characters to participate, at least lightly, in gay sex is probably Joe Buck, the *Midnight Cowboy* (1969) played by Jon Voight. He's a street hustler who hits on women, but he goes home with a male pickup (and then beats him up). The question remains whether he continued to hustle men. The "winner" of the award for "first," though, was finally settled in 1971, when Peter Finch in *Sunday, Bloody Sunday* was nominated as best actor. The British film, about a love triangle where the object of affection is a bisexual man, was also the first mainstream movie to feature a kiss of a sexual nature between two men. For an *American*-made movie, the winner is a tie: Al Pacino and Chris Sarandon, both nominated for their performances in *Dog Day Afternoon* (1975). Pacino plays a gay man who robs a bank in order to finance boyfriend Sarandon's sex change operation. Pacino plays it mostly straight (forgive the pun), but Sarandon's one scene is a touching interchange between a cross-dresser and his loving but disturbed partner. Other nominated portrayals of characters whose homosexuality or bisexuality is not genuinely in dispute include: John Hurt, *Midnight Express* (1978, supporting actor); Bette Midler, *The Rose* (1979, actress); James Coco, *Only When I Laugh* (1981, supporting actor); John Lithgow, *The World According to Garp* (1982, supporting actor; actually, he's a transsexual); Robert Preston, *Victor/Victoria* (1982, supporting actor); Tom Courtenay, *The Dresser* (1983, actor); Cher, *Silkwood* (1983, supporting actress); William Hurt, *Kiss of the Spider Woman* (1985, actor); Whoopi Goldberg, *The Color Purple* (1985, actress); Margaret Avery, *The Color Purple* (1985, supporting actress); Bruce Davison, *Longtime Companion* (1990, supporting actor; the first nominated performer to play an AIDS-afflicted character); Tommy Lee Jones, *JFK* (1991, supporting actor); Stephen Rea, *The Crying Game* (1992, actor); Jaye Davidson, *The Crying Game* (1992, supporting actor); Tom Hanks, *Philadelphia* (1993, actor); Greg Kinnear, *As Good As It Gets* (1997, supporting actor).

Q. ... openly gay character in a film, the portrayal of which received an Oscar?

A. Acknowledging the criteria specified above, the first was William Hurt in *Kiss of the Spider Woman* (1985, best actor). The only other "gay" recipient is Tom Hanks, *Philadelphia* (1993, best actor). Neither Hurt nor Hanks is, in real life, homosexual.

Q. ... openly gay person to receive an Academy Award?

A. Again, this is something more of a trick question than intended. Much has been written about Laurence Olivier's bisexuality, although he was not outwardly gay at the time he won his Oscars (best actor and best picture, *Hamlet*, 1948). The same has been said of Oscar nominees Cary Grant, James Dean, and Montgomery Clift and Oscar winners John Gielgud and Charles Laughton. Director George Cukor (best director, *My Fair Lady*, 1965), admired for directing "women's" pictures, was reportedly known to be gay among the Hollywood community, even though it was not common knowledge to the public at large. Rumors persist about other Oscar winners. A 1997 issue of *Esquire* magazine suggested that Kevin Spacey's (best supporting actor, *The Usual Suspects*, 1994) homosexuality was the worst-kept secret in Hollywood, and there has been widespread speculation about one two-time best actress winner. Moreover, best actor nominee Nigel Hawthorne (*The Madness of King George*, 1995) and *Crying Game* (1992) supporting actor nominee Jaye Davidson have discussed their homosexuality frankly, and Rock Hudson (*Giant*, 1956, actor) gained instant legendary status by being the first former Oscar nominee to publicly announce that he was gay and had AIDS; none of them ever won an award, however. Other winners in nonmajor categories are fairly openly acknowledged as gay—Irving Berlin, composer of best song "White Christmas," and Peter Allen, coauthor of best song "Arthur's Theme," both won— but probably the first Oscar recipient for whom hiding his sexuality was not an issue is Robert Epstein, documentarian of *The Times of Harvey Milk* (1985) and *Common Threads: Stories from the Quilt* (1990).

Q. ... **person to be nominated for an Oscar for playing a character of the opposite sex? To win?**
A. John Lithgow, *The World According to Garp*

(1982, supporting actor). He played transsexual Roberta Muldoon; he lost to Louis Gossett Jr. for *An Officer and a Gentleman*. The following year, Linda Hunt won the best supporting actress Oscar playing Billy Kwan in *The Year of Living Dangerously*. Unlike with Lithgow, however, no reference was made of the fact that the actor and the character were of different genders. Jaye Davidson was nominated as supporting actor for *The Crying Game* (1992), playing a cross-dresser. There was no dispute that he was a man, however.

Race, Ethnicity, and National Origin

Q. ... African-American to win an Oscar?

A. Hattie McDaniel, *Gone with the Wind* (best supporting actress, 1939). She was also the first black to be nominated for an Oscar. (Her acceptance speech was written by the studio.) Other African-American performers who received Oscars: James Baskett (honorary) as Uncle Remus in *Song of the South* (1947); Sidney Poitier, best actor, *The Lilies of the Field* (1963); Louis Gossett Jr., best supporting actor, *An Officer and a Gentleman* (1982); Whoopi Goldberg, best supporting actress, *Ghost* (1990); Cuba Gooding Jr., best supporting actor, *Jerry Maguire* (1996). No African-American woman has ever won the Oscar in the leading actress category.

Q. ... African-American performer to be nominated in a leading role?

A. Dorothy Dandridge, *Carmen Jones* (1954).

Q. ... African-American director to receive a best director nomination?

A. John Singleton, *Boyz N the Hood* (1991).

Q. ... film with a predominantly black cast to receive an Oscar nomination?
A. *Hallelujah*, nominated for best director (King Vidor), 1929/30.

Q. ... year in which two or more black performers were nominated?
A. 1972, when both Cicely Tyson and Paul Winfield from *Sounder*, and Diana Ross from *Lady Sings the Blues*, received leading nominations. None won. In 1985, three more African-Americans were in competition: Whoopi Goldberg, Oprah Winfrey, and Margaret Avery, all from *The Color Purple*. Again, none turned out a winner.

Q. ... black performer to be nominated in two separate acting categories?
A. Morgan Freeman, who was nominated for supporting actor for *Street Smart* (1987), and for leading actor in *Driving Miss Daisy* (1989). He was also nominated a third time for best actor—*The Shawshank Redemption* (1994). Since Freeman, Whoopi Goldberg and Denzel Washington have each been nominated in both leading and supporting categories. Washington was the first black performer to receive three acting nominations—*Cry Freedom*, supporting actor, 1987; *Glory*, supporting actor (win), 1989; *Malcolm X*, actor 1992.

Q. ... black to present the best picture award?
A. Ralph Bunche at the 1950 awards, presented on March 29, 1951. Dr. Bunche himself won the 1950 Nobel Peace Prize.

Q. ... Asian to be nominated for an acting Oscar?
A. Depending on how you define your terms, Miyoshi Umeki, *Sayonara* (1957, supporting actress), is the first Asian to win. Arguably, Yul Brynner (best actor, *The King and I*, 1956) and Ben Kingsley (best actor, *Gandhi*, 1982), who were both

born in Asia (on an island off of Siberia and in India, respectively) and of at least one native parent, might also qualify. The only other Asians to have been nominated for an acting Oscar are: Sessue Hayakawa, *The Bridge on the River Kwai* (1957, supporting actor); Mako, *The Sand Pebbles* (1966, supporting actor); Noriyuki "Pat" Morita, *The Karate Kid* (1984, supporting actor); and Dr. Haing S. Ngor, *The Killing Fields* (1984, supporting actor [w]). No Asian has ever been nominated in a leading category. Perhaps Asia's greatest star, Toshiro Mifune—who appeared in the Oscar-winning Japanese films *Rashomon* and *Seven Samurai*—was never nominated, nor did he ever receive an honorary award. He died in 1997.

Q. ... year that minorities outnumbered Anglos in a single acting category?
A. 1984, when Haing S. Ngor [w], Noriyuki "Pat" Morita, and Adolph Caesar were up against Ralph Richardson and John Malkovich. It also marked the first time that a black and an Asian were in direct competition in acting.

Q. ... full-blooded Native American to be nominated for playing a Native American?
A. Chief Dan George, *Little Big Man* (1970, supporting actor). The only other nominee is Graham Greene, *Dances with Wolves* (1990, supporting actor).

Q. ... year in which all 10 leading acting nominees were Americans?
A. 1985.

Q. ... foreign language film nominated in any category?
A. *La Grande Illusion* (best picture, 1939; France). The only other foreign language films to be nominated for best picture are: *Z* (1969; Alge-

ria); *The Emigrants* (1972; Sweden); *Cries and Whispers* (1973; Sweden); and *Il Postino (The Postman)* (1995; Italy).

Q. **... foreign-language film to win an award in a general competitive category?**
A. *Marie-Louise* (1945), for its screenplay.

Q. **... non-Hollywood (non-American-made) film nominated for best picture?**
A. *The Private Life of King Henry VIII* (UK; 1932/33).

Q. **... performer from a foreign-made film to win an acting Oscar?**
A. Charles Laughton, *The Private Life of King Henry VIII* (UK; 1932/33).

Q. **... foreign-born performer to win an Oscar?**
A. Perhaps surprisingly, perhaps not, there is no dearth of foreign-*born* Oscar nominees, and winners, particularly in the early years. Although first-ever best actor winner Emil Jannings claimed to have been born in Brooklyn, N.Y., records indicate he was born in Switzerland; three of the first four best actress winners—Norma Shearer, Marie Dressler, even "America's Sweetheart" Mary Pickford—were Canadian-born; and the third best actor winner, George Arliss, was born in London, England.

Q. **... foreign language film to win a writing Oscar?**
A. *Marie-Louise* (1945, French). The only other foreign language writing winners are *Divorce, Italian Style* (1962, Italian) and *A Man and a Woman* (1966, French). *The Red Balloon* (1956), a short film that won a writing award, has no actual dialogue, although there is background conversation in French. *The Godfather* movies have substantial passages of Italian, and much of the dialogue in

Dances with Wolves is spoken in the Lakota Sioux language.

Q. **... song from a foreign film to win best song?**
A. "Never on Sunday," from *Never on Sunday* (1960, Greece).

Q. **... performer to win an acting Oscar for a foreign language film?**
A. Sophia Loren, best actress, *Two Women* (1961, Italy). Other performers who have won acting Oscars for a largely non-English-language performance include: Robert De Niro, best supporting actor, *The Godfather Part II* (1974; every line he speaks, except for "I'll make him an offer he can't refuse," is in Italian); Meryl Streep, best actress, *Sophie's Choice* (1981; large portions of her performance are in German and Polish); Haing S. Ngor, best supporting actor, *The Killing Fields* (1985; playing an interpreter, he speaks a good deal of Vietnamese in the movie); Marlee Matlin, best actress, *Children of a Lesser God* (1986; American Sign Language); and Graham Greene, best supporting actor, *Dances with Wolves* (1990; Sioux). *Dances with Wolves* nominees Kevin Costner and Mary McDonnell also spoke Sioux, although not as much as Greene.

Q. **... best director nominee for a foreign language film?**
A. Federico Fellini, *La Dolce Vita* (1961, Italy). Although it took a little while for the process to get started, the 1960s was the beginning of a fertile period for nominating foreign language directors. Other nominees include: Pietro Germi, *Divorce, Italian Style* (1962, Italy); Federico Fellini, *8½* (1963, Italy); Hiroshi Teshigahara, *Woman of the Dunes* (1965, Japan); Claude Lelouche, *A Man and a Woman* (1966, France); Gillo Pontecorvo, *The*

Battle of Algiers (1968, Italy); Costa-Gavras, *Z* (1969, Algeria); Federico Fellini, *Satyricon* (1970, Italy); Jan Troell, *The Emigrants* (1972, Sweden); Ingmar Bergman, *Cries and Whispers* (1973, Sweden); Bernardo Bertolucci, *Last Tango in Paris* (1973, France/Italy; 1973 was the first year in which two best director nominations were given to foreign language films); François Truffaut, *Day for Night* (1974, France); Federico Fellini, *Amarcord* (1975, Italy); Ingmar Bergman, *Face to Face* (1976); Lina Wertmuller, *Seven Beauties* (1976, Italy); Eduardo Molinaro, *La Cage aux Folles* (1979, France); Wolfgang Petersen, *Das Boot* (1982, Germany); Ingmar Bergman, *Fanny and Alexander* (1983, Sweden); Akira Kurasawa, *Ran* (1985, Japan); Lasse Hallstrom, *My Life As a Dog* (1987, Sweden); Krzysztof Kieslowski, *Red* (1994, Switzerland/France/Poland); Michael Radford, *Il Postino (The Postman)* (1995, Italy). Radford's nomination is interesting because he is a native English speaker who could only receive financing for his film from Italian investors, who required that the film be made in the Italian language. Jean Renoir, director of the first foreign language best picture nominee, *La Grande Illusion*, received his only directing nomination for *The Southerner* (1975), which was in English.

Q.   ... year in which all of the best director nominees were foreign-born?
A.   The year was 1987: Bernardo Bertolucci, *The Last Emperor* (Italian; winner); Lasse Hallstrom, *My Life As a Dog* (Swedish); Adrian Lyne, *Fatal Attraction*, and John Boorman, *Hope and Glory* (British); and Norman Jewison, *Moonstruck* (Canadian).

Q.   ... foreign language film to receive a record six Oscar nominations?

A. *Das Boot* (1982), followed the next year by *Fanny and Alexander* (1983). *Das Boot* received no awards, *Fanny* won for foreign language film, cinematography, and art direction. *Das Boot* is also unique in that it was *not* nominated for best foreign language film, so all of its nominations were in categories directly competitive with all other films.

Q. ... **performer to receive acting nominations for both foreign language and English language performances?**

A. Marlon Brando had just won his second Oscar when he was nominated again for *Last Tango in Paris* (1973) in which more than half his dialogue was spoken in French. Ingrid Bergman received three Oscars in English before her final nomination, for *Autumn Sonata* (1978), which was completely in her native Swedish. Robert De Niro's primarily Italian language performance in *The Godfather Part II* (1974) was followed by his all-English work as Travis Bickle in *Taxi Driver* (1976).

African-Americans at the Oscars

Beginning with Hattie McDaniel, who was the first black nominee *and* the first winner, African-Americans have slowly increased their numbers in the nominations for major-category Oscars. Thankfully, it is no longer considered newsworthy when an African-American is nominated or wins.

Actor nominees

Sidney Poitier, *The Defiant Ones* (1958)
Sidney Poitier, *The Lilies of the Field* (1963) [w]
James Earl Jones, *The Great White Hope* (1970)
Paul Winfield, *Sounder* (1972)
Dexter Gordon, *'Round Midnight* (1986)

Morgan Freeman, *Driving Miss Daisy* (1989)
Denzel Washington, *Malcolm X* (1992)
Laurence Fishburne, *What's Love Got to Do with It* (1993)
Morgan Freeman, *The Shawshank Redemption* (1994)

Actress nominees

Dorothy Dandridge, *Carmen Jones* (1954)
Diana Ross, *Lady Sings the Blues* (1972)
Cicely Tyson, *Sounder* (1972)
Diahann Carroll, *Claudine* (1974)
Whoopi Goldberg, *The Color Purple* (1985)
Angela Bassett, *What's Love Got to Do with It* (1993)

Supporting actor nominees

Rupert Crosse, *The Reivers* (1969)
Louis Gossett Jr., *An Officer and a Gentleman* (1982) [w]
Adolph Caesar, *A Soldier's Story* (1994)
Morgan Freeman, *Street Smart* (1987)
Denzel Washington, *Cry Freedom* (1987)
Denzel Washington, *Glory* (1989) [w]
Jaye Davidson, *The Crying Game* (1992)
Samuel L. Jackson, *Pulp Fiction* (1994)
Cuba Gooding Jr., *Jerry Maguire* (1996) [w]

Supporting actress nominees

Hattie McDaniel, *Gone with the Wind* (1939) [w]
Ethel Waters, *Pinky* (1949)
Ethel Waters, *The Member of the Wedding* (1952)
Juanita Moore, *Imitation of Life* (1959)
Beah Richards, *Guess Who's Coming to Dinner* (1967)
Margaret Avery, *The Color Purple* (1985)
Oprah Winfrey, *The Color Purple* (1985)

Whoopi Goldberg, *Ghost* (1990) [w]
Marianne Jean-Baptiste, *Secrets & Lies* (1996)

Director nominee

John Singleton, *Boyz N the Hood* (1991)

Other Assorted Taboos and Odd Records

Q. ... X-rated film to receive a best picture nomination?

A. *Midnight Cowboy* (1969). The rating system was still new, and X did not necessarily imply pornographic. Its official rating was later reduced to R. No NC-17 film has ever received a best picture nomination.

Q. ... male Oscar nominee to be fully frontally nude in a film?

A. Jaye Davidson, *The Crying Game* (1993, supporting actor).

Q. ... performer playing an alcoholic/drug addict to receive an Oscar nomination?

A. During the heyday of the Production Code, topics such as drug addition were too controversial to be addressed outright (despite a great tolerance for casual upper-class alcoholism in films from the '30s). Depending on what standard you employ, you could say that William Powell in *The Thin Man* (1934) was the first actor portraying an alcoholic to be nominated for an Oscar. Other actors portraying alcoholics to win in the early days include Thomas Mitchell in *Stagecoach* (1939) and James Stewart in *The Philadelphia Story* (1940). (Stewart, though technically not playing an alcoholic in the film, won the award owing in part to his riotous drunk scene.) Ray Milland in *The Lost Weekend* (1945) won for the first "issue" film about alcoholism, where a dipsomaniac was the main character. The first person playing an actual junkie to receive an Oscar nomination is Frank Sinatra in *The Man with the Golden Arm* (1955).

Q. ... films nominated for major Oscars to have one of the following serious themes: cannibalism, pedophilia, lesbianism, psychoanalysis?

A. Cannibalism was the shocking secret in *Suddenly Last Summer* (1959); a married-but-chaste teenaged girl who is the object of seduction attempts was the controversial premise for *Baby Doll* (1955); an accusation of lesbianism against a teacher was the explicit topic of *The Children's Hour* (1961), a remake of *These Three* (1936) which, due to the Production Code, was changed to adultery; and the first best picture nominee to be "about" psychoanalysis is the romantic, overwrought melodrama *Spellbound* (1945).

Q. ... stunt man to receive an Oscar?

A. Yakim Canutt, honorary (1966). In an age where lots of actors make hay over doing some of the own stunts, Canutt, one of the greatest stuntmen of his day, did everyone else's. His honorary award is the first one ever presented to a stuntman for stunts (John Wayne was a former stuntman). The only other stunt recipient is Hal Needham, who won a technical award for designing and developing a car and crane.

Q. ... out-and-out sequel to be nominated for best picture?

A. *The Bells of St. Mary's* (1945; sequel to *Going My Way*, 1944). Earlier movies that capitalized on prior films, without actually being sequels, include *The Broadway Melody of 1936* (1935), a best picture nominee that followed in the shoes of best picture winner *The Broadway Melody* (1928/29); and *Madame Curie* (1943) which coasted on the success of 1942's *Mrs. Miniver* by reuniting its stars, Greer Garson and Walter Pidgeon, in another tearful prestige picture.

Q. ... sequel to win for best picture?
A. *The Godfather Part II* (1974; sequel to *The Godfather*, 1972). In the case of both *Going My Way* and *The Godfather*, the originals won a best picture award.

Q. ... remake to win for best picture?
A. *Ben-Hur* (1959). Cecil B. DeMille had made a silent version in 1925.

Q. ... blind Oscar winner?
A. Stevie Wonder, for the song "I Just Called to Say I Love You" from *The Woman in Red* (1984).

Q. ... performer to receive three Oscars?
A. Walter Brennan, all for best supporting actor: *Come and Get It* (1936), *Kentucky* (1938), and *The Westerner* (1940).

Q. ... director to receive three Oscars?
A. Frank Capra, who was as prolific as Brennan during the same period, also winning in alternate years: *It Happened One Night* (1934), *Mr. Deeds Goes to Town* (1936), and *You Can't Take It with You* (1938).

Q. ... performer to be nominated in leading and supporting categories?
A. Fay Bainter, leading actress, *White Banners,* and supporting actress, *Jezebel* (both 1938).

Q. ... winner in a leading acting category to be later nominated in a supporting category?
A. Overall (and for women) it was Jennifer Jones, best actress winner in 1943 for *The Song of Ber-*

nadette and nominated the next year for supporting actress in *Since You Went Away*. For men, it was Victor McLaglen, best actor winner, *The Informer* (1935); best supporting actor nominee, *The Quiet Man* (1952).

Q.   ... **person to win an acting Oscar for his or her film debut?**
A.   Gale Sondergaard, *Anthony Adverse* (1936). She was also the first woman to receive the supporting actress award.

First-timers

Who says there's no such thing as an overnight success? After Sondergaard, a number of actors have won Oscars for their debut film, or in their first year as a film actor. At least one explanation for this oddity is that audiences hadn't had a chance to get bored by the actor's tricks; they were still fresh enough that Academy voters were able to believe they had a lot ahead of them. Consider: Of the following 19 performers, only five were able to parlay their early win into a subsequent nomination, and *none* has ever won two acting awards.

Actor winners

Yul Brynner
Ben Kingsley
Geoffrey Rush

Actress winners

Shirley Booth
Julie Andrews
Barbra Streisand
Marlee Matlin

Supporting actor winners

Harold Russell
Timothy Hutton
Haing S. Ngor

Supporting actress winners

Gale Sondergaard
Mercedes McCambridge
Eva Marie Saint
Jo Van Fleet
Miyoshi Umeki
Estelle Parsons
Tatum O'Neal
Anna Paquin

Q. ... person to receive consecutive Oscars?

A. Luise Rainer, best actress, *The Great Ziegfeld* (1936) and *The Good Earth* (1937). Other first consecutive-year Oscar winners (excluding multiple-recipients in a single year) in the major categories are:

• Actor: Spencer Tracy, *Captains Courageous* (1937) and *Boys Town* (1938).

• Picture (to the producer): David O. Selznick, *Gone with the Wind* (1939) and *Rebecca* (1940).

• Director and screenplay: Joseph L. Mankiewicz, *A Letter to Three Wives* (1949) and *All About Eve* (1950).

• Supporting actor: Jason Robards, *All the President's Men* (1976) and *Julia* (1977). (No supporting actress has ever received consecutive Oscars.)

Q. ... category in which all the nominees were from the same studio?

A. Best actress, 1931/32: all the nominees were

from MGM. In 1974, Paramount repeated the feat in the category of best costume design.

Q. ... year in which all best picture nominees were in color?

A. 1956. The nominees were *Around the World in 80 Days* [w], *Friendly Persuasion, Giant, The King and I,* and *The Ten Commandments.*

Q. ... team to be nominated for directing?

A. Jerome Robbins and Robert Wise, *West Side Story* (1961). They also won. Interestingly, neither mentioned the other in his acceptance speech. There was only one other directing team ever nominated: Warren Beatty and Buck Henry, *Heaven Can Wait* (1978).

Q. ... person to present himself with an Oscar?

A. Walt Disney, in 1936.

Q. ... person to receive a posthumous Oscar?

A. Douglas Fairbanks (a commemorative award) in 1939.

Q. ... performer nominated for an Oscar posthumously?

A. Jeanne Eagels, *The Letter* (1928/29).

Q. ... performer to receive a posthumous award for acting?

A. Peter Finch, best actor, *Network* (1976). He's also the *only* posthumous winner to date.

Q. ... academy Award winner to die?

A. Joseph Farnham, best title writing 1927/28. He died two years later.

Last rites

Perhaps no aspect of Oscar presentation is more suspect than the old-timer who gets nominated late in his career; any win is seen as a sympathy prize. Of course, you could argue there's nothing wrong with that; how many times has the Academy had to contend with the disingenuous surprise of commentators asking, "How could you never have awarded X an Oscar after so many great performances?" After all, aren't we all *glad* to see Henry Fonda win, finally? The following performers all won an Oscar for their final film, or were nominated posthumously:

- Jeanne Eagels (posthumous nominee for actress)
- James Dean (two posthumous nominations for actor)
- Spencer Tracy (posthumous nominee for actor)
- Peter Finch (posthumous winner for actor)
- Ralph Richardson (posthumous nominee for supporting actor)
- Massimo Troisi (posthumous nominee for actor)

Special mention. Henry Fonda who won the best actor award for what was generally acknowledged to be his last film; indeed, he died five months later.

The Ceremony: High Kitsch, High Drama

SPEECH! SPEECH!

The humor and camp of the Oscars is, at least in part, the fun of the three-plus-hour show. Despite the best efforts of the show's producers, the Oscarcast is hardly known for its witty banter. Maybe that's why the best hosts—and often the best presenters—have never themselves been Oscar nominees. There are different skills involved in being a fluid MC and a gifted thespian; a difference between acting a character and being yourself on stage; a difference between preparation and surprise.

The Oscars may be derided for the overlong, gushing lists of names no one has ever heard of, but you cannot deny that if you get beyond the lists themselves, much of the time there's a beautiful sentiment underneath. What follows are selections over the years from some of my favorite banter, some memorable acceptance speeches, some amusing introductions, and impromptu hosting jobs:

Quiz: The Ceremony

Q. **What presentation ran the longest? The shortest?**

A. The 1997 ceremony ran three hours and 47 minutes—33 minutes longer than the best picture winner that year, *Titanic*. A close second is the 1983 program, which lasted three hours and 42 minutes. (In the early days, it took far less time to hand out the awards—five to ten minutes at the first ceremony.)

Q. What two performers to win Oscars since 1970 are the only ones who wore eyeglasses from the time they left their seats all the way through their time at the podium?

A. Art Carney (best actor, *Harry and Tonto*, 1974) and Marlee Matlin (best actress, *Children of a Lesser God*, 1986).

Q. Who did Muhammad Ali "spar" with at the 1976 Oscarcast?

A. Sylvester Stallone.

Q. Who was Clint Eastwood pinch-hitting for at the 1972 Oscars when he was forced to improvise an introduction?

A. Charleton Heston. Heston arrived momentarily to relieve an obviously rattled Eastwood.

Q. When was the Oscarcast first televised? Over what network?

A. The Oscars have been broadcast on television since 1952, beginning with NBC. The ceremony appeared on NBC a total of 12 times, it has aired on ABC a total of 34 times as of 1997 and has appeared on ABC every year since 1975.

Q. Only once were the two leading performer Oscars in one year presented for actors portraying real-life, living people. What was the year, who were the actors, and what real-life people did they play?

A. In 1980, Loretta Lynn was in the audience watching Sissy Spacek accept the best actress award for *Coal Miner's Daughter*, in which Spacek portrayed Lynn; that same year, Jake LaMotta looked on from the Dorothy Chandler Pavilion as Robert De Niro won best actor for portraying LaMotta in *Raging Bull*.

Q. **Where has the Academy Award ceremony most often occurred?**
A. Twenty-four times it has been held at the Dorothy Chandler Pavilion. Other popular spots are: the RKO Pantages Theater (11 times); the Santa Monica Civic Auditorium (8); The Biltmore Hotel (8); the Shrine Auditorium (8); the Ambassador Hotel (6); Graumann's Chinese Theater (3); the Academy Theater (1); and Roosevelt Hotel (1). (For the first five years of broadcasting on television, the ceremony was cohosted out of the NBC Century Theater in New York City.) In the spring of 1998, soon after the 1997 awards were given, the Academy announced plans to finally build its own auditorium for the ceremonies.

Q. **Who has hosted the Oscar ceremony the most times?**
A. Bob Hope, who hosted 18 times between 1939 and 1977. Other multiple hosts of note include Billy Crystal (6 times), Johnny Carson (5), Jack Lemmon (4), and David Niven (3).[3]

Q. **How many one-armed push-ups did Jack Palance do when he won best supporting actor in 1991 for *City Slickers*?**
A. Four.

Q. **Best costume design winner Lizzy Gardiner (*The Adventures of Priscilla, Queen of the Desert*) had the most eye-catching dress in the history of the**

---

[3] In 1968, 1969, and 1970, the ceremony was hosted by "the friends of Oscar," a definition which numbered in the dozens. None of these "friends" is included in this list.

Oscars in 1994. Out of what unconventional material was the dress made?
A.   Her outfit was comprised of American Express gold cards.

Q.   **When were the most awards handed out? The fewest?**
A.   The year when the fewest awards were presented is an easy answer—in 1928/29, there were fewer categories (only one writing award), fewer multiple winners (no film won more than one Oscar, and each category had only one recipient), no special awards, and fewer overall nominees accepting the seven trophies. Figuring out "the most" is more challenging, depending on whether you count all the individual plaques, statuettes, certificates, technical winners, and honorary awards. The year with the most categories—and therefore the most individual films to be nominated in a competitive category—was 1956, when there were 27 separate categories (the design awards were still divided into black-and-white and color, there were three writing trophies, and best foreign language film was made competitive for the first time).

Q.   **How many times did best director winner Jonathan Demme say "uh" or "um" during his acceptance speech in 1991?**
A.   It's difficult to count them all during the lengthy speech, because he sometimes slurred together an "um" and the beginning of another word, but they number at least 90.

Q.   **Who was the first African-American woman to serve as an Oscar presenter? Who was the first African-American to perform a nominated song?**
A.   In both instances, the answer is Dorothy Dandridge, a presenter in 1954 (the same year she was

nominated as best actress for *Carmen Jones*) and performer in 1956.

Q. When was the first time an Oscar-winning black performer presented an Academy Award to another black performer? Who were the individuals involved?

A. 1990, when Denzel Washington, the previous year's winner for best supporting actor for *Glory*, presented the best supporting actress award to Whoopi Goldberg for *Ghost*.

Q. In what years were the ceremonies delayed for flooding, for an assassination, and for an assassination attempt?

A. 1937; 1968; and 1980. The awards, of course, took place the following calendar year. In 1968, the ceremony was postponed until the day after Martin Luther King Jr.'s funeral; in 1980, newly elected President Reagan was shot at by John Hinckley, and as President Reagan was a former actor and had prerecorded a greeting to the Academy, it was deemed appropriate to delay until his health was better established.

Q. What director did Jeremy Irons mention in his acceptance speech for *Reversal of Fortune* (1990)?

A. David Cronenberg. Cronenberg directed Irons in *Dead Ringers*, which many had anticipated would draw Irons an Oscar nomination (it did not; the same fate befell Jeff Goldblum in Cronenberg's *The Fly*). Irons obviously felt that giving credit where it is due is the most significant thing an acceptance speech can offer.

Q. Who is Jack Valenti?

A. The white-maned, tight-jawed president of the Motion Picture Association of America—which has no *direct* relation to the Academy—is the man in charge of the "ratings" board. He has been called "Hollywood's ambassador to Washington," owing largely to his D.C. connections (he served as LBJ's press secretary) and the existence of the MPAA as an internal industry watchdog charged with policing the film industry. Exactly why he is afforded a platform at almost every ceremony remains a mystery.

Q. **Who are those well-dressed strangers who often seem to be sitting next to the celebrities?**
A. If you think it's hard to sit still watching the Oscars at home, imagine what it is like being in the audience, wondering if your name is going to be called. So even the nominees get up to go to the bathroom and stretch their legs and such. Those sartorial strangers are basically glorified ushers who take the seats of all the celebrities who storm out in a huff or go backstage to accept their awards, so that the camera doesn't let folks at home know that not everyone will take the Academy's choices sitting down.

Q. **Name at least two *presenters* who received standing ovations.**
A. In 1978, John Wayne, whose battle with cancer had been covered in the press, appeared to present the best picture award. Within three months, he had died. Sean Connery received two standing ovations in 1987—the first occurring when he appeared to present the award for best special effects. (Several minutes later, he won the best supporting actor trophy.) There may have been more, but certainly these are two of the most memorable. (N.B.—In 1992, Bob Hope got a standing ovation as nothing more than an audience member when the former multiple Oscar host was recognized by Billy Crystal. Christopher Reeve received two

standing ovations when he appeared to introduce a film clip about socially conscious movies.)

Q. Standing ovations are normally reserved for actors, directors, and producers; name the winner of a *screenplay* award who received a standing ovation.

A. Billy Bob Thornton, best adapted screenplay, *Sling Blade* (1996). Thornton also directed and starred in the simple, prosaically elegant morality play, which was the sleeper hit of 1996. His victory over the more favored Anthony Minghella for *The English Patient* also added to the suspense about who would win the best actor award, for which Thornton was also nominated. (He lost to Geoffrey Rush in *Shine*.)

Q. Who sang "Talk to the Animals" at the 1967 Oscars?

A. Sammy Davis Jr.

Q. Has any winner ever been booed?

A. Yes, on several unwelcome occasions, including during Vanessa Redgrave's "Zionist hoodlums" speech for winning in *Julia* (1977), and when Orson Welles won his only Oscar, for co-writing the screenplay of *Citizen Kane* (1941).

Q. Who rejected the best actor award on behalf of Marlon Brando when he won for *The Godfather* (1972)? Why did he say he was turning it down?

A. Sasheen Littlefeather rejected on his behalf as a protest for the poor treatment of Native Americans in Hollywood. *She* was booed, too, though she obviously was not a "winner."

Q. Why did George C. Scott turn down his Oscar for *Patton* (1970)?

A. Allegedly, Scott was embarrassed by his own cutthroat campaigning for *Anatomy of a Murder*

(1959), and hated considering himself in competition with his fellow nominees. (His rejection of it, though, remains suspicious. The following year, he was nominated again, and did *not* publicly announce his rejection; and later the same year as *Patton*, he *accepted* an Emmy award.)

Quiz: A Little Levity

Q. **Name the presenter, host, honoree or sore loser responsible for the following quotes.**

- **"Good evening, Hollywood phonies."**
  A. Chevy Chase.

- **"It's not as sexy, perhaps, as best picture or best director, but still, it is one of the most beloved and anxiety-producing categories at Oscar parties across the country, because as we all know, whoever gets this one right inevitably goes on to win the pool."**
  A. Ron Silver, presenting best documentary feature (with Phoebe Cates) at the 1990 awards.

- **"I guess you didn't think it was possible for anyone to overdress for this affair."**
  A. A flamboyantly decorated Bette Midler, before presenting the best song award at the 1980 Oscars.

- **"I have it on good authority that Cher will in fact be dressed. She apparently has decided against the simple but elegant wardrobe of dress shields and Odor-Eaters and is going for the full body covering."**
  A. Chevy Chase, mocking Cher's well-known skimpy outfits.

- *"Jerry Maguire* is a moving and funny American film which accomplishes an impossible task: It makes you feel sorry for an agent."
  A. Steve Martin, introducing one of the 1996 best picture nominees.

- "Before I came I went to visit Jane Austen's grave in Winchester Cathedral, to pay my respects, you know, and tell her about the grosses."
  A. Emma Thompson, accepting her best adapted screenplay award for *Sense and Sensibility* (1995).

- "Now, I'm nominated tonight, and I realize I'm not exactly the odds-on favorite. But I traveled 13,000 miles to be here for this—I come from the other side of the planet. And if they read out someone else's name instead of mine, it's not gonna be pretty."
  A. Host Paul Hogan (1986).

- "I think *The Godfather Part II* has an excellent chance of winning. Neither Mr. Price nor Mr. Waterhouse has been seen in days."
  A. A traditional Bob Hope one-liner, in 1974.

- "You've just provided me with the makings of one hell of a weekend in Dublin."
  A. Daniel Day-Lewis, winning for best actor (*My Left Foot*, 1989).

- "There are directors who know everything about human behavior and nothing about the camera. There are directors who know camera angles, camera lenses, camera sprockets, and depth of focus but who are totally igno-

rant of the human condition. We have *all* of these directors with us tonight."
A.   Walter Matthau and Jack Lemmon, presenting the best director award at the 1981 Oscars.

* "Tonight is the night we honor people for individual achievement and also for bodies of work, and looking at this crowd some of your bodies have had a lot of work."
A.   Billy Crystal, hosting the 1992 awards.

Graciousness, Honesty, and Class

* "I have a lot of people to thank and I'm going to be one of those people that tries to mention a lot of names, because I know just two seconds ago my mother and father went berserk and I'd like to give some other mothers and fathers that opportunity."
A.   Meryl Streep, accepting her best actress award for *Sophie's Choice* (1981).

* "I'm so surprised. It's true I didn't prepare anything. I thought Lauren was going to get it, and I think she deserves it."
A.   Juliette Binoche, the surprise supporting actress winner, defeating the favorite Lauren Bacall (1996).

* "I consider this woman the greatest actress in the English language."
A.   F. Murray Abraham, seconds before announcing that Geraldine Page had won as best actress for *The Trip to Bountiful* (1985).

* "As a messenger, peer, and movie lover, I stand here tonight to tell you five nominees the best news of all: You have moved me, moved

**the Academy, moved the people; your per-
formances took us somewhere we have never
been, somewhere strange and familiar, and we
are changed forever by that glimpse, that moment, that intimacy, and that surrender, all of
it etched in celluloid."**

A.   Jodie Foster, presenting the best actor award
at the 1989 ceremony, and proving that a presenter doesn't need to be funny, and that a great
actress can convey a sincere sentiment quite
movingly.

• **"Omigod, the winner is George C. Scott!"**
A.   Goldie Hawn, presenting the best actor
award in 1970. Scott had already announced that
he would not accept the award.

• **"As George C. Scott didn't get around to saying last year, thank you."**
A.   Helen Hayes, in 1971.

• **"When I was 19 years old, I was the number-
one star of the world for two years; when I
was 40 nobody wanted me—I couldn't get a
job."**
A.   Mickey Rooney, expressing some bitterness
on receiving his honorary award in 1982.

• **"I'd also thank Tom Hanks, Max von Sydow,
Edward James Olmos, and my good friend
Gene Hackman for their wonderful work,
even if they didn't vote for me. . . . I didn't
vote for you guys either."**
A.   Dustin Hoffman, on winning as best actor
for *Rain Man* (1988).

- "There's only one thing that's missing for me tonight and that is having Tom Hulce standing by my side."

A. F. Murray Abraham, praising his *Amadeus* costar.

Naked Sentiment

- "Well, it looks like you all hated me so much that you have given me this award for it, and I'm loving every minute of it. And all I can say is I've loved being hated by you."

A. Louise Fletcher, best actress for her villainous performance as Nurse Ratched in *One Flew Over the Cuckoo's Nest* (1975). Fletcher then proceeded to sign her acceptance to her deaf parents.

- "It's very easy for people to trivialize what we do sometimes and they do it in ways of saying, 'Well, if it's such a big deal, how come nobody remembers who last year won the Oscar.' Well, I've got a real flash for you: I will never forget what happened here tonight; my family will never forget what happened here; my Native American brothers and sisters around the country, especially the Lakota Sioux, will never forget; people I went to school with will never forget."

A. Kevin Costner, stammering over his acceptance for best picture for *Dances with Wolves* in 1990.

- "I know that my work in this case is magnified by the fact that the streets of heaven are too crowded with angels. We know their names. They number a thousand for each one of the red ribbons that we wear here tonight. They finally rest in the warm embrace of the

gracious creator of us all, a healing embrace
that cools their fevers, that clears their skin,
and allows their eyes to see a simple, self-
evident commonsense truth that is made man-
ifest by the benevolent creator of us all. It was
written down on paper by wise men, tolerant
men, in the city of Philadelphia 200 years
ago.''
A.   Tom Hanks, winning his first Oscar playing
a gay AIDS victim in *Philadelphia* (1993).

Three Beautiful Speeches

1.   Laurence Olivier was nominated for best actor
in 1978 (for *The Boys from Brazil*), but he was a
long shot, especially considering that he was to
receive an honorary award at the same ceremony.
After an introduction by Cary Grant, he delivered
the following address. (I remember as a child, after
the speech my mother, who was not one for star-
gazing or even much of a movie fan, turned to me
and said: "*That's* why he's considered the greatest
actor in the world.")

> *Oh, dear friends, am I supposed to speak
> after that? Cary, my dear old friend for
> many a year, from the earliest years of either
> of us working in this country. Thank you for
> that beautiful citation and the trouble you
> have taken to make it and all the warm gen-
> erosities in it. Mr. President and governors
> of the Academy, committee members, fel-
> lows, my very noble and approved good
> masters, my colleagues, my friends, my fel-
> low students. In the great wealth, the great
> firmament of your nation's generosities, this*

*particular choice may perhaps be found by
future generations as a trifle eccentric, but
the mere fact of it—the prodigal, pure human kindness of it—must be seen as a beautiful star in that firmament, which shines
upon me at this moment—dazzling me a little, but filling me with the warmth of the ex-
traordinary elation, the euphoria that
happens to so many of us at the first breath
of the majestic glow of a new tomorrow.
From the top of this moment, in the solace,
in the kindly emotion that is charging my
soul and my heart at this moment, I thank
you for this great gift, which lends me such
a very splendid part of this, your glorious
occasion. Thank you.*

2. There has probably never been a more touching impromptu sentiment expressed at the Oscars
than this tribute by William Holden to his dear
friend and former costar Barbara Stanwyck at the
1977 ceremony: "Before Barbara and I present
this next award, I'd like to say something. Thirty-
nine years ago this month, we were working on a
film together called *Golden Boy*, and it wasn't going well because I was going to be replaced. But
due to this lovely human being [touching Stanwyck's arm] and her interest and understanding,
and her professional integrity, and her encouragement and above all her generosity, I am here tonight." Stanwyck, shaken and moved, responded
only with "Oh, Bill!" and fell into his arms.

3. Four years later, on accepting her honorary
award the year after Holden's death, Stanwyck
concluded by saying: "I loved [Bill Holden] very
much and I miss him. He always wished I would

get an Oscar, and so tonight, my golden boy, you got your wish.''

. . . AND THE GREATEST SINGLE MOMENT IN OSCAR HISTORY

That's a pretty definitive statement, but one I feel confident would be backed up by anyone who saw it: the audience reaction immediately after the following five words: "Ladies and gentlemen: Christopher Reeve." The *Superman* star was paralyzed in a horse-riding accident in 1995, and his appearance at the Academy Awards ceremony the next year was probably the most emotional, least affected tribute to the human spirit the Oscars have ever been witness to. A standing ovation began immediately, and continued unabated for well over a minute. After Reeve introduced a tribute to films dealing with social issues, he received a *second* standing ovation.

There wasn't a dry eye in the house.

And the Winner is . . .

Presenting the best picture Oscar wasn't always the greatest honor at the Oscars; occasionally over the years, best picture hasn't even been the last award presented that evening (once it was even followed by the arcane scientific and technical categories). Yet a list of best picture presenters is something of a who's who of top Hollywood talent over the years, and whether they realized it at the time or not, the following people are among a select group: they have presented the best picture award more than once.

Two-time presenters

Eric Johnston
Gary Cooper
Frank Capra*
Warren Beatty
Sidney Poitier
Al Pacino †

Three-time presenter

Elizabeth Taylor**

Four-time presenter

Audrey Hepburn

Five-time presenter

Jack Nicholson‡

Missing you

Not every Oscar trophy gets the red carpet treatment. Sure, everyone says they treat their awards nicely or want to put them under glass, but some end up at strange ends, or at least in peculiar places. Do you know what happened to each of the following winners' Oscar?

• Alice Brady wasn't present to accept her best supporting actress award in 1937—only the sec-

---

*The greatest time gap between multiple best picture presentations: first in 1938, again in 1983.

†Copresenter with Robert De Niro in 1994.

**In 1991, copresented the award with Paul Newman.

‡Copresenter with Warren Beatty in 1989; the only person to present the best picture award in consecutive years (1976 and 1977).

ond time the category was handed out—but *someone* did: He walked to the podium, accepted it on her behalf, and disappeared, and neither he nor the Oscar were ever seen again. Brady got a replacement, but she died within two years.

• Spencer Tracy grudgingly agreed to lend his Oscar for *Boys Town* to the orphanage that bore its name.

• Vivien Leigh was scheduled to be a presenter at the Oscars, but had a nervous breakdown instead. While she was in the hospital, thieves broke into her home and stole valuables, including her Oscar.

• Ernest Borgnine's best actor trophy was destroyed in a house fire; the Academy supplied a replacement.

• In his autobiography, Marlon Brando claims that he lost track of his Oscar for *On the Waterfront*, not having seen it or having any idea as to its whereabouts for decades.

• Shelley Winters's Oscar for *The Diary of Anne Frank* resided for some time at the shrine to Anne Frank in Amsterdam.

• Harold Russell, the handless veteran who won two Oscars (one for supporting actor, one honorary) for *The Best Years of Our Lives*, auctioned off one of his awards in 1991 in order to pay for his wife's surgery.

• Barry Fitzgerald's Oscar was handed out during World War II, and so was made of plaster—at least until he bumped it with a golf club and knocked its head off. He got a metal replacement.

• Best screenplay winner John Osborne, one of the pioneers of the "Angry Young Man" cinema to emerge from England in the late '50s and early

'60s, was so destitute he sold his Oscar to raise money.

• According to legend, Woody Allen has never picked up any of his Oscars from the Academy, and they remain waiting for him. Of course, George C. Scott and Marlon Brando (the second time around, at least) made it clear they did not even want the invitation.

• Jimmy Stewart's Oscar for *The Philadelphia Story* spent years on display in his father's hardware store window back in Indiana.

For the record. The Academy does not condone selling Oscars, and has a standing rule that anyone who doesn't want it anymore can sell it back to the Academy . . . for one dollar. That hasn't prevented Russell, Osborne, and others from auctioning off their Oscars, sometimes for tens of thousands of dollars.

Part III
Trivia by Decade

The '20s and '30s: Growing Pains

THE ACADEMY TAKES ITS FIRST STEPS

The Academy itself was officially founded as a California nonprofit corporation on May 4, 1927, by a few dozen Hollywood power-hitters. It had its origins as a labor dispute mechanism, but quickly blossomed into an institution interested in improving the image of the movie business through a structured, formal organization. Douglas Fairbanks was its first president and founder, along with wife Mary Pickford, studio honcho Louis B. Mayer, designer Cedric Gibbons, and others. The creation of the award itself occurred within a week of its establishment, at a banquet on May 11, 1927, when Mayer suggested that the Academy and the industry bring itself artistic distinction by handing out self-congratulatory awards to its industry fellows.

Gibbons, an MGM art director, hastily sketched the design of the statuette that would become an enduring icon of quality, ego, kitsch, and glamour—a naked man holding a sword, standing atop a reel of film whose five spokes signified the five original branches of the Academy (actors, directors, producers, writers, and technicians). The statuette was sculpted by George Stanley in 1928. For a few years, the statuette was cast in bronze with gold plating; it has had its current makeup since 1930. The reel base was Belgian black marble until 1945, when the base was made of metal. During World

War II, from 1942 through 1944, plaster statuettes were given. These were replaced with metal ones when the materials became available again after the war. The size of the base was standardized from the 1945 ceremony till the present.

THE AWARDING CEREMONY: WORKING OUT THE KINKS

The first awards were presented on May 16, 1929, but there were kinks to be worked out. Some categories lasted only one or two years; others stuck around in slightly renamed formats. For example, names for the individual writing awards have varied from ''screenplay'' and ''original story'' to ''story and screenplay based on material not previously published or produced,'' and ''interior decoration'' developed into ''art direction (including set decoration),'' and ''sound recording'' became merely ''sound.''

There was always bound to be a little self-dealing worked into the self-congratulations. Gibbons himself received more Oscar nominations (and arguably more wins) that anyone else in Academy history, including the second award ever presented in the ''interior decoration'' (later ''art direction'') category. Louis B. Mayer could claim the second best picture winner, *The Broadway Melody*, and Pickford won the second best actress trophy presented (for *Coquette*—it was her only nomination and win ever, although she did receive a honorary award in 1975).

⚙ Oscar's Statistics

Height: 13½ inches
(10½ inches of Oscar, 3 inches of base)
Base diameter: 5¼ inches

Weight: 8½ pounds
Design copyrighted: September 2, 1941
Materials: Britannia metal alloy, then copper-, nickel-, silver- and 24-karat gold-plated.

DO I HEAR A SECOND OF THAT MOTION?

The nomination procedure also has its share of detractors from early in the Academy's history. The first year, the list of winners was announced without reference to the nominees, and the awards not presented until three months later; and for several years, the details of the winners' lists weren't much of a secret: from 1932/33 through 1935, the Academy actually announced not only the winners, but who placed and showed in the polling. Thus, in 1935, although *Mutiny on the Bounty* took best picture honors, its director, Frank Lloyd, came in fourth out of four. Paul Muni, not an official nominee in 1935 for his performance in *Black Fury*, came in second in the voting behind winner Victor McLaglen, besting the other "real" nominees for best actor Charles Laughton, Clark Gable, and Franchot Tone, all from *Mutiny on the Bounty*.

A related problem with the awards has been that the number of nominees in each category, which did not become standardized in the major categories (at five each) until around 1944. In the '20s and '30s, anywhere from three to ten films or performers might be in contention in any given year. Indeed, lists of nominees in the early days were unofficial and irregular. For instance, in 1928/29, the nominees were *all* "unofficial," the Academy announcing only the winners; and from 1932/33–1935, the published list of nominees was often limited to the top three finishers, who were then identified by who came in second and third place.

The lack of true secrecy at the Oscars became problematic as the years went on. Best actress winner Luise Rainer did not even show up to the ceremony her first year as a nominee—until the studio found out she was the winner and had her rousted from bed to accept, despite her protests. She arrived at the hotel ballroom less than an hour before receiving the trophy.

The Academy began its questionable policy of trumping competitive awards by bestowing honorary ones almost from the first moment of its existence. Charlie Chaplin, nominated for best comedy direction the first year of the Oscars, later had his name all but removed from the competition when the Academy wrote him to say it would be awarding him a special award "for versatility and genius in writing, acting, directing and producing *The Circus*." The comedy direction award went to Lewis Milestone for *Two Arabian Knights* instead. And Louis B. Mayer took the unheard-of step of counseling the panel of judges *against* awarding the "artistic quality of production" trophy to MGM's own hit, *The Crowd*, arguing that rival studio Fox's *Sunrise* conveyed a more noble message—which, after all, was one of the purposes of the Academy in the first place. Indeed, in the early days, the Academy was well-known for undertaking such acts best described as just plain goofy. (Not to say it hasn't continued to do so . . .) The Academy had the feel of a playhouse more than a dour institution, a self-congratulatory industry activity rather than a world-watched media event.

THE TIMES, THEY ARE A-CHANGIN'

For the first several years of the Oscars, the Academy couldn't even decide upon consistent names for the assorted categories. Although production, actor, actress, director, cinematography, and interior decoration survived intact over many years, others underwent changes from the outset: Three writing awards were presented the first year (for "adaptation," "original story," and "title writing"), one in the second ("writing achievement"), and two in the third (the same as the first year, with the deletion of "title writing"). The advent of sound triggered the addition of music, song, and sound recording categories; and the popularity of one- and two-reel comedy films, including Disney's cartoons, created a market for short film awards.

The Great Depression had as much an effect on the Academy as changes in technology. The musical became a popular staple during the '30s, with so-called "white telephone" pictures—lightweight social comedies about the idle rich getting slowly snockered in their tuxedos and ball gowns—and splashy musicals the ideal tonic to widespread unemployment and privation. Escapism became the watchword of America, and Hollywood responded in kind: For several years, the "dance direction" category was set up to reward camera-choreographers like Hermes Pan and Busby Berkeley whose inventive, showy musical numbers made them household names in their own right. The Depression and its focus on the workingman may have also contributed to the short-lived "assistant director" category, and may also have accounted for why movie "extras" were given voting privileges for several years.

But no change in the Oscars has had a more lasting effect than the addition in 1936 of supporting acting categories. In 1934, Frank Morgan received a best actor nomination for his performance in *The Affairs of Cellini*, even though his part was secondary to that of Fredric March as Cellini. Despite widespread acclaim for Morgan's work, the size of his part compared against those of Clark Gable in *It Happened One Night* and William Powell in *The Thin Man* made him an unlikely winner. The acting branch eventually succeeded in creating the supporting categories to reward featured players. Successful implementation of the distinction, however, proved less than a stunning achievement: During the first year of the supporting categories, Stuart Erwin, the star of the football comedy *Pigskin Parade*, was nominated for his "supporting" performance, while Spencer Tracy, who received third billing in *San Francisco*, was in the running for best actor.

Quiz: Trivia from the '20s and '30s

Q. **At the first Oscar presentation, a dinner at the Hollywood Roosevelt Hotel, the awards were passed out in about five minutes, and only one person gave an acceptance speech. Who hosted the first ceremony? Who made the speech?**
A. Academy president Douglas Fairbanks served as MC; Darryl Zanuck made the only speech.

Q. **Although sound films had arrived before the first best picture Oscar was handed out, they were deemed ineligible for best picture. But what was the first sound film to receive any nomination, and in what category?**
A. Warner Brothers's *The Jazz Singer* (1927/28) lost to best picture winner *Wings* in the only category for which it was nominated: best engineering effects. It did receive a special award.

Q. **In what category did the award go not to the individuals responsible for any one film but to the studio department, from the start of the awards until 1969?**
A. The winners for best sound went to sound departments, often in the name of the department head.

Q. **Although the statuette's official name has always been "the Academy Award of Merit," stories about how it came to be known by the familiar moniker "Oscar" are competing and plentiful. Which of the following is *not* an actual expla-**

nation offered for the notoriously nicknamed little man?

a. Bette Davis claimed that she named it after
her ex-husband, Harmon Oscar Nelson Jr.

b. Margaret Herrick, the Academy's librarian,
allegedly exclaimed when she saw the statuette, "Why, he resembles my uncle Oscar!"

c. Silent screen star Mabel Normand, overlooked in the first year of balloting, was re-
ported as saying that the male-dominated
Academy "Has so many men lacking in
taste, their idea of a good actress is a drag
queen named Oscar."

d. Columnist Sidney Skolsky maintained that
the name originated from an old music hall
joke: "Will you have a cigar, Oscar?"

A. Choice c is a complete fabrication.

Q. Whichever of the above stories is true, it is generally undisputed that the first printed reference
to "Oscar" occurred in Skolsky's column on
March 18 of what year?
A. 1934.

Q. What performer received a wooden statuette in
1937?
A   The award was presented to Edgar Bergen and
Charlie McCarthy.

Q. To whom were seven miniature statuettes
awarded that same year?
A. Walt Disney, commemorating the achievement
of the first all-animated film, *Snow White and the
Seven Dwarfs* (1938).

Q. Of the first 12 best picture winners, match the
broad genre of film (or significant subplot) with
the number of best picture trophies the genre
received.

a.	Western	i.	Four
b.	War/rebellion	ii.	Three
c.	Musical	iii.	Two
d.	Biopic	iv.	Two
e.	Comedy	v.	One

A. a.-iii. or iv.; b.-i.; c.-iii. or iv.; d.-v.; e.-ii. The war/rebellion movies proved exceedingly popular (*Wings, All Quiet on the Western Front, Mutiny on the Bounty,* and *Gone with the Wind*). The other genres are: comedies (*Grand Hotel, It Happened One Night, You Can't Take It with You*), musicals (*The Broadway Melody, The Great Ziegfeld*), Westerns (*Cimarron, Cavalcade*), and biopic (*The Life of Emile Zola*).

Q. **In what year did Shirley Temple receive a miniature version of the Oscar?**
A. 1934; she was five years old at the time. She was never in competition for an Oscar.

Q. **Who was the first person to reject his Oscar in protest?**
A. Dudley Nichols, writer of *The Informer* (1935).

Q. **The Golden Age of Hollywood certainly was that: Name the year that the following films— all Oscar-nominated—were released: *Gone with the Wind; The Wizard of Oz; Dark Victory; Ninotchka; Wuthering Heights; Stagecoach; Beau Geste; Juarez; Goodbye, Mr. Chips; Young Mr. Lincoln; Mr. Smith Goes to Washington; Gunga Din; Intermezzo; Love Affair; The Private Lives of Elizabeth and Essex; Of Mice and Men.***
A. 1939, a year that, arguably, has never been surpassed.

Q. **In 1930/31, three of the films nominated for original story starred the same actor, although none**

proved to be the winner. Who was the actor?
A.   James Cagney.

Q.   **What *wunderkind* producer and head of production at MGM died of pneumonia in September of 1936, at age 37?**
A.   Irving Thalberg. His widow, Norma Shearer, remained in seclusion until the night of the 1936 Oscar ceremony, in which she was nominated for appearing in the last film Thalberg personally produced, *Romeo and Juliet.* (They both lost to *The Great Ziegfeld.*) Thalberg personally won the best picture award twice: for *Grand Hotel* (1931/32) and *Mutiny on the Bounty* (1936)—the later award coming only six months before his demise. Subsequent films continued to attribute their conception and implementation to Thalberg, including *The Good Earth* (1936) and *Goodbye, Mr. Chips* (1939)—a British production released by MGM *three years* after Thalberg's death. The Irving G. Thalberg Memorial Award came about practically before the producer's body was cold, and has been presented most years since 1937 to the producer whose body of work (especially over the preceding year) deserves individual recognition. It is voted on by the Board of Governors of the Academy.

Q.   **Who designed the Thalberg award, and what does it represent?**
A.   It was designed by Gibbons in 1937 as a solid bronze head of Thalberg, resting on a black marble base. It weights 10¾ pounds and is 9 inches tall. The award is the only trophy presented that is *not* a replica of ol' Oscar himself.

Q.   **What three performers each won two Oscars in the '30s, never to win again? What legendary star won one Oscar, and received two more nominations in the '30s, only never to be nomi-**

nated again? What director won three Oscars in the '30s, never to win again?

A. Luise Rainer, Spencer Tracy, and Bette Davis each won twice. Clark Gable, an enduring star until the 1960s, received three nominations (and one win), never to be in contention again. Frank Capra was the much-lauded director. Walter Brennan won three supporting actor Oscars, although he won one in the 1940s. Garbo, the biggest star of her day, was winless after four nominations. She retired from film completely by 1942, at age 36.

Q. **Nobel profession: Who is the only Nobel laureate to win an Academy Award?**

A. George Bernard Shaw, for his adaptation of *Pygmalion* (1938). He won the Nobel Prize for literature in 1925. Other future Nobel Prize winners who were nominated for writing Oscars include: John Steinbeck (original motion picture story, *Lifeboat*, 1944; *A Medal for Benny*, 1945; best story and screenplay, *Viva Zapata!*, 1952), and Jean-Paul Sartre (best motion picture story, *The Proud and the Beautiful*, 1956).

Q. **Who was the only "Oscar" winner in the '20s and '30s not to know he won an "Oscar"?**

A. Joseph Farnham, winner for best title writing (presented only the first year of the awards), who died two years after he won—and before the name "Oscar" came into use.

Q. **Especially in the early years, categories of awards were presented then abruptly discontinued. Name at least three categories that lasted five years or less—all of which were gone by 1937.**

A. The six fleeting categories were:

• Artistic quality of production (also known as

unique and artistic picture; presented in 1927/28 only).

• Comedy direction (1927/28 only).

• Engineering effects (1927/28 only).

• Title writing (1927/28 only). It applied only to silent films, which were essentially gone by the second year of the Oscars.

• Assistant director (1933–1937). The nominees the first year were all submitted by each studio; each studio was also guaranteed one winner.

• Dance direction (1935–1937). Probably the most famous stager of dance sequences, Busby Berkeley, never won.

Q. What "tied" best actor award was not a tie in fact? Who really won?
A. Wallace Beery was credited with a "tie" for Fredric March as best actor (1931/32)—even though he was one vote shy of March's total. Under the Academy rules at the time, a margin of error of three votes was permitted to determine "ties." The tie in 1968—when Barbra Streisand and Katharine Hepburn shared the best actress honors—was therefore the only legitimate tie in a major category in Oscar history.

Q. What film marks the only time that the best director award was given to a film that was not also nominated for best picture?
A. Frank Lloyd's win for *The Divine Lady* (1928/29). (Half-credit if you said Lewis Milestone won for directing *Two Arabian Knights* in the first year of the Oscars, but the category was actually called "comedy direction," and it was discontinued the following year.)

Q. Beginning a trend of honorary consolation prizes, what great director of the silent era re-

ceived an honorary Oscar in 1935 (his only one; not even a nomination!), and never went on to make another motion picture?

A. D. W. Griffith.

Q. Name the only film to win the best picture award and not receive a single other nomination.

A. *Grand Hotel* (1931/32). Only two other films, *The Broadway Melody* (1928/29) and *Mutiny on the Bounty* (1935), won the Oscar without winning any other awards. Interestingly enough, all were produced by MGM.

Q. What distinction do Douglas Fairbanks, William C. DeMille (Cecil's brother), Will Rogers, and Irvin S. Cobb share?

A. They all were to be the *only* Oscar presenters during the first few years of the awards, handing out every statuette.

Q. How many Oscar nominations did the original *King Kong* (1933) receive?

A. One of the seminal films of Hollywood, and even today with its comparatively cheesy special effects, one of the most inexplicably entertaining, failed to draw a single Oscar nomination.

Q. When Lionel Barrymore won the Oscar for *A Free Soul* (1930/31), he defeated Fredric March in a part based on Lionel's brother, John. What was the name of March's film?

A. *The Royal Family of Broadway.*

Q. Who was the first posthumous nominee for an Oscar in any category?

A. Gerald Duffy, who was nominated for best title writing in the first year of the awards. His mother accepted his "honorable mention" scroll as a runner-up.

OSCAR HIGHLIGHTS AND LOWLIGHTS
OF THE DECADE

- **What a night**. February 23, 1939. The same night of the eleventh Oscar ceremony, Peter Fonda, future best actor and screenwriter nominee, was born.

- **Get your story straight.** *The Way of All Flesh* and *The Last Command,* previously listed by the Academy as best picture nominees in the historic first year (1927/28), are not currently listed on the official Academy list of best picture nominees. Similar discrepancies plagued much of the early years of the Oscars, especially during the second year of the awards (1928/29) when all of the nominees were ''unofficial,'' only the winners being formally announced. The ''nominees'' for this year were instead considered only the films under consideration by the Academy.

- **The Great Kate Count, part I**. Katharine Hepburn received two Oscar nominations as best actress, for *Alice Adams* (1935) and a win for *Morning Glory* (1932/33).

···

THE WINNERS
1927/28

Production—*Wings*
Artistic Quality of Production*—*Sunrise*

---

*Given this year only.

Direction—Frank Borzage, *Seventh Heaven*
Comedy Direction*—Lewis Milestone, *Two Arabian Knights*
Actor—Emil Jannings, *The Last Command* and *The Way of All Flesh*
Actress—Janet Gaynor, *Seventh Heaven, Street Angel*, and *Sunrise*
Original Story—*Underworld*
Adaptation—*Seventh Heaven*
Title Writing*—*The Fair Co-ed, Telling the World* and *Laugh, Clown, Laugh*
Cinematography—*Sunrise*
Interior Decoration—*The Tempest* and *The Dove*
Engineering Effects—*Wings**
Special Awards—*The Jazz Singer*; Charles Chaplin for *The Circus*

1928/29

Production—*The Broadway Melody*
Direction—Frank Lloyd, *The Divine Lady, Weary River*, and *Drag*[4]
Actor—Warner Baxter, *In Old Arizona*
Actress—Mary Pickford, *Coquette*
Writing Achievement—*The Patriot*
Cinematography—*White Shadows in the South Seas*
Interior Decoration—*The Bridge of San Luis Rey*

1929/30

Production—*All Quiet on the Western Front*
Direction—Lewis Milestone, *All Quiet on the Western Front*
Actor—George Arliss, *Disraeli*
Actress—Norma Shearer, *The Divorcée*
Writing Achievement—*The Big House*
Cinematography—*With Byrd at the South Pole*

---

*Given this year only.
[4] Earlier records indicated that Lloyd's Oscar was for *The Divine Lady* only, but the Academy now lists all three of his films from that year.

Interior Decoration—*King of Jazz*
Sound Recording—*The Big House*

1930/31

Picture—*Cimarron*
Direction—Norman Taurog, *Skippy*
Actor—Lionel Barrymore, *A Free Soul*
Actress—Marie Dressler, *Min and Bill*
Writing Original—*The Dawn Patrol*
Writing Adaptation—*Cimarron*
Cinematography—*Tabu*
Interior Direction—*Cimarron*

1931/32

Picture—*Grand Hotel*
Direction—Frank Borzage, *Bad Girl*
Actor—Fredric March, *Dr. Jekyll and Mr. Hyde*; Wallace Beery, *The Champ*
Actress—Helen Hayes, *The Sin of Madelon Claudet*
Original Story—*The Champ*
Writing Adaptation—*Bad Girl*
Cinematography—*Shanghai Express*
Interior Decoration—*Transatlantic*
Sound Recording—*Bad Girl*
Short Subject (Cartoon)—*Flowers and Trees*
Short Subject (Comedy)—*The Music Box*
Short Subject (Novelty)—*Wrestling Swordfish*
Special Award—Walt Disney, for creating Mickey Mouse

1932/33

Picture—*Cavalcade*
Direction—Frank Lloyd, *Cavalcade*
Actor—Charles Laughton, *The Private Life of Henry VIII*
Actress—Katharine Hepburn, *Morning Glory*
Original Story—*One Way Passage*
Writing Adaptation—*Little Women*

Cinematography—*A Farewell to Arms*
Interior Decoration—*Cavalcade*
Sound Recording—*A Farewell to Arms*
Short Subject (Cartoon) —*The Three Little Pigs*
Short Subject (Comedy)—*So This Is Harris*
Short Subject (Novelty)—*Krakatoa*

1934

Picture—*It Happened One Night*
Direction—Frank Capra, *It Happened One Night*
Actor—Clark Gable, *It Happened One Night*
Actress—Claudette Colbert, *It Happened One Night*
Original Story—*Manhattan Melodrama*
Writing Adaptation—*It Happened One Night*
Cinematography—*Cleopatra*
Film Editing—*Eskimo*
Interior Decoration—*The Merry Widow*
Sound Recording—*One Night of Love*
Score—*One Night of Love*
Song—"The Continental," *The Gay Divorcée*
Short Subject (Cartoon) —*The Tortoise and the Hare*
Short Subject (Comedy) —*La Cucaracha*
Short Subject (Novelty)—*City of Wax*
Special Award—Shirley Temple

1935

Picture—*Mutiny on the Bounty*
Direction—John Ford, *The Informer*
Actor—Victor McLaglen, *The Informer*
Actress—Bette Davis, *Dangerous*
Original Story—*The Scoundrel*
Screenplay—*The Informer*
Cinematography—*A Midsummer Night's Dream*
Film Editing—*A Midsummer Night's Dream*
Interior Decoration—*The Dark Angel*
Sound Recording—*Naughty Marietta*
Score—*The Informer*

Song—"Lullaby of Broadway," *The Gold Diggers of 1935*
Short Subject (Cartoon) —*Three Orphan Kittens*
Short Subject (Comedy) —*How to Sleep*
Short Subject (Novelty) —*Wings over Mount Everest*
Special Award—D. W. Griffith

1936

Picture—*The Great Ziegfeld*
Direction—Frank Capra, *Mr. Deeds Goes to Town*
Actor—Paul Muni, *The Story of Louis Pasteur*
Actress—Luise Ralner, *The Great Ziegfeld*
Supporting Actor—Walter Brennan, *Come and Get It*
Supporting Actress—Gale Sondergaard, *Anthony Adverse*
Original Story—*The Story of Louis Pasteur*
Screenplay—*The Story of Louis Pasteur*
Cinematography—*Anthony Adverse*
Film Editing—*Anthony Adverse*
Interior Decoration—*Dodsworth*
Sound Recording—*San Francisco*
Score—*Anthony Adverse*
Song—"The Way You Look Tonight," *Swing Time*
Short Subject (Cartoon)—*The Country Cousin*
Short Subject (One-reel)—*Bored of Education*
Short Subject (Two-reel)—*The Public Pays*
Short Subject (Color)—*Give Me Liberty*
Special Awards—*The March of Time*; *The Garden of Allah*

1937

Picture—*The Life of Emile Zola*
Direction—Leo McCarey, *The Awful Truth*
Actor—Spencer Tracy, *Captains Courageous*
Actress—Luise Rainer, *The Good Earth*
Supporting Actor—Joseph Schildkraut, *The Life of Emile Zola*
Supporting Actress—Alice Brady, *In Old Chicago*

Original Story—*A Star Is Born*
Screenplay—*The Life of Emile Zola*
Cinematography—*The Good Earth*
Film Editing—*Lost Horizon*
Interior Decoration—*Lost Horizon*
Sound Recording—*The Hurricane*
Score—*One Hundred Men and a Girl*
Song—"Sweet Leilani," *Waikiki Wedding*
Short Subject (Cartoon)—*The Old Mill*
Short Subject (One-reel)—*The Private Life of the Gannetts*
Short Subject (Two-reel)—*Torture Money*
Short Subject (Color)—*Penny Wisdom*
Irving G. Thalberg Award—Darryl F. Zanuck

1938

Picture—*You Can't Take It with You*
Direction—Frank Capra, *You Can't Take It with You*
Actor—Spencer Tracy, *Boys Town*
Actress—Bette Davis , *Jezebel*
Supporting Actor—Walter Brennan, *Kentucky*
Supporting Actress—Fay Bainter, *Jezebel*
Original Story—*Boys Town*
Screenplay—*Pygmalion*
Cinematography—*The Great Waltz*
Film Editing—*The Adventures of Robin Hood*
Interior Decoration—*The Adventures of Robin Hood*
Sound Recording—*The Cowboy and the Lady*
Original Score—*The Adventures of Robin Hood*
Score—*Alexander's Ragtime Band*
Song—"Thanks for the Memory," *The Big Broadcast of 1938*
Short Subject (Cartoon)—*Ferdinand the Bull*
Short Subject (One-reel)—*That Mothers Might Live*
Short Subject (Two-reel)—*Declaration of Independence*
Irving G. Thalberg Memorial Award—Hal B. Wallis

Special Awards—Deanna Durbin; Mickey Rooney; Walt Disney (for *Snow White and the Seven Dwarfs*)

1939

Picture—*Gone with the Wind*
Direction—Victor Fleming, *Gone with the Wind*
Actor—Robert Donat, *Goodbye, Mr. Chips*
Actress—Vivien Leigh, *Gone with the Wind*
Supporting Actor—Thomas Mitchell, *Stagecoach*
Supporting Actress—Hattie McDaniel, *Gone with the Wind*
Original Story—*Mr. Smith Goes to Washington*
Screenplay—*Gone with the Wind*
Cinematography (Black and White)—*Wuthering Heights*
Cinematography (Color)—*Gone with the Wind*
Film Editing—*Gone with the Wind*
Interior Decoration—*Gone with the Wind*
Sound Recording—*When Tomorrow Comes*
Original Score—*The Wizard of Oz*
Score—*Stagecoach*
Song—"Over the Rainbow," *The Wizard of Oz*
Special Effects—*The Rains Came*
Short Subject (Cartoon)—*The Ugly Duckling*
Short Subject (One-reel)—*Busy Little Bears*
Short Subject (Two-reel)—*Sons of Liberty*
Irving G. Thalberg Memorial Award—David O. Selznick
Special Awards—Douglas Fairbanks; Jean Hersholt; Judy Garland (outstanding juvenile performer); William Cameron Menzies (use of color in *Gone with the Wind*)

....

The '40s: America, America

THE LIFE OF A PATRIOT

As in America itself, the decade of the 1940s was a complex and volatile time in Hollywood—a fact that the industry only exacerbated by trying to pretend for so long it was not. There's no denying that the reason for the controversies relate directly to World War II. It didn't start out that way; America was still in the grip of the Depression, and had not established itself as a world power. Most European nations lacked the luxury of neutrality, and their movies tended to be more spirited and proactive. But in America, for the first two years at least, Hollywood would have none of it.

That changed in December 1941, when the U.S. was drawn inextricably into the fray with the bombing of Pearl Harbor. It was no longer acceptable to be evasive—we now had to choose sides. Movies are largely about marketing, of course, so the studios were quick to jump on the bandwagon and give the people what they wanted.

By and large, the "prestige" pictures of the era dealt primarily with the war, and tended toward shameless propaganda; they were serious (even stuffy), courageous films about how the Allies were brave, understood sacrifice, and would prevail because, damn it, they were *right!* Three of the best picture winners that decade—

Mrs. Miniver (1942), *Casablanca* (1943), and *The Best Years of Our Lives* (1946)—dealt with war, its human toll, and its immediate aftermath. (*Casablanca* in particular was a marvelous reflection of American ambivalence, with bar owner Rick perfectly embodying the spirit of the nation—anxious to stay apart, but compelled by a sense of duty to get involved.) Countless other films also dealt with the war both directly and indirectly. Laurence Olivier's *Henry V* (1946), one of Shakespeare's most rousing, jingoistic plays, was released just in time to capitalize on the Nazi defeat. Olivier received a special Oscar for his masterful adaptation. Gary Cooper received his first best actor trophy for portraying Sergeant Alvin York, a World War I hero, in *Sergeant York*—one of the first anti-isolationist films made in Hollywood that decade.

There's a dark side to patriotism, of course, which the industry seemed ill-prepared to deal with at the time. (It would be more than 20 years before an Oscar winning best picture—*Patton*—would openly criticize a WWII hero.) Hedda Hopper, Louella Parsons, and the studios themselves were desperate to make Hollywood out to be the artistic and cultural bellwether of the world. America's victory on the battlefields implied superiority in all walks of life, so naturally show business was expected to dominate as well. It wasn't enough that the French had invented cinema, or that many of its early acknowledged geniuses—Eisenstein, Murnau, von Sternberg, Renoir, von Stroheim, Reifenstahl—worked in foreign languages, or that some of the most influential directors *in* Hollywood were themselves émigrés from Europe; you had to be an *American* to win an Oscar. When *Hamlet* received the best picture award in 1948, based on the outcry you'd think Hitler himself had produced it, and Britain was an *ally!* Eventually things settled down, but there's no denying the impact the war had on the film industry.

WE HAVE ISSUES

As the news of the Holocaust spread throughout the world, the plight of the Jews came into sharp focus; suddenly, the war wasn't just about fascism, but anti-Semitism as well. The result was that "issues" pictures tended to find their audience—and accolades—in great number in the 1940s as well: not only was anti-Semitism dealt with (*Gentlemen's Agreement*, 1947; best picture [w+]), but also alcoholism (*The Lost Weekend*, 1945; best picture [w+]) and political corruption (*All the King's Men*, 1949; best picture [w+]), all of which scored big (they each have their dated qualities by today's standards, but were controversial at the time). As the Academy was founded in part as a public relations device, the idea that Hollywood would so publicly embrace "important" movies is perhaps not surprising. Dour dramas have always fared better than enjoyable comedies (although in the '50s and '60s musicals did remarkably well). Additional "issues" films that were nominated for best picture but lost out include: the American dust bowl (*The Grapes of Wrath*, 1940; best director [w+]), mob violence (*The Ox-Bow Incident*, 1943; picture [n+]), psychoanalysis (*Spellbound*, 1945; picture [n+]), racism (*Crossfire*, 1947; picture [n+]), and mental illness (*The Snake Pit*, 1948; picture [n+]).

Truly great movies, of course, don't need to be "about" issues in order to be *about issues*. Indeed, the tendency of message pictures to send not only the message but the resolution itself is the weakest part of "issues" movies. Films like *A Letter to Three Wives* (1949) and *All the King's Men* (1949) are all the better because they aren't cleanly resolved to everyone's satisfaction in 90 minutes. The '40s was an incredible period of interesting and diverse moviemaking (happy escapism was even more popular than other film genres, although not as honored by Oscar), and the future of film looked to be as diverse and challenging.

But a storm was brewing in Hollywood, and the source was a senator from Wisconsin named Joseph McCarthy. The Red Scare, the first and strongest symptom of the Cold War, had all America looking under their beds for communists, and the alarmism rattled by Congress to that effect was one of the most shameful black marks in American history. The chilling effect of the McCarthy era was destined to cool off the brilliance promised by Hollywood's maturation during the '40s, and result in a period of lightweight fluff and damning innovation—the '50s would prove to be the decade of the bipolar film community, and Oscar went along for the ride.

FILM FATALE

There was a trickle-down effect from the war as well, leading to the immigration in even greater numbers of skilled craftsmen and genuine artists from Europe, and not surprisingly, they had their own worldview that was not necessarily as perky as Hollywood's. The backlash against rabid patriotism turned out to be unbridled cynicism, borne with the advent of the Cold War; one remarkable thing about Hollywood was how the two were able to coexist, successfully. Foreign-born directors like Billy Wilder, Fritz Lang, and Jacques Tourneur, and some revolutionary Americans like John Huston and Nicholas Ray, were closely associated with the style of moviemaking known as *film noir*. *Noir* films began to gain currency in the United States after World War II, although they had been around longer. It wasn't until the late '40s, however—and really, not until the '50s—that this specialized genre came into its own. The elements of *film noir*, I have often maintained, are immutable. You can have noirish style, but without the catalogue of components, you just can't be genuine *film noir*. These components are: the *femme fatale*, a spiderlady whose sexuality makes her attractive, but whose inherent badness necessarily leads to trouble; a cynical, hard-boiled, always unattached antihero, who refers to women as "broads" or "dames," has a menial but over-glamorized job, wears a hat, and always has a light; an urban setting, usually with wet, slick-looking streets; a sad ending; a malaise that accompanies the inevitability of corruption; of course black-and-white film (or chiaroscuro lighting, full of shadows and slivers of light), and lots of night scenes—after all, *film noir* means "black movie."

Not surprisingly, the canon of *films noir* is more impressive and varied than most jingoistic war films. The two main reasons for this fact are fairly obvious. First, the number of *films noir* produced is more numerous than war pictures, for reasons of simple economics: The Venetian blinds cost far less than an airplane. Second, they have stood the test of posterity better because they are less tied to a particular era. There's a universality to the themes in *film noir* that transcends a specific year.

Also somewhat predictably, *film noir* fared less well with the Oscars than the happily concluded counterparts. Given a choice between the touching, prosaic bravery of a handless war vet (*The Best Years of Our Lives*) or the dark, unwelcome ending of an adulterous relationship that results in murder and scandal (*The Postman Always Rings Twice*), can you imagine Hollywood going any other way? At least the hesitation of the Academy to reward this important genre of films didn't prevent directors from making them, and sharing them with generations of moviegoers—and moviemakers—to come.

Quiz: Oscar Trivia from the 1940s

Q. *Casablanca, Mrs. Miniver*, and *The Best Years of Our Lives* may have won best picture for dealing with WWII, but can you name at least five best picture *nominees* to address the war?

A. Other include: *Foreign Correspondent, The Great Dictator*, and *The Long Voyage Home* (all 1940); *Blossoms in the Dust* and *Hold Back the Dawn* (1941); *The Invaders* and *Wake Island* (1942); *The Human Comedy, In Which We Serve, Watch on the Rhine*, and *The More the Merrier* (1943—the latter a comedy about the housing shortage in Washington, D.C., during the war); *Since You Went Away* (1944); *Battleground* and *Twelve O'Clock High* (1949).

Q. **What was the first *noir* film nominated for best picture?**
A. John Huston's *The Maltese Falcon* (1941), taken from Dashiell Hammett's hard-boiled detective yarn, is probably the first. Other important, Oscar-nominated *films noir* released during the '40s are *Double Indemnity* (1944; picture [n+]), *Laura* (1944; director [n+]), *Mildred Pierce* (1945; actress [w+]), *The Killers* (1946; director [n+]), *Crossfire* (1947; picture [n+]), and *Kiss of Death* (1947; supporting actor [n+]).

Q. **What cornball character seen in low-budget serialized comedies got started as an Academy Award–nominated performance in a respectable film?**
A. Ma Kettle (supporting actress nominee Marjorie Main), who first appeared in *The Egg and I* (1947). Although Celeste Holm won the Oscar, Main parlayed the part into a full-blown franchise.

Q. **Who, upon taking full control of RKO in 1948 (after holding a large stake in the company), became the first individual ever to wholly own an entire Hollywood studio?**
A. Howard Hughes.

Q. **What was unique about the Oscar statuettes handed out between 1941 and 1944?**

A.   As a way to save on metals for the war effort, the statuettes were made of plaster. After the war, winners could exchange them for metal ones.

Q. **For what short film did Frank Sinatra receive an Oscar?**
A.   *The House I Live In* (1945). The film about the virtues of tolerance received a special award for almost everyone associated with it, including the director (Mervyn LeRoy), the songwriting team, the screenwriter (Albert Maltz, later imprisoned as one of the Hollywood Ten), and star Sinatra.

Q. **In what year did both sets of art design and cinematography awards—black-and-white and color—go, for the first time, to two British productions, and what were the films?**
A.   *Great Expectations* and *Black Narcissus*, both released in 1947.

Q. **When was the first Oscar ceremony broadcast over radio?**
A.   1944, on the ABC network.

Q. **Which studio became the last of the original big seven studios to finally take home a best picture award? In what year?**
A.   United Artists, which finally won best picture for *Rebecca* in 1940.

Q. **After the success of *Snow White and the Seven Dwarfs* (1938), Walt Disney released three absolute classics that next decade. What were they and what did they win for?**
A.   *Pinocchio* (1940), *Dumbo* (1941), and *Fantasia* (1941), the latter an animated film of music that astounded adults, wowed children, and won Oscars. *Pinocchio* won for song and original score, *Dumbo* for scoring of a musical, and two special awards were presented to *Fantasia*.

Q. **Hard-boiled novelist Raymond Chandler was twice nominated for writing screenplays. What were the films?**

A. *Double Indemnity* (1944) and *The Blue Dahlia* (1946).

Q. **What U.S. Supreme Court ruling in 1948 greatly impacted the studio mogul?**

A. The U.S. Supreme Court ruled that "vertical integration"—the system by which the studios produced, distributed, and exhibited movies—was an antitrust violation, and directed them to divest themselves of at least one aspect of the process (most abandoned exhibition, leasing their product to independent cinemas). Although the studios weathered the problem for a while, by the '60s the era of the studio mogul had all but passed.

Q. **In the '40s, the Academy required Academy membership to be eligible to nominate and vote in the ceremony. How did this influence the balloting?**

A. It dropped the number of those with ballots from 9,000 to around 1,500.

Q. **True or false: The Academy instigated its "sealed envelope" policy from the very first year of the ceremonies.**

A. False. The habit began in 1940. Although it originally met with some derision in the press, the suspense generated by the idea makes the envelope one of Oscar's most enduring draws.

Q. **What is the only foreign film studio to have won the best picture award without an American co-producer or distributor?**

A. J. Arthur Rank, which, along with Two Cities, released *Hamlet* (1948). Rank is also the only studio in history to win only one best picture award.

Q. **What noteworthy backstage event happened in 1946 when Olivia de Havilland won the Oscar for best actress?**
A. De Havilland's estranged sister (and previous winner) Joan Fontaine extended a congratulatory hand to the honoree—only to have de Havilland pull back and turn away. The snub made as much news as the win.

Q. **For what film did Richard Rodgers receive his only Oscar—and only nomination?**
A. *State Fair* (1943), for which he composed (with Oscar Hammerstein II) the song "It Might As Well Be Spring."

Q. **What precipitated the resignation of Academy president Bette Davis?**
A. She resigned after suggesting that the 1941 awards, to be handed out soon after the attack on Pearl Harbor, be opened to the public and serve as a fund-raiser for the war effort. (When the Oscars moved to the spacious Shrine Auditorium in 1946, the Academy had enough extra seats to sell them to the public.) The Board of Governors rejected the suggestion, and Davis resigned in a fit of pique.

Q. **In 1947, Broadway joined Hollywood in celebrating its own with the establishment of the Tony Awards—giving a whole generation of actors a second shot at winning another trophy. Below are the names of performers who won Oscars for particular parts. In each case, the *part* also won the stage actor a Tony. Name which ones also won the Tony personally, and which ones stole the film role from another performer. (For extra credit, name the person who played the role on Broadway.)**

a. José Ferrer, *Cyrano de Bergerac* (stage, 1947; screen, 1950)

b. Vivien Leigh, *A Streetcar Named Desire* (stage, 1948; screen, 1951)

c. Shirley Booth, *Come Back, Little Sheba* (stage, 1950; screen, 1952)

d. Grace Kelly, *The Country Girl* (stage, 1951; screen, 1954)

e. Rex Harrison, *My Fair Lady* (stage, 1957; screen, 1964)

f. Anne Bancroft, *The Miracle Worker* (stage, 1960; screen, 1962)

g. Paul Scofield, *A Man for All Seasons* (stage, 1962; screen, 1966)

h. Elizabeth Taylor, *Who's Afraid of Virginia Woolf?* (stage, 1963; screen, 1965)

i. Jack Albertson, *The Subject Was Roses* (stage, 1965; screen, 1968)

j. Katharine Hepburn, *The Lion in Winter* (stage, 1966; screen, 1968)

k. Joel Grey, *Cabaret* (stage, 1967; screen, 1972)

l. Maggie Smith, *The Prime of Miss Jean Brodie* (stage, 1968; screen, 1969)

A. The following actors all *repeated* their stage success with an Oscar win: a.; c.; e.; f.; g.; i.; k. These performers all managed to steal a championship part away from the person who originated it: b. (Jessica Tandy played Blanche DuBois on Broadway); d. and h. (Uta Hagen created the roles that won both Kelly and Taylor their Oscars); j. (Rosemary Harris originated the bravura part of Eleanor of Aquitaine); l. (Zoe Caldwell played the role on stage).

Quiz: Trivia About the Most Notoriously Overlooked Contender Ever

In 1940, Orson Welles, 24 and fresh off his phenomenal stint on radio (in 1938, his *War of the Worlds* broadcast made front-page headlines) and Broadway theater (a modern-dress *Julius Caesar* was among his towering achievements) but with no film experience, got a contract from RKO that 20-year veterans would have envied: choice of project, choice of cast and crew, absolute final cut. He spent a year fielding projects, starting and abandoning several, until he came upon a screenplay by Herman J. Mankiewicz, retooled it, got legendary cinematographer Gregg Toland involved, and produced what was hailed at the time, and more than 60 years later remains, one of the greatest films of all time: *Citizen Kane*, a technical marvel, astoundingly acted, and a dramatically compelling achievement. Hollywood's top directors admitted that Welles had all but rewritten film grammar. From that start, *Citizen Kane* was hailed as a landmark film, but it was a financial disaster.

Q. **Why did the film not achieve the financial success that seemed inevitable from the reviews?**
A.   The film's story, a thinly veiled treatment of the life of publisher William Randolph Hearst, angered Hearst, who refused to allow any of his newspapers to advertise it, and who threatened to sanction any theater-owners who screened the film by refusing their advertising. In pretelevision days, the cinemas couldn't afford to lose display ads, and the boycott worked. Hearst's Hollywood hatchet woman, Louella Parsons, also trashed the film in her column, having a greater impact than even the best review could hope for.

Q. How many Oscar nominations did the film receive and what were they for?
A.   It was nominated for nine Oscars: picture, director, actor, original screenplay, cinematography, score, film editing, art direction, and sound.

Q. How many Oscars did it ultimately win?
A.   Only one, for its screenplay, cowritten by Welles and Herman J. Mankiewicz.

Q. What record did Welles set in the Oscar books with this film?
A.   He became the first person to receive four nominations for a single film: as producer, director, actor, and writer.

Q. How many additional Oscars and nominations did Welles receive in his career?
A.   The following year (1942), *The Magnificent Ambersons* got Welles another nomination as producer of a best picture nominee. Welles himself was never again nominated, even for acting, although he did receive an honorary award in 1970.

OSCAR HIGHLIGHTS AND LOWLIGHTS OF THE DECADE

- **The rising storm**. On November 28, 1947, director Edward Dmytryk was fired from RKO for refusing to "name names" before the House Un-American Activities Committee, when asked "Are you now or have you ever been a member of the Communist Party?" Dmytryk's already released film, *Crossfire*, received five Oscar nominations, including best picture and best director, but won none.

- **The Great Kate Count, part II**. Katharine Hepburn received two more Oscar nominations as best actress, for *The Philadelphia Story* (1940) and *Woman of the Year* (1942), bringing her total count to four.

....

THE WINNERS

1940

Picture—*Rebecca*
Direction—John Ford, *The Grapes of Wrath*
Actor—James Stewart, *The Philadelphia Story*
Actress—Ginger Rogers, *Kitty Foyle*
Supporting Actor—Walter Brennan, *The Westerner*
Supporting Actress—Jane Darwell, *The Grapes of Wrath*
Original Story—*Arise, My Love*
Original Screenplay—*The Great McGinty*
Screenplay—*The Philadelphia Story*
Original Score—*Pinocchio*
Song—"When You Wish Upon a Star," *Pinocchio*

1941

Picture—*How Green Was My Valley*
Direction—John Ford, *How Green Was My Valley*
Actor—Gary Cooper, *Sergeant York*
Actress—Joan Fontaine, *Suspicion*
Supporting Actor—Donald Crisp, *How Green Was My Valley*
Supporting Actress—Mary Astor, *The Great Lie*
Original Story—*Here Comes Mr. Jordan*
Original Screenplay—*Citizen Kane*
Screenplay—*Here Comes Mr. Jordan*

Scoring of a Dramatic Picture—*All That Money Can Buy*
Scoring of a Musical Picture—*Dumbo*
Song—"The Last Time I Saw Paris," *Lady Be Good*
Irving G. Thalberg Memorial Award—Walt Disney

1942

Picture—*Mrs. Miniver*
Direction—William Wyler, *Mrs. Miniver*
Actor—James Cagney, *Yankee Doodle Dandy*
Actress—Greer Garson, *Mrs. Miniver*
Supporting Actor—Van Heflin, *Johnny Eager*
Supporting Actress—Teresa Wright, *Mrs. Miniver*
Original Story—*The Invaders*
Original Screenplay—*Woman of the Year*
Screenplay—*Mrs. Miniver*
Scoring of a Dramatic or Comedy Picture—*Now, Voyager*
Scoring of a Musical Picture—*Yankee Doodle Dandy*
Song—"White Christmas," *Holiday Inn*
Irving G. Thalberg Memorial Award—Sidney Franklin

1943

Picture—*Casablanca*
Direction—Michael Curtiz, *Casablanca*
Actor—Paul Lukas, *Watch on the Rhine*
Actress—Jennifer Jones, *The Song of Bernadette*
Supporting Actor—Charles Coburn, *The More the Merrier*
Supporting Actress—Katina Paxinou, *For Whom the Bell Tolls*
Original Story—*The Human Comedy*
Original Screenplay—*Princess O'Rourke*
Screenplay—*Casablanca*
Scoring of a Dramatic or Comedy Picture—*The Song of Bernadette*
Scoring of a Musical Picture—*This Is the Army*

Song—"You'll Never Know," *Hello, Frisco, Hello*
Irving G. Thalberg Memorial Award—Hal B. Wallis

1944

Picture—*Going My Way*
Direction—Leo McCarey, *Going My Way*
Actor—Bing Crosby, *Going My Way*
Actress—Ingrid Bergman, *Gaslight*
Supporting Actor—Barry Fitzgerald, *Going My Way*
Supporting Actress—Ethel Barrymore, *None But the Lonely Heart*
Original Story—*Going My Way*
Original Screenplay—*Wilson*
Screenplay—*Going My Way*
Scoring of a Dramatic or Comedy Picture—*Since You Went Away*
Scoring of a Musical Picture—*Cover Girl*
Song—"Swinging on a Star," *Going My Way*
Irving G. Thalberg Memorial Award—Darryl F. Zanuck

1945

Picture—*The Lost Weekend*
Direction—Billy Wilder, *The Lost Weekend*
Actor—Ray Milland, *The Lost Weekend*
Actress—Joan Crawford, *Mildred Pierce*
Supporting Actor—James Dunn, *A Tree Grows in Brooklyn*
Supporting Actress—Anne Revere, *National Velvet*
Original Story—*The House on 92nd Street*
Original Screenplay—*Marie-Louise*
Screenplay—*The Lost Weekend*
Scoring of a Dramatic or Comedy Picture—*Spellbound*
Scoring of a Musical Picture—*Anchors Aweigh*
Song—"It Might As Well Be Spring," *State Fair*

1946

Picture—*The Best Years of Our Lives*
Direction—William Wyler, *The Best Years of Our Lives*
Actor—Fredric March, *The Best Years of Our Lives*
Actress—Olivia De Havilland, *To Each His Own*
Supporting Actor—Harold Russell, *The Best Years of Our Lives*
Supporting Actress—Anne Baxter, *The Razor's Edge*
Original Story—*Vacation from Marriage*
Original Screenplay—*The Seventh Veil*
Screenplay—*The Best Years of Our Lives*
Scoring of a Dramatic or Comedy Picture—*The Best Years of Our Lives*
Scoring of a Musical Picture—*The Jolson Story*
Song—"On the Atchison, Topeka, and Sante Fe," *The Harvey Girls*
Irving G. Thalberg Memorial Award—Samuel Goldwyn

1947

Picture—*Gentleman's Agreement*
Direction—Elia Kazan, *Gentleman's Agreement*
Actor—Ronald Colman, *A Double Life*
Actress—Loretta Young, *The Farmer's Daughter*
Supporting Actor—Edmund Gwenn, *Miracle on 34th Street*
Supporting Actress—Celeste Holm, *Gentleman's Agreement*
Original Story—*Miracle on 34th Street*
Original Screenplay—*The Bachelor and the Bobby-Soxer*
Screenplay—*Miracle on 34th Street*
Scoring of a Dramatic or Comedy Picture—*A Double Life*
Scoring of a Musical Picture—*Mother Wore Tights*
Song—"Zip-A-Dee-Doo-Dah," *Song of the South*

1948

Picture—*Hamlet*
Direction—John Huston, *The Treasure of the Sierra Madre*
Actor—Laurence Olivier, *Hamlet*
Actress—Jane Wyman, *Johnny Belinda*
Supporting Actor—Walter Huston, *The Treasure of the Sierra Madre*
Supporting Actress—Claire Trevor, *Key Largo*
Motion Picture Story—*The Search*
Screenplay—*The Treasure of the Sierra Madre*
Scoring of a Dramatic or Comedy Picture—*The Red Shoes*
Scoring of a Musical Picture—*Easter Parade*
Song—"Buttons and Bows," *The Paleface*
Irving G. Thalberg Memorial Award—Jerry Wald

1949

Picture—*All the King's Men*
Direction—Joseph Mankiewicz, *A Letter to Three Wives*
Actor—Broderick Crawford, *All the King's Men*
Actress—Olivia de Havilland, *The Heiress*
Supporting Actor—Dean Jagger, *Twelve O'Clock High*
Supporting Actress—Mercedes McCambridge, *All the King's Men*
Motion Picture Story—*The Stratton Story*
Screenplay—*A Letter to Three Wives*
Story and Screenplay—*Battleground*
Scoring of a Dramatic or Comedy Picture—*The Heiress*
Scoring of a Musical Picture—*On the Town*
Song—"Baby, It's Cold Outside," *Neptune's Daughter*

Chapter
Nine

The '50s: Television Be Damned!

THE BOOB TUBE: IT'S THE *PICTURES* THAT GOT SMALL

The decline of the "B" picture—the second feature, often produced by minor studios and featuring lesser actors in easily pigeonholed potboilers—is largely attributable to a homebound cathode ray tube that became known as television. Radio might have been entertaining in its own way, but it was no competition for the excitement of the movies. When movies, New York–style theater productions, live made-for-TV dramas, and sports could be beamed directly into the living room—well, this was cause for concern to the movie moguls. (Worse yet: most early television originated from New York, not Hollywood.) Suddenly, families were not coming in droves to the cinema anymore, and the movies needed to counteract this trend.

The proposed solution came when Twentieth Century-Fox debuted its new process known as CinemaScope. Before that time, a film's aspect ratio (the relationship between the height of the screen image and its width) was 1.33:1—about the proportion of a postage stamp on its side, or the standard TV screen. CinemaScope was a wide-screen format that increased the visual information that could appear on film. The first movie released in CinemaScope, the Richard Burton biblical epic *The Robe* (1953), was a hit, but it wasn't long before all the studios were jumping on the bandwagon, and all were anxious to make their own wide-screen epic (and develop their own wide-screen format: VistaVision, Warner Scope, Panavision, Todd-AO, even the short-lived multiscreen process, Cinerama).

In truth, the wide-screen process had been conceived almost a century before, and was even experimented with in the '20s; it was only when the studios became desperate for a gimmick that they resorted to reviving the idea, with the hope of attracting a curious audience. (Other efforts to get bodies into the seats are fondly remembered if in fact short-lived, including 3-D glasses, which had a meteoric rise in late 1952 followed by an equally speedy fall—it was gone by 1954.) In fact, although *The Robe* came out in September of 1953 (and was the top-grossing film of the year), it was a latecomer, a Western with Alan Ladd, that won the cinematography award. *Shane*, which helped revitalize and repopularize the Western, used the panoramic landscape vistas that the CinemaScope delivered and supersaturated Technicolor to create a standard for all mythic tales of the proud, quiet loner that future Westerns would emulate.

Westerns weren't the only beneficiaries of the newly rediscovered technology. The popularity of CinemaScope led to a resurgence in all forms of flashy movies. Musicals like *An American in Paris* (1951) and *Gigi* (1958), and stately, fun, or exotic locales, from the days of the Roman Empire (*The Ten Commandments*, 1956) to a tropical Oriental village (*The Bridge on the River Kwai*, 1957), also helped make movies the spectacle they always could be.

THE PRODUCTION CODE LOSES ITS TEETH

Not all films or topics seemed ideally suited for the flashy CinemaScope, however. Sweeping, all-color films like *Around the World in 80 Days, The Ten Command-*

ments, and *Giant* might fit nicely in with wide-screen, but what about black-and-white comedies, character pieces, and lower-budget movies? How could *they* compete with television?

Otto Preminger solved that problem, also in 1953, when he bucked the Breen Office, the entity that enforced the oppressive Production Code, and released his comedy *The Moon Is Blue* without the seal of approval. Until that time, the conventional wisdom was that no film lacking the Breen Office nod had a chance commercially. Whether Preminger realized that controversial subject matter, the kind that couldn't be handled on TV, was ripe for generating business or just thought a thumbing of his nose at Hollywood was long overdue is uncertain. What *is* certain is that *The Moon Is Blue*, which bandied about *verboten* words such as "virgin," became a smash, made a star out of leading lady Maggie McNamara, and harbingered the fall of the Production Code. In fact, Preminger's next film, *The Man with the Golden Arm* (1955), also failed to get the Breen Office okay, but distributors didn't care—they soaked up the story of a heroin addict, which proved to be extremely popular. This was just the beginning: nominations for a "nympho" (*The Bachelor Party*), actresses portraying women "of easy virtue" winning three consecutive best actress trophies (*The Three Faces of Eve, I Want to Live!, Room at the Top*, 1957–59), and the endorsement of adulteress Ingrid Bergman (best actress for *Anastasia*, 1956; she also presented the best picture award to *Gigi* in 1958) all singled the decline of censorship by decade's end. Preminger, who never won an Oscar, ended up as perhaps the single most influential figure in the development of the scope of film topics to come out of the 1950s.

Quiz: Trivia from the '50s

Q. **What was the first best picture winner that was adapted from a television program?**

A. *Marty* (1955). The Paddy Chayefsky television show starred Rod Steiger as the homely, lonely New Yorker looking for love with a plain Jane. Ernest Borgnine got the lead in the feature film, which won Oscars for best picture, best director, best screenplay (an adaptation category) for Chayefsky, and best actor.

Q. **Who was the first TV-trained performer to win an Oscar?**

A. Eva Marie Saint, best supporting actress, *On the Waterfront* (1954). Other Oscar winners and nominees had appeared on television (before and since), but Saint was the first one who got her start there.

Q. **Who was the first Oscar winner to star in a winner for best foreign language film?**

A. Anthony Quinn. Quinn already had a supporting actor Oscar for *Viva Zapata!* (1952) when he won a second time for *Lust for Life* (1956); that same year, he appeared in Fellini's *La Strada*, the best foreign language film winner. (1956 was also the first year that foreign language films received a competitive Oscar; until then, the winner was selected by committee.)

Q. **Name at least two of the writer-directors known as the Hollywood Ten.**

A. Here's the complete list: Edward Dmytryk, Adrian Scott, Herbert Biberman, Dalton Trumbo, Ring Lardner Jr., Albert Maltz, John Howard Lawson, Lester Cole, Alvah Bessie, and Samuel Ornitz.

Q. **What two leading Oscar winners saw their chances at winning dimmed, if only momentarily, by the suggestion of Communist ties?**

A. José Ferrer, *Cyrano de Bergerac*, and Judy Holliday, *Born Yesterday*, both in 1950. Ferrer was eventually summoned to testify before HUAC with no ill effects, and the charge against Holliday was frivolous enough that it went away almost as quickly as it was made.

Q. What Woody Allen–starring film about the Mc-Carthy era was written by a former blacklisted screenwriter?
A. *The Front* (1976), by Walter Bernstein. The plot involved a blacklisted screenwriter who got his nebbishy friend (Allen) to be a "front" for him—to sign his name to screenplays so that the writer could keep working. Bernstein's seriocomic screenplay was nominated for an Oscar. (A subsequent film by Bernstein about McCarthyism, *The House on Carroll Street*, was less well-received when released in 1988.)

Q. What was Hitchcock's only best director nomination for a color film?
A. *Rear Window* (1954). His other four nominations, all for black-and-white films, are *Rebecca* (1940), *Lifeboat* (1944), *Spellbound* (1945), and *Psycho* (1960).

Q. Why did best supporting actor nominee Brandon de Wilde ("Come back, Shane! Shane! Come back!") not attend the ceremony in the year of his only nomination?
A. The 10-year-old's parents did not tell him he was nominated; he found out four years after the fact. (His costar, Jack Palance, was also nominated, despite having only a few dozen lines.)

Q. What film which received the best screenplay award included contributions made by a nonprofessional writer who happened to be the authors' bridge partner?
A. *Sunset Boulevard* (1950). Longtime collaborators Billy Wilder and Charles Brackett credited

buddy D. M. Marshman for making useful suggestions about the script, and awarded him with a co-writing credit (and, eventually, an Oscar).

Q. **What two films bracketed the '50s by kicking off the decade with the most-ever nominations, and closing it with the most-ever wins?**
A. *All About Eve* (1950) received a still-unbeaten (though eventually tied) 14 nominations; *Ben-Hur* (1959) won a record-setting 11 Oscars (also later tied).

Q. **For what film did Henry Fonda receive his second Oscar nomination?**
A. If you said *On Golden Pond*, you're quite a bit off. Fonda's second nomination was not for acting, but for producing best picture nominee *Twelve Angry Men* (1957).

Q. **What best actor winner was nominated for his screenplay for *The Horse's Mouth* in 1958?**
A. Alec Guinness.

Q. **For what television sitcom were Oscar-nominated screenwriters Joe Connelly and Bob Mosher (for the sentimental 1955 film *The Private War of Major Benson*) better known?**
A. *Leave It to Beaver*.

Q. **Who is the only person to have received four Oscars in one evening?**
A. Walt Disney, who in 1953 walked away with the awards for documentary feature (*The Living Desert*), documentary short (*The Alaskan Eskimo*), short film (*Bear Country*), and cartoon (*Toot, Whistle, Plunk and Boom*). Disney received the awards personally, even though he was not the individual responsible for each production.

Q. **What film remains, to this day, the only one to win both the Oscar for best picture and the Palme d'Or at the Cannes Film Festival?**
A. *Marty* (1955).

Q. **When did the Academy first air a television program in which they read off the list of nominees?**
A. The experiment was first pursued in 1954 and 1955, but each time it was considered a fiasco, and was discontinued. The practice reemerged in 1986, when the network morning shows provided a convenient format.

Q. ***The Red Balloon*** **(1956), a French film in which writer-director Albert Lamorisse's six-year-old son chases a big, willful balloon through Montmartre, won the best original screenplay award. What was unusual about its victory in this category?**
A. In addition to being only 35 minutes in length, the film contained no dialogue.

Q. **After a few bit parts, James Dean stormed onto the American screen with searing performances in several mid-'50s films. He received two Oscar nominations as best actor. For what films was he nominated, and what is unique about his nominations?**
A. He was cited for *East of Eden* (1955) and *Giant* (1956), but both nominations were posthumous: He died in a car crash on September 30, 1955, after only *Eden* had been released. His third film, *Rebel Without a Cause* (1955), received two acting nominations, for supporting costars Natalie Wood and Sal Mineo.

Q. **What honorary award got its start during the 1956 Oscar ceremony?**
A. The Jean Hersholt Humanitarian Award, given to those in the industry who put others before them-

selves—apparently a rare enough occurrence in Hollywood that it merits winning an Oscar.

Q. Who invented the idea of "cameo" screen appearances, and for what film?
A. Mike Todd, the Broadway impresario who made his producing debut with *Around the World in 80 Days* (1956). He lured some of Hollywood's top stars to appear in small parts by playing to their egos. (Some of those "cameos" actually outpulled supporting actor winner Anthony Quinn, who had fewer than 10 minutes of screen time in *Lust for Life*.) *Around the World* went on to win best picture.

Q. What category did the Academy introduce in 1948?
A. Costume design.

Q. What Oscar-winning team (director and writer) of *On the Waterfront*—a film about a man who rats out his buddies—testified before HUAC, admitting to leftist sympathies and pointing fingers at their friends' Communist ties?
A. Director Elia Kazan and writer Budd Schulberg. Writer Clifford Odets and actors Sterling Hayden, Larry Parks, and Marc Lawrence also testified before Congress and were warmly welcomed back to Hollywood. Among those blacklisted for refusing to testify: directors Jules Dassin, Joseph Losey, and Robert Rossen; writers Carl Foreman, Abe Burrows, Dorothy Parker, Lillian Hellman, and Dashiell Hammett; and actors Will Geer, Howard DaSilva, Jeff Corey, Dorothy Comingore, Lionel Stander, Anne Revere, and Gale Sondergaard.

Q. What Oscar-winning director said of Katharine Hepburn: "She's the greatest amateur actress in the world, most of whose performances, though remarkably effective, are fake."
A. Joseph L. Mankiewicz, whose clashes with best actress winner Katharine Hepburn on the set

of *Suddenly, Last Summer* (1959) were well-reported. (Kate allegedly spat at her director when filming ended.) Hepburn got the last laugh, though, receiving her eighth nomination for the film, while Mankiewicz went unnoticed by the Academy.

Oscar-nominated films that began as television shows

• *Marty* (1955) isn't the only movie nominated for best picture to start out as a TV show—but it is one of only a handful, and the only one to eventually walk away the winner. Filmdom was slow to steal *directly* from television, at least in sophisticated, Oscar-friendly ways, but the following movies, nominated for Academy Awards (some were winners), had their start on the boob tube.

• *The Bachelor Party* (1957). A talky melodrama from the team that did *Marty*, trying to capitalize on a prior television success. (Supporting actress [n].)

• *Twelve Angry Men* (1957). Reginald Rose's teleplay got the platinum treatment with the socially conscious Henry Fonda producing the claustrophobic jury room drama for the silver screen, with an incredible cast (Lee J. Cobb, E. G. Marshall, Jack Klugman, etc.) and enlisting newcomer Sidney Lumet to direct it. The result was one of the tightest dramas of the decade. (Picture [n+].)

• *Judgment at Nuremberg* (1961). *Playhouse 90* may well have been the apex of television's Golden Age, as evidenced by its lasting impact on films as well. Abby Mann's *Playhouse 90* TV script got rewritten into a big, lengthy, star-studded presentation that was just as stuffy as all Stanley Kramer films, but its genuinely important subject matter—the trial of Nazi judges—helped it to a best picture nomination. (Actor [w], picture [n+].)

• *Days of Wine and Roses* (1962). Jack Lemmon and Lee Remick gave strong performances in this dark alcoholism drama directed by, of all people, Blake Edwards. It also had originally appeared on *Playhouse 90*. (Actor [n+].)

• *The Miracle Worker* (1962). Although it started as a Broadway play, it made it to TV before the big screen. Its film and Broadway star, Anne Bancroft, defeated Remick in *Wine and Roses* for the Oscar that year. (Actress [w], picture [n+].)

• *Charly* (1968). Cliff Robertson starred in the telefilm of *Days of Wine and Roses*, and was miffed he wasn't tapped for the film version. To remedy this, he bought the rights to a short story by Daniel Keyes called ''Flowers for Algernon'' which had been adapted for TV. The film version, *Charly*, won Robertson an Oscar as best actor. (Actor [w].)

• *A Man Called Charlie Brown* (1970). Although *Peanuts* was already a popular comic strip, this feature-length cartoon was an offshoot of the popular TV special *Merry Christmas, Charlie Brown*. (Song score [n].)

• *Superman* (1978). Like *Charlie Brown*, *Superman* had a history that predates its TV roots, but the cameo appearance in the movie by Noel Neill, who played Lois Lane on the 1950s syndicated program, tied the two together. *Batman* (1989), *Batman Returns* (1992), and *Batman Forever* (1995), also Oscar-nominated, owe almost nothing to the campy TV series. (Score [n+].)

• *Star Trek—The Motion Picture* (1979), *Star Trek IV: The Voyage Home* (1986), and *Star Trek: First Contact* (1996). Probably the first successful film series to feature the original TV cast transporting their small-screen personas to the silver screen. (*The Motion Picture*: art direction [n+]; *The Voyage Home*: cinematography [n+]; *First Contact*: makeup [n].)

• *The Muppet Movie* (1979), *The Great Muppet Caper* (1981), and *The Muppets Take Manhattan* (1984). Starting out on PBS and proceeding to a great run in syndication, the amusing puppets produced usually reliable, hummable songs. (*Movie*: song [n+]; *Caper*: song [n]; *Manhattan*: song score [n].)

• *Pennies from Heaven* (1981). Dennis Potter's brilliant, challenging series made for British TV gets transported to America in the persona of Steve Martin in an ambitious but not wholly successful adaptation. (Adapted screenplay [n+].)

• *The Untouchables* (1987). Eliot Ness was a real-life crime-fighter, but the '50s series with Robert Stack is what sold this Brian De Palma film. Sean Connery's aggressively delicious, Oscar-winning performance sold audiences. (Supporting actor [w+].)

• *The Addams Family* (1991) and *Addams Family Values* (1993). Charles Addams's laconically morbid clan was a cult favorite in the '60s on TV, and regained some prominence, buoyed by the talents of Anjelica Huston and Raul Julia in the tailor-made roles of Morticia and Gomez. (*Addams Family*: costumes [n]; *Addams Family Values*: art direction [n].)

• *The Fugitive* (1993). The only TV-based film other than *Marty* and *Twelve Angry Men* to be nominated for best picture, and the only one based on a regular weekly series instead of a dramatic special. The Harrison Ford thriller managed to condense the episodic quality of the series into less than two and a half hours, but the brilliance of the film was its updating of *Les Misérables*, with Oscar winner Tommy Lee Jones the relentless Javert pursuing the innocent hero Valjean (Ford). (Supporting actor [w], picture [n+].)

• *Maverick* (1994)—James Garner's tongue-in-cheek TV Western was far more entertaining than this lame tribute, despite the efforts of Mel Gibson, Jodie Foster, and Garner himself. (Costumes [n].)

PAINT IT BLACK

Even if the studios were wary of the boob tube, there was one popular show being broadcast on television that kept Hollywood pinned to the screen. In March of 1951, the House Un-American Activities Committee hearings, now undertaken in the second incarnation and chaired by Joseph McCarthy, continued its investigation of Communism, centering on Hollywood. The presence of the cynical *film noir* school and the furious emphasis on reborn patriotism fueled the mania. ''Are you now or have you ever been'' became the refrain that everyone with even slightly leftist leanings dreaded, because everyone knew what your choices were: Take the Fifth, be held in contempt of Congress, pay a fine, go to prison . . . and never work in Hollywood again; or rat out all your friends and enjoy—for a while, at least—a normal career. By the time Red-baiting had more or less run its course, 212 people had been blacklisted, including some of the most potent behind-the-scenes talent Hollywood had to offer.

The net effect of this concern over extreme controversy was that the Academy seemed to bend over backward to reward "standard" entertainments. When *An American in Paris* defeated such powerhouse competition as *A Streetcar Named Desire* and *A Place in the Sun* for best picture of 1951, the crowd didn't react nearly as warmly as they might have had the harder, more realistic films taken the prize. The remainder of the decade was an infuriating roller-coaster of spectacular epics (*Ben-Hur*) and likable if essentially ordinary musicals (*Gigi*) and middlebrow comedies (*Marty*), along with hard-hitting dramas on the cutting edge (*On the Waterfront*). It was a prolific period of experimentation and playing it safe, radicals and reactionaries which has never quite been matched. What is undeniable, however, is that despite the studios' best efforts at getting Americans out of their easy chairs, Hollywood began to lose its grip on the moviemaking process. By 1958, the big studios were responsible for only about a third of the films being produced, and independent production companies seemed to be on their way to making a mark.

Here are some notable blacklist black marks on the Academy:

- *Broken Arrow* (1950). Its best screenplay nomination was originally attributed to Michael Blankfort, a writer who "fronted" for blacklisted screenwriter Albert Maltz. Maltz was bestowed with official credit by the Academy in 1991.

- *Roman Holiday* (1953). Ian McLellan Hunter was originally listed as the winner for best motion picture story, but he, too, was merely a "front" for blacklisted writer Dalton Trumbo. In 1992, Trumbo's credit was restored by the Academy.

- *The Brave One* (1956). The original author credited with the Oscar was Robert Rich, which was a pseudonym for the blacklisted Dalton Trumbo.

The award was finally properly presented to Trumbo in 1975.

- *Friendly Persuasion* (1956). The author of the best motion picture story nominee was Michael Wilson (whose name did not even appear on the print of the film). Wilson was deemed ineligible for Oscar consideration because he refused to "name names" before the HUAC. An attempt to credit the film, but not the author, was abortive, and the nomination was later formally withdrawn.

- *The Bridge on the River Kwai* (1957). In a masterstroke of the ridiculous, the original author of the book *Kwai*, Pierre Boulle, was credited with the screenplay as well—even though the French Boulle spoke little English. The actual authors, Carl Foreman and Michael Wilson, were both blacklisted. In 1984, Wilson and Foreman (both already deceased) were given Oscar credit.

- *The Defiant Ones* (1958) and *Inherit the Wind* (1960). "Nathan E. Douglas," one of the authors credited with both of these screenplays, was a pseudonym for blacklisted writer Nedrick Young. (His coauthor on both was Harold Jacob Smith.) Young was given posthumous credit: for the best story and screenplay award for *The Defiant Ones*, and best screenplay based on material from another medium nomination for *Inherit the Wind*.

OSCAR HIGHLIGHTS AND LOWLIGHTS OF THE DECADE

- **The Academy is not pink.** A rule enacted in 1956 forbade an Oscar nomination to anyone who refused to testify before the HUAC or otherwise to respond to a subpoena, or who admitted to membership in the Communist Party. Two years later, the rule was repealed.

- **Who ya votin' for, honey?** 1956 best picture nominee *Giant*, starring Elizabeth Taylor, lost to *Around the World in 80 Days*, produced by Taylor's husband, Mike Todd. Best actor winner Yul Brynner costarred with nominee Deborah Kerr in *The King and I* and with winner Ingrid Bergman in *Anastasia*.

- **It's not about awards.** Although he was not personally nominated as producer, Burt Lancaster's production company won the best picture award for *Marty* (1955).

- **An early retirement.** 1954's best actress winner, Grace Kelly, followed up her win by appearing in *To Catch a Thief* (1955), filmed on location in Monaco. She met the principality's monarch, Prince Rainer, and in 1956 they married, with Princess Grace abandoning Hollywood forever (although *The Swan* was released after her wedding).

- **The Great Kate Count, part III**. Katharine Hepburn received four Oscar nominations as best actress this decade, for *The African Queen* (1951), *Summertime* (1955), *The Rainmaker* (1956), and *Suddenly Last Summer* (1959), bringing her total count to eight.

THE WINNERS

1950

Picture—*All About Eve*
Direction—Joseph L. Mankiewicz, *All About Eve*
Actor—Jose Ferrer, *Cyrano de Bergerac*
Actress—Judy Holliday, *Born Yesterday*
Supporting Actor—George Sanders, *All About Eve*
Supporting Actress—Josephine Hull, *Harvey*
Motion Picture Story—*Panic in the Streets*
Screenplay—*All About Eve*
Story and Screenplay—*Sunset Boulevard.*
Song—"Mona Lisa," *Captain Carey, U.S.A.*
Scoring of a Dramatic or Comedy Picture—*Sunset Boulevard*
Scoring of a Musical Picture—*Annie Get Your Gun*
Irving G. Thalberg Memorial Award—Darryl F. Zanuck

1951

Picture—*An American in Paris*
Direction—George Stevens, *A Place in the Sun*
Actor—Humphrey Bogart, *The African Queen*
Actress—Vivien Leigh, *A Streetcar Named Desire*
Supporting Actor—Karl Malden, *A Streetcar Named Desire*
Supporting Actress—Kim Hunter, *A Streetcar Named Desire*
Motion Picture Story—*Seven Days to Noon*
Screenplay—*A Place in the Sun*
Story and Screenplay—*An American in Paris*

Song—"In the Cool, Cool, Cool of the Evening," *Here Comes the Groom*
Scoring of a Dramatic of Comedy Picture—*A Place in the Sun*
Scoring of a Musical Picture—*An American in Paris*
Irving G. Thalberg Memorial Award—Arthur Freed
Honorary Foreign Language Film Award—*Rashomon* (Japan)

1952

Picture—*The Greatest Show on Earth*
Direction—John Ford, *The Quiet Man*
Actor—Gary Cooper, *High Noon*
Actress—Shirley Booth, *Come Back, Little Sheba*
Supporting Actor—Anthony Quinn, *Viva Zapata!*
Supporting Actress—Gloria Grahame, *The Bad and the Beautiful*
Motion Picture Story—*The Greatest Show on Earth*
Screenplay—*The Bad and the Beautiful*
Story and Screenplay—*The Lavender Hill Mob*
Song—"High Noon (Do Not Forsake Me, Oh My Darlin')," *High Noon*
Scoring of a Dramatic or Comedy Picture—*High Noon*
Scoring of a Musical Picture—*With a Song in My Heart*
Irving G. Thalberg Memorial Award—Cecil B. DeMille
Honorary Foreign Language Film Award—*Forbidden Games* (France)

1953

Picture—*From Here to Eternity*
Direction—Fred Zinnemann, *From Here to Eternity*
Actor—William Holden, *Stalag 17*
Actress—Audrey Hepburn, *Roman Holiday*
Supporting Actor—Frank Sinatra, *From Here to Eternity*

Supporting Actress—Donna Reed, *From Here to Eternity*
Motion Picture Story—*Roman Holiday*
Screenplay—*From Here to Eternity*
Story and Screenplay—*Titanic*
Song—"Secret Love," *Calamity Jane*
Scoring of a Dramatic or Comedy Picture—*Lili*
Scoring of a Musical Picture—*Call Me Madam*
Irving G. Thalberg Memorial Award—George Stevens

1954

Picture—*On the Waterfront*
Direction—Elia Kazan, *On the Waterfront*
Actor—Marlon Brando, *On the Waterfront*
Actress—Grace Kelly, *The Country Girl*
Supporting Actor—Edmond O'Brien, *The Barefoot Contessa*
Supporting Actress—Eva Marie Saint, *On the Waterfront*
Motion Picture Story—*Broken Lance*
Screenplay—*The Country Girl*
Story and Screenplay—*On the Waterfront*
Scoring of a Dramatic or Comedy Picture—*The High and the Mighty*
Scoring of a Musical Picture—*Seven Brides for Seven Brothers*
Song—"Three Coins in the Fountain," *Three Coins in a Fountain*
Honorary Foreign Language Film Award—*Gate of Hell* (Japan)

1955

Picture—*Marty*
Direction—Delbert Mann, *Marty*
Actor—Ernest Borgnine, *Marty*
Actress—Anna Magnani, *The Rose Tattoo*
Supporting Actor—Jack Lemmon, *Mister Roberts*
Supporting Actress—Jo Van Fleet, *East of Eden*

Motion Picture Story—*Love Me or Leave Me*
Screenplay—*Marty*
Story and Screenplay—*Interrupted Melody*
Scoring of a Dramatic or Comedy Picture—*Love Is a Many-Splendored Thing*
Scoring of a Musical Picture—*Oklahoma!*
Song—"Love Is a Many-Splendored Thing," *Love Is a Many-Splendored Thing*
Honorary Foreign Language Film Award—*Samurai, The Legend of Musashi* (Japan)

1956

Picture—*Around the World in 80 Days*
Direction—George Stevens, *Giant*
Actor—Yul Brynner, *The King and I*
Actress—Ingrid Bergman, *Anastasia*
Supporting Actor—Anthony Quinn, *Lust for Life*
Supporting Actress—Dorothy Malone, *Written on the Wind*
Motion Picture Story—*The Brave One*
Original Screenplay—*The Red Balloon*
Adapted Screenplay—*Around the World in 80 Days*
Scoring of a Dramatic or Comedy Picture—*Around the World in 80 Days*
Scoring of a Musical Picture—*The King and I*
Song—"Whatever Will Be, Will Be (Que Será, Será)," *The Man Who Knew Too Much*
Foreign Language Film—*La Strada* (Italy)
Irving G. Thalberg Memorial Award—Buddy Adler

1957

Picture—*The Bridge on the River Kwai*
Direction—David Lean, *The Bridge on the River Kwai*
Actor—Alec Guinness, *The Bridge on the River Kwai*
Actress—Joanne Woodward, *The Three Faces of Eve*
Supporting Actor—Red Buttons, *Sayonara*
Supporting Actress—Miyoshi Umeki, *Sayonara*

Story and Screenplay Written Directly for the Screen—*Designing Woman*

Screenplay Based on Material from Another Medium—*The Bridge on the River Kwai*

Score—*The Bridge on the River Kwai*

Song—"All the Way," *The Joker Is Wild*

Foreign Language Film—*The Nights of Cabiria* (Italy)

1958

Picture—*Gigi*

Direction—Vincente Minelli, *Gigi*

Actor—David Niven, *Separate Tables*

Actress—Susan Hayward, *I Want to Live!*

Supporting Actor—Burl Ives, *The Big Country*

Supporting Actress—Wendy Hiller, *Separate Tables*

Story and Screenplay Written Directly for the Screen—*The Defiant Ones*

Screenplay Based on Material from Another Medium—*Gigi*

Scoring of a Dramatic or Comedy Picture—*The Old Man and the Sea*

Scoring of a Musical Picture—*Gigi*

Song—"Gigi," *Gigi*

Foreign Language Film—*My Uncle* (France)

Irving G. Thalberg Memorial Award—Jack L. Warner

1959

Picture—*Ben-Hur*
Direction—William Wyler, *Ben-Hur*
Actor—Charlton Heston, *Ben-Hur*
Actress—Simone Signoret, *Room at the Top*
Supporting Actor—Hugh Griffith, *Ben-Hur*
Supporting Actress—Shelley Winters, *The Diary of Anne Frank*
Story and Screenplay Written Directly for the Screen—*Pillow Talk*
Screenplay Based on Material from Another Medium—*Room at the Top*
Scoring of a Dramatic or Comedy Picture—*Ben-Hur*
Scoring of a Musical Picture—*Porgy and Bess*
Song—"High Hopes," *A Hole in the Head*
Foreign Language Film—*Black Orpheus* (France)

Chapter
Ten

The '60s: So Long to the Studios...
Sort Of

BIG IS BIG, AND ART IS ART

Beginning in the '40s and continuing through the '50s, the majors enjoyed a stranglehold on virtually all film production, distribution, and exhibition; in the '60s, their control over stars' careers waned, their monopoly of film production and distribution had ended, and the era of the dictatorial mogul was fading fast, and by the 1960s was all but a memory.

But the big studios never really went away. There's no denying that the "studio system" finally died, but as the rest of Hollywood entered a new era, Fox, Paramount, and company found new ways to keep their thumbs in the pie. Indeed, the legacy of the studios' transformation remains with us even today, as we tend to divide films into "indie" and "studio" pictures; "art" vs. "product." The studios of the '60s continued to produce memorable movies with that slick veneer and broad, universal sentimentality. Remarkably, more musicals won the best picture Oscar in the '60s—four—than in all other decades combined.

That was a perfect example of how the studios were filling one particular need, while international and "art house" films began to make inroads into popular culture. *L'Avventura* is simply not everyone's cup of tea, and the glamorous, spectacular entertainments with the perfect, classy stars of old were still around appeal to "the establishment."

But starting in the late '50s with the release of *Room at the Top,* a variation of Italian neorealism began to creep into English language films. This frank, brutal, usually grim genre of drama from Britain became known as "Angry Young Man" cinema, and ushered in a romance between international films and the Academy. The '60s would also signal the first decade in which an acting trophy was given to a foreign language performance, the first time since 1939 that a foreign language film was nominated for best picture, and an incredible surge of films (mostly from Europe—especially Italy—but some from Japan) competing in the "regular" Oscar categories. In 1966 alone, two best actress nominees, one best director nominee, one screenplay nominee, and six nominees in assorted design and scoring categories were from foreign language films.

Even many of the English language films were touching on areas that weren't considered "appropriate" for the studios themselves (even if the studios buckled under to the promise of money and distributed them). Abortion (*Alfie, The L-Shaped Room*), race relations (*Lilies of the Field, In the Heat of the Night, Guess Who's Coming to Dinner*), rape (*Two Women*), and many other issues of current and pressing interest to the public bullied their way into movie theaters with a force and regularity unheard of in prior decades. Other genres of film that began to take hold during a decade when anything goes included:

- the French New Wave, or *nouvelle vague*
- Cold War political thrillers
- psychological dramas
- allegorical art house films, especially from Bergman, Antonioni, and Fellini

The tension between the "established" studio-style filmmakers and the Young Turks of cinema was nowhere more vividly reflected than in the Academy Awards races. When presented in 1965 with a choice between *My Fair Lady* and *Dr. Strangelove*, the way an Academy member voted clearly suggested an allegiance to the old ways or the new, and there were many desperate to cling to the old ways. Because as much as the nation was in a state of upheaval, the studios continued to produce escapism. (It worked during the Depression, so there was no reason to think it wouldn't work again during Hippiedom.) Most of the '60s reflects an uneasy tension between the "new" facts and the old—the nominations for the new might flow like wine, but the wins were few and far between—until 1967, when *The Graduate* won the best director Oscar. It was up for many more awards than it actually won, but this sole victory marked a turning point for the Academy: Counterculture, when framed in a white suburban environment, became not only artistically meritorious but also big box office. And *The Graduate* was released by upstart Embassy Pictures—the first time an American-made film took the prize without any help from a major studio. Two years later, when *Easy Rider* became one of the most financially successful films of all time (and earned Oscar nominations for its hippie-trippie screenplay by Peter Fonda, Dennis Hopper, and Terry Southern, and Jack Nicholson's drawling, druggy supporting performance), the truth seemed inevitable: "Alternative" filmmaking had finally arrived, and Oscar had validated it.

📽 The studio tally

The calculation of wins for each studio has altered somewhat with the changes in the industry. The seven big studios from the early days of the Oscars—Columbia, Metro-Goldwyn-Mayer, Paramount, Twentieth Century-Fox, United Artists, Universal, and Warner Brothers—released most of the films in the United States at the time, and produced most of them in-house as well. With the deterioration of the studio system, studios became less involved in the actual production of films, and instead were more involved in financing and distribution. The effect is that independent production companies "make" the movies, but the still-existing studios have the privilege of attaching their names to them. The first time two of the major studios collaborated on a best picture nominee was when Twentieth Century-Fox and Warner Brothers both had distribution/production credit for *The Towering Inferno* (1974). They lost to Paramount's *The Godfather Part II*.

In addition to the studios named above, the other studios responsible for Oscar-winning films are RKO, J. Arthur Rank (in conjunction with Two Cities), and Orion. The only other "minor" studios (or other production sources) ever to receive best picture Oscar nominations without distribution association with one of the majors are: First National (*Five Star Final*, 1931/32; *Flirtation Walk*, 1934); Republic Pictures (*The Quiet Man*, 1952); Allied Artists (*Friendly Persuasion*, 1956; *Cabaret*, 1972); Romulus Films (*Room at the Top*, 1959); Avco-Embassy Pictures (*Becket*, 1965; *The Lion in Winter*, 1968; *A Touch of Class*, 1973); Cinema V (*Z*, 1969); Svensk Filmindustri (*The Emigrants*, 1972); New World Pictures (*Cries and Whispers*, 1973); Island Alive (*Kiss of the Spider Woman*, 1985); Cinecom (*A Room with a View*, 1986); Miramax (*My Left Foot*, 1981; *The Crying Game*, 1992; *The Piano*, 1993; *Pulp Fiction*, 1994; *Il Postino [The Postman]*, 1995; *The English Patient*, 1996; *Good Will Hunting*, 1997); Gramercy (*Four Weddings and a Funeral*, 1994).

A watershed year occurred in 1996 when four of the five best picture nominees were from independent studios: Miramax (winner, *The English Patient*), Gramercy (*Fargo*), Fine Line Features (*Shine*), and October Films (*Secrets & Lies*); the fifth nominee was *Jerry Maguire*, from Columbia/TriStar.

Making an authoritative list of the Oscars "won" by each studio which "made" them, therefore, is not a clear-cut procedure. What follows, however, accurately reflects which studios have been, at a minimum, closely affiliated with each best picture Oscar winner.

• **Columbia**. Total best picture wins: 12.
Best picture winners: *It Happened One Night* (1934); *You Can't Take It With You* (1938); *All the King's Men* (1949); *From Here to Eternity* (1953); *On the Waterfront* (1954); *The Bridge on the River Kwai* (1957); *Lawrence of Arabia* (1962); *A Man for All Seasons* (1966); *Oliver!* (1968); *Kramer vs. Kramer* (1979); *Gandhi* (1982); *The Last Emperor* (1987).

• **Metro-Goldwyn-Mayer (MGM)**. Total best picture wins: 8.
Best picture winners: *Broadway Melody* (1928/29); *Grand Hotel* (1931/32); *Mutiny on the Bounty* (1935); *The Great Ziegfeld* (1936); *Gone with the Wind** (1939); *Mrs. Miniver* (1942); *An American in Paris* (1951); *Ben-Hur* (1959).

---

*Selznick International, although technically a production company and not a studio—its two winning films, *Gone with the Wind* (1939) and *Rebecca* (1940), were released through MGM and UA, respectively—holds a particular distinction in that David O. Selznick was once head of MGM (he was married to Mayer's daughter Irene). His independence in establishing his own studio led to him later claim that

- **Orion**. Total best picture wins: 4.
Best picture winners: *Amadeus* (1984); *Platoon* (1986); *Dances with Wolves* (1990); *The Silence of the Lambs* (1991).

- **Paramount**. Total best picture wins: 11.
Best picture winners: *Wings* (1927/28); *Going My Way* (1944); *The Lost Weekend* (1945); *The Greatest Show on Earth* (1952); *The Godfather* (1972); *The Godfather Part II* (1974); *Ordinary People* (1980); *Terms of Endearment* (1983); *Forrest Gump* (1994); *Braveheart* (1995); *Titanic* (1997).

- **J. Arthur Rank**. Total best picture wins: 1.
Best picture winner: *Hamlet* (1948).

- **RKO**.* Total best picture wins: 2.
Best picture winners: *Cimarron* (1930/31); *The Best Years of Our Lives* (1946).

- **Twentieth Century-Fox**. Total best picture wins: 8.
Best picture winners: *Cavalcade* (1932/33); *How Green Was My Valley* (1941); *Gentleman's Agreement* (1947); *All About Eve* (1950); *The Sound of Music* (1965); *Patton* (1970); *The French Connection* (1971); *Titanic* (1997).

- **United Artists**. Total best picture wins: 12.
Best picture winners: *Rebecca** (1940); *Marty* (1955); *Around the World in 80 Days* (1956); *The Apartment* (1960); *West Side Story* (1961); *Tom Jones* (1963); *In the Heat of the Night* (1967); *Midnight Cowboy* (1969); *One Flew Over the*

"*Gone with the Wind* is not an MGM picture." Selznick was the only producer to win two consecutive best picture awards—his only wins. Of the two other most famous independent producers of the '30s, '40s, and '50s—Otto Preminger and Samuel Goldwyn—only Goldwyn won a best picture Oscar, for *The Best Years of Our Lives* (1946), released through RKO.

Cuckoo's Nest (1975); *Rocky* (1976); *Annie Hall* (1977); *Rain Man* (1988).

• **Universal**. Total best picture wins: 5.
Best picture winners: *All Quiet on the Western Front* (1929/30); *The Sting* (1973); *The Deer Hunter* (1978); *Out of Africa* (1985); *Schindler's List* (1993).

• **Warner Brothers**. Total best picture wins: 6.
Best picture winners: *The Life of Emile Zola* (1937); *Casablanca* (1943); *My Fair Lady* (1964); *Chariots of Fire* (1981); *Driving Miss Daisy* (1989); *Unforgiven* (1992).

GRAY LADY DOWN

The 1960s also heralded the end of dual awards in the color and black-and-white categories, in 1966. (The distinction was temporarily abandoned earlier, for one year, in 1957.) The decision would seem to be a consequence of the predominance of color films and the increasingly spartan b&w choices, but was that really true? Many of the lower-budget films of the era continued to be in black-and-white (as they are today), and many directors, especially from the New Wave, preferred to work with the chiaroscuro effect of a monochromatic pallette. Although there no doubt were fewer black-and-white films, what is probably as true was that there were fewer films that the Academy felt like honoring. After all, the b&w dividing line has always had the effect of diluting the value of the awards by increasing their number, and though the decision was fair, after a while the Academy probably just got tired of having to come up with ten nominees, leading to such dubious nominations as *The Oscar* for color costumes, or *Period of Adjustment* competing with *The Pigeon That Took Rome* for b&w art direction . . . or maybe they just got tired of feeling obligated to nominate Edith Head (sometimes more than once) every damn year.

Quiz: Trivia from the '60s

Q. **What four musicals won the best picture Oscar during the 1960s?**
A.   *West Side Story* (1961), *My Fair Lady* (1964), *The Sound of Music* (1965), and *Oliver!* (1968).

Q. **What was the first New Wave film to receive an Oscar nomination?**
A.   *The 400 Blows* (1959). François Truffaut and his coauthor were nominated for story and screenplay and lost, offensively enough, to *Pillow Talk*. Other early New Wave screenplay nominees include *Hiroshima, Mon Amour* (1960; story and screenplay) and *Last Year at Marienbad* (1962; story and screenplay). Although it is not generally considered a New Wave film, director Jacques Demy's *The Umbrellas of Cherbourg* (1965) actually is part of the movement—it's just that Demy's aesthetic was for musicals rather than gangster and coming-of-age films. *Umbrellas* received a best foreign language film nomination in 1964 (the year it was submitted by France), and four other nominations (including story and screenplay) in 1965. Until *Das Boot* in 1982, *The Umbrellas of Cherbourg* held the record for the most nominations for a foreign language film.

Q. **Name at least three Westerns that were best picture nominees. (More Westerns were nominated in the 1960s than in any other single decade.)**
A.   The 11 Westerns nominated for best picture are: *In Old Arizona* (1928/29), *Cimarron* (1930/31) [w], *Stagecoach* (1939), *The Ox-Bow Incident* (1943), *High Noon* (1952), *Shane* (1953), *The Al-*

amo (1960), *How the West Was Won* (1963), *Butch Cassidy and the Sundance Kid* (1969), *Dances with Wolves* (1990) [w], and *Unforgiven* (1992) [w]. If you mentioned *Midnight Cowboy*, deduct 10 points.

Q. **What was the last best picture nominee to be shot in black-and-white?**
A. *Schindler's List* (1993), *Raging Bull* (1980), *Lenny* (1974), and *The Last Picture Show* (1971) used all or predominantly black-and-white photography for a particular effect, even though color films had dominated the market for several years. The last black-and-white film nominated for best picture at a time when there were still separate awards handed out for color and black-and-white categories (cinematography, art direction, costumes) was *Who's Afraid of Virginia Woolf?* (1966). Elizabeth Taylor is also the last leading actress to receive an award for a black-and-white film. Best actor Robert De Niro in *Raging Bull* and supporting winners Cloris Leachman and Ben Johnson from *The Last Picture Show* are the b&w winners from their categories.

Q. **When was the first year that the Oscars were broadcast in color?**
A. 1967, on ABC.

Q. **What film served as the inspiration for 1960's best picture *The Apartment*, when writer-director Billy Wilder became obsessed over the guy who owned the apartment where sexual liaisons took place?**
A. *Brief Encounter* (1946).

Q. **Name the only major production studio never to win a best picture Oscar.**
A. Walt Disney. Individually, it has received only two best picture nominations—for *Mary Poppins* (1964) and *Beauty and the Beast* (1991)—although

its subsidiaries, which include Hollywood Pictures, Touchstone Pictures, and Caravan Pictures (and its distribution arm, Buena Vista), have produced several more best picture–nominated films, including *Quiz Show* (1994). (Several subsidiaries of Sony/ Columbia—TriStar and Sony Pictures Classics— and Twentieth Century-Fox's Fox Searchlight have also received best picture nominations.)

Q. **What extremely popular, Oscar-winning documentary feature was also nominated for film editing by Scorsese perennial Thelma Schoonmaker?**
A. *Woodstock* (1970). Her editorial assistant on the film was Martin Scorsese himself.

Q. **What were the names of the competing street gangs in *West Side Story*?**
A. The Jets and the Sharks. The Sharks were the Puerto Ricans, the Jets the Italians.

Q. **What two best actress winners accepted their awards in high-fashion ... pajamas?**
A. Julie Christie (*Darling*, 1965) and Barbra Streisand (*Funny Girl*, 1968).

Q. **What Oscar-winning picture gets its title from the telephone number of the leading character?**
A. *Butterfield 8* (actress, 1960) The title originates from the now-antiquated policy of referring to a telephone exchange by using the first two letters of the prefix (here, BU) in the number. Thus "BUtterfield 8" would be "288."

Q. **What film was nominated as best foreign language film in 1966, two years before it received nominations for its writing and direction (1968)?**
A. *The Battle of Algiers*. It occurred because of the odd Academy rules concerning submission of foreign language films for eligibility. Similar bon-

ers can be found, usually in lesser categories,
throughout Oscar history.

Q. **Who was the first person to win an Oscar for
makeup?**
A.   William Tuttle received an honorary Oscar for
The 7 Faces of Dr. Lao (1964). The only other
recipient of an honorary makeup award was John
Chambers for *Planet of the Apes* (1968). It became
a regular competitive category in 1981.

Q. **What actor best known for playing a villain on
the campy TV series *Batman* received an Oscar
nomination for best supporting actor as a con
man, opposite Bette Davis?**
A.   Victor Buono, for *What Ever Happened to
Baby Jane?* (1962). He played "King Tut" on *Batman*.

Q. **"Liz and Dick" (Taylor and Burton) were about
the most exciting and glamorous thing to happen
to Hollywood—and the Oscars—in the '60s.
Their films together tended to be fairly popular,
although on occasion critically acclaimed. Name
at least three movies in their Oscar-nominated
(and sometimes Oscar-winning) *oeuvre* of the
decade.**
A.   They kicked off the decade with the big, ter-
rible epic *Cleopatra* (1963; picture [n+]). Despite
the attention focused on the two top stars, it was
costar Rex Harrison who received the only acting
nomination. Their pairings continued with *The
V.I.P.'s* (1963; supporting actress [w]), *The Sandpiper* (1965; song [w]), *Who's Afraid of Virginia
Woolf?* (1966; picture [n+]), and *The Taming of
the Shrew* (1967; costumes [n+]). Their last three
films, *Dr. Faustus, The Comedians*, and finally, the
aptly titled *Boom!*, justly received no Oscar nominations of any kind.

Q. Who are the only two codirectors to share an Oscar, and for what film?

A. Jerome Robbins and Robert Wise, for *West Side Story* (1961). Neither mentioned the other in his acceptance speech. The only other codirector nominees ever are Warren Beatty and Buck Henry for *Heaven Can Wait* (1978).

Q. In what category in 1963 were all the nominees foreign-born?

A. Supporting actress.

Q. Audrey Hepburn had her singing voice dubbed in *My Fair Lady*, and failed to net a nomination. For what film (in which she was nominated as best actress) did she sing the popular best song winner?

A. *Breakfast at Tiffany's*. The song was "Moon River."

Q. What two films received the most Oscar nominations in history *without* winning best picture?

A. *Who's Afraid of Virginia Woolf?* (1966), which netted five awards, and *Mary Poppins* (1965), six wins—each out of 13 nominations—but best picture not among them. *Becket* (1965) and *Reds* (1981) each clocked 12 nominations without the ultimate victory.

Q. What Oscar-winning film went by the title *Meet Whiplash Willie* in Britain?

A. *The Fortune Cookie* (supporting actor, 1966). Walter Matthau played the (British) title character, a shady ambulance-chasing lawyer.

Q. What was the first film to be nominated for best foreign language film and best picture in the same year?

A. *Z* (1969).

Q. **What Henry Mancini–scored cartoon character won his first animated short Oscar in the 1960s?**
A.   The Pink Panther, for *The Pink Phink* (1964).

🎞 James at 19

A relic of the '60s Cold War, or an icon of universal appeal? The most successful movie franchise in history began in 1962, when Sean Connery breathed the words, "My name is Bond . . . James Bond" for the first time in *Dr. No*, and things haven't been the same since: 18 "official" features (i.e., those produced by Cubby Broccoli and company), one "official" spoof (*Casino Royale*), and one "unofficial" remake of *Thunderball* starring, of all people, Sean Connery (*Never Say Never Again*). James hasn't fared as well at the Oscars as one might expect—not a single nomination for the major awards—but he's turned in a respectable showing: nine nominations doled out over about half of the films, two early wins, millions of fans, and millions more dollars. Nominations and wins include:

- *Goldfinger* (1964): sound effects [w]
- *Thunderball* (1965): visual effects [w]
- *Diamonds Are Forever* (1971): sound [n]
- *Live and Let Die* (1973): song [n]
- *The Spy Who Loved Me* (1977): art direction [n], song [n], original score [n]
- *Moonraker* (1979): visual effects [n]
- *For Your Eyes Only* (1981): song [n]

OSCAR HIGHLIGHTS AND LOWLIGHTS
OF THE DECADE

- **In English, please**. In 1962, three of the best story and screenplay nominees were for foreign language films.

- **Telling the good guys from the bad guys**. All of the (evil) Romans in *Spartacus* are played by Britons—or at least actors with British accents; all of the (good) slaves are played by Americans.

- **The Great Kate Count, part IV**. Katharine Hepburn received three more Oscar nominations as best actress, for *Long Day's Journey into Night* (1962), and two back-to-back wins, for *Guess Who's Coming to Dinner* (1967) and *The Lion in Winter* (1968). Her three wins set a record in the leading performer category (it tied Walter Brennan's), and her total nominations were a staggering eleven.

THE WINNERS

1960

Picture—*The Apartment*
Direction—Billy Wilder, *The Apartment*
Actor—Burt Lancaster, *Elmer Gantry*
Actress—Elizabeth Taylor, *Butterfield 8*
Supporting Actor—Peter Ustinov, *Spartacus*
Supporting Actress—Shirley Jones, *Elmer Gantry*
Screenplay Written Directly for the Screen—*The Apartment*

Screenplay Based on Material from Another Medium—*Elmer Gantry*
Cinematography (Black and White)—*Sons and Lovers*
Cinematography (Color)—*Spartacus*
Scoring of a Dramatic or Comedy Picture—*Exodus*
Scoring of a Musical Picture—*Song Without End*
Original Song—"Never on Sunday," *Never on Sunday*
Foreign Language Film—*The Virgin Spring* (Sweden)
Jean Hersholt Humanitarian Award—Sol Lesser
Honorary Awards—Gary Cooper; Stan Laurel; Hayley Mills (outstanding juvenile performance for *Polyanna*)

1961

Picture—*West Side Story*
Direction—Robert Wise and Jerome Robbins, *West Side Story*
Actor—Maximilian Schell, *Judgment at Nuremberg*
Actress—Sophia Loren, *Two Women*
Supporting Actor—George Chakiris, *West Side Story*
Supporting Actress—Rita Moreno, *West Side Story*
Story and Screenplay Written Directly for the Screen—*Splendor in the Grass*
Screenplay Based on Material from Another Medium—*Judgment at Nuremberg*
Cinematography (Black and White)—*The Hustler*
Cinematography (Color)—*West Side Story*
Scoring of a Dramatic or Comedy Picture—*Breakfast at Tiffany's*
Scoring of a Musical Picture—*West Side Story*
Song—"Moon River," *Breakfast at Tiffany's*
Foreign Language Film—*Through a Glass Darkly* (Sweden)
Irving G. Thalberg Memorial Award—Stanley Kramer
Jean Hersholt Humanitarian Award—George Seaton

1962

Picture—*Lawrence of Arabia*
Direction—David Lean, *Lawrence of Arabia*

Actor—Gregory Peck, *To Kill a Mockingbird*
Actress—Anne Bancroft, *The Miracle Worker*
Supporting Actor—Ed Begley, *Sweet Bird of Youth*
Supporting Actress—Patty Duke, *The Miracle Worker*
Story and Screenplay Written Directly for the Screen—*Divorce, Italian Style*
Screenplay Based on Material from Another Medium—*To Kill a Mockingbird*
Cinematography (Black and White)—*The Longest Day*
Cinematography (Color)—*Lawrence of Arabia*
Musical Score (Substantially Original)—*Lawrence of Arabia*
Scoring of Music (Adaptation or Treatment)—*The Music Man*
Original Song—"Days of Wine and Roses," *Days of Wine and Roses*
Foreign Language Film—*Sundays and Cybele* (France)
Jean Hersholt Humanitarian Award—Steve Broidy

1963

Picture—*Tom Jones*
Direction—Tony Richardson, *Tom Jones*
Actor—Sidney Poitier, *Lilies of the Field*
Actress—Patricia Neal, *Hud*
Supporting Actor—Melvyn Douglas, *Hud*
Supporting Actress—Margaret Rutherford, *The V.I.P.'s*
Screenplay Based on Material from Another Medium—*Tom Jones*
Story and Screenplay Written Directly for the Screen—*How the West Was Won*
Cinematography (Black and White)—*Hud*
Cinematography (Color)—*Cleopatra*
Music Score (Substantially Original)—*Tom Jones*
Scoring of Music (Adaptation or Treatment)—*Irma La Douce*

Original Song—"Call Me Irresponsible," *Papa's Delicate Condition*
Foreign Language Film—*8½* (Italy)
Irving G. Thalberg Memorial Award—Sam Spiegel

1964

Picture—*My Fair Lady*
Direction—George Cukor, *My Fair Lady*
Actor—Rex Harrison, *My Fair Lady*
Actress—Julie Andrews, *Mary Poppins*
Supporting Actor—Peter Ustinov, *Topkapi*
Supporting Actress—Lila Kedrova, *Zorba the Greek*
Story and Screenplay Written Directly for the Screen—*Father Goose*
Screenplay Based on Material from Another Medium—*Becket*
Cinematography (Black and White)—*Zorba the Greek*
Cinematography (Color)—*My Fair Lady*
Music Score (Substantially Original)—*Mary Poppins*
Scoring of Music (Adaptation or Treatment)—*My Fair Lady*
Song—"Chim Chim Cher-ee," *Mary Poppins*
Foreign Language Film—*Yesterday, Today and Tomorrow* (Italy)

1965

Picture—*The Sound of Music*
Direction—Robert Wise, *The Sound of Music*
Actor—Lee Marvin, *Cat Ballou*
Actress—Julie Christie, *Darling*
Supporting Actor—Martin Balsam, *A Thousand Clowns*
Supporting Actress—Shelley Winters, *A Patch of Blue*
Story and Screenplay Written Directly for the Screen—*Darling*
Screenplay Based on Material from Another Medium—*Doctor Zhivago*
Cinematography (Black and White)—*Ship of Fools*

Cinematography (Color)—*Doctor Zhivago*
Music Score (Substantially Original)—*Doctor Zhivago*
Scoring of Music (Adaptation or Treatment)—*The Sound of Music*
Song—"The Shadow of Your Smile," *The Sandpiper*
Foreign Language Film—*The Shop on Main Street* (Czechoslovakia)
Irving G. Thalberg Memorial Award—William Wyler
Jean Hersholt Humanitarian Award—Edmund L. DePatie

1966

Picture—*A Man for All Seasons*
Direction—Fred Zinnemann, *A Man for All Seasons*
Actor—Paul Scofield, *A Man for All Seasons*
Actress—Elizabeth Taylor, *Who's Afraid of Virginia Woolf?*
Supporting Actor—Walter Matthau, *The Fortune Cookie*
Supporting Actress—Sandy Dennis, *Who's Afraid of Virginia Woolf?*
Story and Screenplay Written Directly for the Screen—*A Man and a Woman*
Screenplay Based on Material from Another Medium—*A Man for All Seasons*
Cinematography (Black and White)—*Who's Afraid of Virginia Woolf*
Cinematography (Color)—*A Man for All Seasons*
Original Music Score—*Born Free*
Scoring (Adaptation or Treatment)—*A Funny Thing Happened on the Way to the Forum*
Original Song—"Born Free," *Born Free*
Foreign Language Film—*A Man and a Woman* (France)
Irving G. Thalberg Memorial Award—Robert Wise
Jean Hersholt Humanitarian Award—George Bagnall

1967

Picture—*In the Heat of the Night*
Direction—Mike Nichols, *The Graduate*
Actor—Rod Steiger, *In the Heat of the Night*
Actress—Katharine Hepburn, *Guess Who's Coming to Dinner*
Supporting Actor—George Kennedy, *Cool Hand Luke*
Supporting Actress—Estelle Parsons, *Bonnie and Clyde*
Screenplay Based on Material from Another Medium—*In the Heat of the Night*
Story and Screenplay Written Directly for the Screen—*Guess Who's Coming to Dinner*
Cinematography—*Bonnie and Clyde*
Original Music Score—*Thoroughly Modern Millie*
Scoring of Music (Adaptation or Treatment)—*Camelot*
Original Song—"Talk to the Animals," *Doctor Doolittle*
Foreign Language Film—*Closely Watched Trains* (Czechoslovakia)
Irving G. Thalberg Memorial Award—Alfred Hitchcock
Jean Hersholt Humanitarian Award—Gregory Peck

1968

Picture—*Oliver!*
Direction—Carol Reed, *Oliver!*
Actor—Cliff Robertson, *Charly*
Actress (tie)—Katharine Hepburn, *The Lion in Winter*; Barbra Streisand, *Funny Girl*
Supporting Actor—Jack Albertson, *The Subject Was Roses*
Supporting Actress—Ruth Gordon, *Rosemary's Baby*
Story and Screenplay Written Directly for the Screen—*The Producers*
Screenplay Based on Material from Another Medium—*The Lion in Winter*
Cinematography—*Romeo and Juliet*

Original Score for a Picture (Not a Musical)—*The Lion in Winter*
Score of a Musical Picture (Original or Adaptation)—*Oliver!*
Original Song—"The Windmills of Your Mind," *The Thomas Crown Affair*
Foreign Language Film—*War and Peace* (Russia)
Jean Hersholt Humanitarian Award—Martha Raye

1969

Picture—*Midnight Cowboy*
Direction—John Schlesinger, *Midnight Cowboy*
Actor—John Wayne, *True Grit*
Actress—Maggie Smith, *The Prime of Miss Jean Brodie*
Supporting Actor—Gig Young, *They Shoot Horses, Don't They?*
Supporting Actress—Goldie Hawn, *Cactus Flower*
Story and Screenplay Based on Material Not Previously Published or Produced—*Butch Cassidy and the Sundance Kid*
Screenplay Based on Material from Another Medium—*Midnight Cowboy*
Cinematography—*Butch Cassidy and the Sundance Kid*
Original Score for a Motion Picture (Not a Musical)—*Butch Cassidy and the Sundance Kid*
Score of a Musical Picture (Original or Adaptation)—*Hello, Dolly!*
Original Song—"Raindrops Keep Fallin' on My Head," *Butch Cassidy and the Sundance Kid*
Foreign Language Film—*Z* (Algeria)
Jean Hersholt Humanitarian Award—George Jessell
Honorary Award—Cary Grant

The '70s: The School for Scandal

WHEN RADICALS REIGNED

If the success of *Easy Rider* in 1969 was the advent of an age when youth-oriented films would dominate the market, then 1970 saw Hollywood jump headlong into controversy and the rebellion of youth, with Oscar following suit. The debut year of the decade saw major nominations for *M*A*S*H* (with its antiwar, anti-God message), *Women in Love* (with its all-male, all-nude wrestling scene), *Five Easy Pieces* (in which the undirected anger of Jack Nicholson leads to the best restaurant scene until *My Dinner with André*), and *The Great White Hope* (dealing with an interracial love). But the biggest controversy of 1970 didn't appear on screen, but on the stage of the Dorothy Chandler Pavilion—or rather, off it. George C. Scott became the first major winner to publicly refuse his Oscar, for best actor in *Patton*.

Scott had rejected the nomination from the outset, and so when he failed to appear no one was a bit surprised—there was no speech, no proselytizing, no righteous indignation. That would have to wait two years, when Marlon Brando became the *second* best actor winner to refuse his Oscar, this time for *The Godfather*—even though he showed up to accept his win in 1954 for *On the Waterfront*. But Brando knew how to make a fuss, and he sent a surrogate: Native American activist Sasheen Littlefeather, in full tribal regalia, shaming the Hollywood community for its treatment of the American Indian.

And this was just the beginning. The '60s may have been when America was in the throes of great change, but there has never been a more turbulent, vocal, and public era for the Oscars than the '70s. The war in Vietnam began to rage in the late '60s, and it took the studios time to catch up. Just as jingoistic WWII films dominated the nominees in the '40s, the 1970s saw *antiwar* films like *Coming Home, The Deer Hunter*, and *Apocalypse Now* (all about Vietnam), *Taxi Driver* (about a disturbed Vietnam vet), and *M*A*S*H* (set during the Korean War but "about" Vietnam nonetheless) win major accolades. (Even *American Graffiti*, a swan song to the innocence of the '50s and early '60s, also hinted at the clouds of dissent on the horizon through the sobering lens of hindsight.)

The age of the "message" movie seemed to have arrived. Not only were films about Vietnam, race relations, and similar sensitive issues now all the rage, but every orphaned liberal cause in Hollywood or politically sensitive topic in the nation seemed to have an Oscar contender: unionism (*Norma Rae*), Watergate (*All the President's Men, The Conversation*), alienation (*Five Easy Pieces, The Last Picture Show, Lenny*), violent crime (*A Clockwork Orange*), postwar trauma (*Taxi Driver*), divorce (*Kramer vs. Kramer, An Unmarried Woman*), frank depictions of sex (*Carnal Knowledge, Last Tango in Paris*), even the evils of television (*Network*). Without a doubt, Hollywood has never been more attuned toward ginning up debate and trying to take its issues "seriously."

The awards ceremony itself did nothing toward curtailing controversy. The '70s will long be remembered for the streaker at the 1974 broadcast, and perhaps most infamously, what may qualify as the most well-known acceptance speech in Oscar history, Vanessa Redgrave's.

Because of her politics, Redgrave had been an object of derision and scorn from many sides, but it reached a scandalous pinnacle at the 1977 Oscar ceremony, when she won an award for best supporting actress for *Julia* while protesters burned her in effigy outside. Her now-notorious speech, more memorable than her Oscar-winning film, actually shows a degree of class—after all, how many of us have been burned in effigy on what should be our best night of the year? In part, she said:

> *I salute you and I pay tribute to you and I think you should be very proud that in the last few weeks you've stood firm and you have refused to be intimidated by the threats of a small bunch of Zionist hoodlums whose behavior is an insult to the stature of Jews all over the world and their great and heroic struggle against fascism and oppression.*

DON'T CALL ME PRETTY BOY

Maybe it was just a side effect of the rebelliousness of the age, but the '70s also saw the rise of the less-than-traditionally-good-looking leading man. "Ethnic" was often the word used to describe popular actors like Dustin Hoffman (*Kramer vs. Kramer*, 1979), Robert De Niro (*The Godfather Part II*, 1974), John Travolta (nominated for *Saturday Night Fever*, 1977), and Al Pacino (nominated for *Serpico*, 1973, and more), but this was also a time when Gene Hackman (*The French Connection*, 1971), Jack Nicholson (*One Flew Over the Cuckoo's Nest*, 1975), and Richard Dreyfuss (*The Goodbye Girl*, 1977) became not only leading actors of the day, but also sex symbols. (Not to say traditionally handsome men disappeared: The decade kicked off with an Oscar nomination for Ryan O'Neal, and Warren Beatty continued to draw crowds and coos.) Also gaining surprise recognition: codgers like John Houseman (best supporting actor, *The Paper Chase*, 1973) and especially

George Burns (best supporting actor, *The Sunshine Boys*, 1975)—the latter going on to star in appealing, popular comedies with young costars like Brooke Shields and John Denver.

Perhaps the most unlikely of all the new stars of a new age, though, was Woody Allen. He had been making his own quirky comedies since the 1960s, but in 1977, his hit *Annie Hall* made him a major force. The film won best picture, as well as actress (Diane Keaton), original screenplay, and director (Allen). His subsequent films made him seem to be an Oscar magnet: In the '70s alone, *Interiors* (nominations for director and screenplay) and *Manhattan* (nominated for screenplay) hit pay dirt; overall, Allen would receive almost 20 nominations, for acting, writing, and directing.

Women began to come into their own, too. Spunky, individualistic working mothers and truly independent women made headway in the Oscar races: grass-roots union organizer Sally Field in *Norma Rae* (1979 [w]), divorcée Jill Clayburgh in *An Unmarried Woman* (1978 [n]), unpredictable, decadent Liza Minnelli in *Cabaret* (1972 [w]), and sharp-tongued Glenda Jackson (*Women in Love*, 1970, and *A Touch of Class*, 1973 [w]). Of course, the traditionally beautiful women of the screen were never the best Oscar contenders anyway—Ava Gardner never won, and Marilyn Monroe was never even nominated.

Okay, so Ingrid Bergman and Grace Kelly won. But when it comes to beauty and to acting, both are on a higher plane than most.

Quiz: Trivia from the '70s

Q.   What actor appeared in only five films, all in the 1970s—and all best picture nominees or winners?

A.   John Cazale. His incredible resume: *The God-*

father (1972 [w]), *The Godfather Part II* (1974 [w]), *The Conversation* (1974 [n]), *Dog Day Afternoon* (1975 [n]), and *The Deer Hunter* (1978 [w]). He died of cancer in 1978.

Q. **Who was the last performer to appear in silent films to win a competitive acting Oscar?**
A. Helen Hayes, who appeared in two silent films before making her first talkie, *The Sin of Madelon Claudet*, and later winning an Oscar again for *Airport* (1970).

Q. **In what industry does Ted Kramer (Dustin Hoffman) work in *Kramer vs. Kramer* (1979)?**
A. Advertising.

Q. **1978's *Heaven Can Wait* was a remake of another Oscar-nominated picture from the 1940s— but *not* the one called *Heaven Can Wait*. What was the name of the original?**
A. *Here Comes Mr. Jordan* (1941).

Q. **Who is the only person to win an acting and a songwriting Oscar?**
A. Barbra Streisand, best actress for *Funny Girl* (1968) and best song (lyricist) for "Evergreen" from *A Star Is Born* (1976).

Q. **Who was the first person to win an Oscar, Tony, and Emmy all in the same year?**
A. Bob Fosse, whose Oscar for *Cabaret* (1972) was probably the capstone in a year that also saw a Tony for directing *Pippin* on Broadway and an Emmy for TV's *Liza with a Z*.

Q. **On what Lillian Hellman memoir was *Julia* (1977) based?**
A. *Pentimento*.

Q. **What are the only Oscar categories in which no women have ever been nominated?**

A.   Cinematography and sound. As some women have been nominated for sound effects editing, and considering that the sound award has only been bestowed individually on the sound engineers (rather than on the studio sound department) since 1969, the cinematography omission seems the more objectionable sin.

Q. **What real-life Nazi hunter was the inspiration for Laurence Olivier's character in *The Boys from Brazil* (1978)?**
A.   Simon Wiesenthal.

Q. **What is the only studio to win three best picture awards in a row, and what years were they won?**
A.   United Artists, who won best picture in 1975 (*One Flew Over the Cuckoo's Nest*), 1976 (*Rocky*), and 1977 (*Annie Hall*).

Q. **What was the greatest difference in ages between two competing nominees in a single category?**
A.   70 years, in 1979—the difference between best supporting actor winner Melvyn Douglas (*Being There*, age 79) and Justin Henry (*Kramer vs. Kramer*, age 9).

Q. **What was the name given by the crew to the mechanical shark in *Jaws* (1975)?**
A.   Bruce.

Q. **What was the first outright horror film to be nominated for best picture?**
A.   *The Exorcist* (1973).

Q. **What Oscar-winning film by David Lean received such a critical drubbing that Lean chose not to work again for 14 years?**
A.   *Ryan's Daughter* (1970). He returned triumphantly with *A Passage to India* (1984).

Q.　**What best song nominee had all of its lyrics in Latin, and what film was it from?**
A.　"Ave Satani" ("Hail Satan"), from *The Omen* (1976).

Q.　**For what film did Ann-Margret receive a best actress Oscar nomination in which she rolled around amid an immense amount of baked beans?**
A.　*Tommy* (1975).

Q.　**Which actress holds the distinction of being the first (and so far only) person to be nominated for an Oscar playing a part based on herself?**
A.　Marsha Mason. Neil Simon's autobiographical *Chapter Two* (1979) is the story of a writer (James Caan) who is conflicted about his love for a woman (Mason) soon after the death of his first wife. Mason was the real-life Mrs. Simon.

Q.　**In what year did four supporting actress nominees have little more than glorified cameos? Who were they and did any of them win?**
A.　1976. That year, Jodie Foster played a small, disturbing part as a 13-year-old prostitute in *Taxi Driver*; Lee Grant was one of dozens of stars aboard a ship in *Voyage of the Damned*; Jane Alexander played a government snitch with a few brief scenes in *All the President's Men*; and the winner, Beatrice Straight, portrayed a dejected wife in *Network*. Straight's one scene, consisting of about 10 lines of dialogue as she recounts the pain of her husband leaving her for a younger woman, lasts about two minutes, and qualifies as the single briefest performance ever to win an Oscar.

Q.　**The fifth supporting actress nominee in 1976, Piper Laurie, has her own distinction: She went longer than any other performer between consecutive nominations for consecutive screen ap-**

pearances. How long was this dry spell and what were the two movies involved?

A.   Laurie got her first Oscar nomination, as best actress, in 1961 for *The Hustler*. She retired from movies the following year before making another film, and emerged from retirement to appear in *Carrie* (supporting actress). She thus waited 15 years between her first nomination and her second, during which time there were no intervening films.

Q.   What best picture nominee has been described as "*Grand Hotel* on an airplane"?
A.   *Airport* (1970).

Q.   Three directors were nominated more than once in the 1970s for both best picture and director. Who are they are and what were the films?
A.   Stanley Kubrick, whose only two films released that decade, *A Clockwork Orange* (1971) and *Barry Lyndon* (1975), were so honored; Bob Fosse, who directed three, *Cabaret* (1972), *Lenny* (1974), and *All That Jazz* (1979); and Francis Ford Coppola, who directed four best film nominees—*The Godfather* (1972), *The Godfather Part II* (1974), *The Conversation* (1974), and *Apocalypse Now* (1979)—all of which were nominated for best director *except* for *The Conversation*. Interestingly, all of Fosse and Coppola's directing nominations are against each other: Fosse won the first round, Coppola the second, and they both lost to Robert Benton's *Kramer vs. Kramer* on the third.

Q.   What adapted screenplay winner from the 1970s later formed the basis for a TV sitcom? What original screenplay winner did the same?
A.   *M*A*S*H* (1970) and *Breaking Away* (1979). (No, *Midnight Express* never even made it past the pilot stage.)

Q.   The life of what legendary rock star was fictionalized in Bette Midler's Oscar-nominated film debut, _The Rose_?
A.   Janis Joplin.

Q.   Who was the first former blacklisted writer to later win a screenplay Oscar under his own name?
A.   Ring Lardner Jr., for _M*A*S*H_ (1970).

Q.   What performer had to be talked into taking his Oscar-winning role by director John Ford?
A.   Ben Johnson, as Sam the Lion in _The Last Picture Show_ (1971). Director Peter Bogdanovich asked Ford to intercede on his behalf after Johnson balked at appearing in a film with what he considered to be too much nudity and foul language.

Q.   In 1974, for the first time in 42 years, all the nominees in a single category were from the same studio: What was the studio and category?
A.   Paramount monopolized the costume design category. The winner was _The Great Gatsby_.

Q.   Which of the last big-time studio moguls finally retired in 1971?
A.   Darryl Zanuck, of Twentieth Century-Fox.

Q.   Which film had the most Oscar wins without winning for best picture?
A.   _Cabaret_ lays claim to that dubious record: eight overall wins (_eight!_) without winning for best picture. (_Star Wars_ comes in a close second with seven wins, all in craft categories.)

Q.   What two famed acting coaches received Oscar nominations for their first- and second-ever film performances?
A.   Lee Strasberg and John Houseman were both nominated for supporting performances, Strasberg for his film debut in _The Godfather Part II_ (1974,

a loss), and Houseman for only his second performance (following a cameo in *Seven Days in May*)
in *The Paper Chase* (1973), a win.

Q. **For what Oscar-nominated film did Princess
Grace of Monaco consider coming out of retirement to perform in?**
A. *The Turning Point* (1977). She was offered her
choice of roles, but Prince Rainier nixed the idea
completely.

Q. **The director's curse: Winning a best director
Oscar isn't always the entree to greater success
(or recognition for years of quality) that it once
was. What four best director winners from the
1970s produced no hits for some time after their
wins?**
A. *Patton*'s Franklin J. Schaffner (1970), *The
Sting*'s George Roy Hill (1973), *Rocky*'s John G.
Avildsen (1976), and *The Deer Hunter*'s Michael
Cimino (1978). All went years between hits (critical or commercial), with only Avildsen eventually
striking it lucky with *The Karate Kid*. Cimino in
particular fell into disfavor after helming what at
the time was the biggest bomb in Hollywood history: *Heaven's Gate*.

Q. **Who won an Oscar portraying a veteran forced
to play Russian roulette?**
A. Christopher Walken, *The Deer Hunter* (1978).

Q. **What best song winner was the best-selling pop-
ular song of the 1970s?**
A. "You Light Up My Life" from *You Light Up
My Life* (1977).

Q. **Beginning in 1970, how many performers won
supporting awards after winning lead Oscars?**
A. Helen Hayes became the first (for *Airport*,
1970). She would be followed by Maggie Smith

and Ingrid Bergman (also in the 1970s), Jack Nicholson (1980s), and Gene Hackman (1990s).

Q. What breed of dog was General Patton embarrassed to learn was not as tough as he imagined?
A.　An English bull terrier. In a memorable scene in *Patton*, the tough-looking pooch is easily scared by a poodle.

Q. What studio went longer than any other between best picture wins—43 years, from *All Quiet on the Western Front* (1929/30) to *The Sting* (1973)?
A.　Universal. Despite its association with such heavy hitters as Steven Spielberg, it has also won the *fewest* best picture Oscars of the original big seven studios.

Q. Which father/child duo won Oscars in the same year? Which father/child acting duo resulted in only the child winning?
A.　Director Francis Ford Coppola gave his dad Carmine a job writing the score to *The Godfather Part II* (1974), and they both won Oscars. Dad Ryan O'Neal gave his nine-year-old daughter Tatum a role in his film, *Paper Moon* (1973); she won, he wasn't even nominated.

Q. Who is the only person to win an Oscar for playing an Oscar loser?
A.　Maggie Smith, in *California Suite* (1978). In the film, she was nominated for best actress, but Smith had to be content to walk away with a supporting actress statuette.

OSCAR HIGHLIGHTS AND LOWLIGHTS OF THE DECADE

- **Green card, please**. *Dersu Uzala*, winner of best foreign language film in 1975, was submitted by the Soviet Union...but was directed by acclaimed Japanese director Akira Kurosawa. Oddly, 20 years later *Il Postino (The Postman)* would be ineligible for best foreign language film because its director, Michael Radford, was English while the producers and stars were Italian and French.

• **The Great Kate Count, part V**. For the first time since the creation of the awards, Katharine Hepburn sat out a decade without receiving a single nomination as best actress.

1970

Picture—*Patton*
Direction—Frankin J. Schaffner, *Patton*
Actor—George C. Scott, *Patton*
Actress—Glenda Jackson, *Women in Love*
Supporting Actor—John Mills, *Ryan's Daughter*
Supporting Actress—Helen Hayes, *Airport*
Story and Screenplay (Based upon Factual Material Not Previously Published or Produced)—*Patton*
Screenplay (Based on Material from Another Medium)—*M*A*S*H*
Original Score —*Love Story*
Original Song Score—*Let It Be*
Song—"For All We Know," *Lovers and Other Strangers*
Foreign Language Film—*Investigation of a Citizen Above Suspicion* (Italy)

Irving G. Thalberg Memorial Award—Ingmar Bergman

1971

Picture—*The French Connection*
Direction—William Friedkin, *The French Connection*
Actor—Gene Hackman, *The French Connection*
Actress—Jane Fonda, *Klute*
Supporting Actor—Ben Johnson, *The Last Picture Show*
Supporting Actress—Cloris Leachman, *The Last Picture Show*
Story and Screenplay (Based upon Factual Material Not Previously Published or Produced)—*The Hospital*
Screenplay (Based on Material from Another Medium)—*The French Connection*
Original Dramatic Score—*Summer of '42*
Scoring: Adaptation and Original Song Score—*Fiddler on the Roof*
Song—"Theme from Shaft," *Shaft*
Foreign Language Film—*The Garden of the Finzi-Continis* (Italy)

1972

Picture—*The Godfather*
Direction—Bob Fosse, *Cabaret*
Actor—Marlon Brando, *The Godfather*
Actress—Liza Minnelli, *Cabaret*
Supporting Actor—Joel Grey, *Cabaret*
Supporting Actress—Eileen Heckart, *Butterflies Are Free*
Story and Screenplay (Based upon Factual Material Not Previously Published or Produced)—*The Candidate*
Screenplay (Based on Material from Another Medium)—*The Godfather*
Original Dramatic Score—*Limelight* (1952)

Scoring: Adaptation and Original Song Score—*Cabaret*
Song —"The Morning After," *The Poseidon Adventure*
Foreign Language Film—*The Discreet Charm of the Bourgeoisie* (France)

1973

Best Picture—*The Sting*
Direction—George Roy Hill, *The Sting*
Actor—Jack Lemmon, *Save the Tiger*
Actress—Glenda Jackson, *A Touch of Class*
Supporting Actor—John Houseman, *The Paper Chase*
Supporting Actress—Tatum O'Neal, *Paper Moon*
Story and Screenplay (Based upon Factual Material Not Previously Published or Produced)—*The Sting*
Screenplay (Based on Material from Another Medium)—*The Exorcist*
Original Dramatic Score—*The Way We Were*
Scoring: Original Song Score and Adaptation—*The Sting*
Song—"The Way We Were," *The Way We Were*
Foreign Language Film—*Day for Night* (France)
Irving G. Thalberg Memorial Award—Lawrence Weingarten

1974

Picture—*The Godfather Part II*
Direction—Francis Ford Coppola, *The Godfather Part II*
Actor—Art Carney, *Harry and Tonto*
Actress—Ellen Burstyn, *Alice Doesn't Live Here Anymore*
Supporting Actor—Robert De Niro, *The Godfather Part II*
Supporting Actress—Ingrid Bergman, *Murder on the Orient Express*
Original Screenplay—*Chinatown*

Screenplay Adapted from Other Medium—*The Godfather Part II*
Original Dramatic Score—*The Godfather Part II*
Scoring: Original Song Score and Adaptation—*The Great Gatsby*
Song—"We May Never Love Like This Again," *The Towering Inferno*
Foreign Language Film—*Amarcord* (Italy)

1975

Picture—*One Flew Over the Cuckoo's Nest*
Direction—Milos Forman, *One Flew Over the Cuckoo's Nest*
Actor—Jack Nicholson, *One Flew Over the Cuckoo's Nest*
Actress—Louise Fletcher, *One Flew Over the Cuckoo's Nest*
Supporting Actor—George Burns, *The Sunshine Boys*
Supporting Actress—Lee Grant, *Shampoo*
Original Screenplay—*Dog Day Afternoon*
Screenplay Adapted from Other Medium—*One Flew Over the Cuckoo's Nest*
Original Score—*Jaws*
Original Song—"I'm Easy," *Nashville*
Scoring: Original Song Score and Adaptation—*Barry Lyndon*
Foreign Language Film—*Dersu Uzala* (U.S.S.R.)
Irving G. Thalberg Memorial Award—Mervyn LeRoy

1976

Picture—*Rocky*
Direction—John G. Avildsen, *Rocky*
Actor—Peter Finch, *Network*
Actress—Faye Dunaway, *Network*
Supporting Actor—Jason Robards, *All the President's Men*
Supporting Actress—Beatrice Straight, *Network*
Screenplay Written Directly for the Screen—*Network*

Screenplay Based on Material from Another Medium—All the President's Men
Original Score—*The Omen*
Original Song Score and Its Adaptation—*Bound for Glory*
Original Song—"Evergreen," *A Star Is Born*
Foreign Language Film—*Black and White in Color* (Ivory Coast)
Irving G. Thalberg Memorial Award—Pandro S. Berman

1977

Picture—Annie Hall
Direction—Woody Allen, *Annie Hall*
Actor—Richard Dreyfuss, *The Goodbye Girl*
Actress—Diane Keaton, *Annie Hall*
Supporting Actor—Jason Robards, *Julia*
Supporting Actress—Vanessa Redgrave, *Julia*
Screenplay Written Directly for the Screen—Annie Hall
Screenplay Based on Material from Another Medium—*Julia*
Original Score—*Star Wars*
Original Song Score and Its Adaptation or Adaptation Score—*A Little Night Music*
Original Song—"You Light Up My Life," *You Light Up My Life*
Foreign Language Film—*Madame Rosa* (France)
Irving G. Thalberg Memorial Award—Walter Mirisch

1978

Picture—*The Deer Hunter*
Direction—Michael Cimino, *The Deer Hunter*
Actor—Jon Voight, *Coming Home*
Actress—Jane Fonda, *Coming Home*
Supporting Actor—Christopher Walken, *The Deer Hunter*
Supporting Actress—Maggie Smith, *California Suite*

Screenplay Written Directly for the Screen—*Coming Home*
Screenplay Based on Material from Another Medium—*Midnight Express*
Original Score—*Midnight Express*
Adaptation Score—*The Buddy Holly Story*
Original Song—"Last Dance," *Thank God It's Friday*
Foreign Language Film—*Get Out Your Handkerchiefs* (France)

1979

Picture—*Kramer vs. Kramer*
Direction—Robert Benton, *Kramer vs. Kramer*
Actor—Dustin Hoffman, *Kramer vs. Kramer*
Actress—Sally Field, *Norma Rae*
Supporting Actor—Melvyn Douglas, *Being There*
Supporting Actress—Meryl Streep, *Kramer vs. Kramer*
Screenplay Written Directly for the Screen—*Breaking Away*
Screenplay Based on Material from Another Medium—*Kramer vs. Kramer*
Original Score—*A Little Romance*
Original Song Score and Its Adaptation—*All That Jazz*
Original Song—"It Goes Like It Goes," *Norma Rae*
Foreign Language Film—*The Tin Drum* (FRG)
Irving G. Thalberg Memorial Award—Ray Stark

The '80s: Return of the Spectacle

ARTS AND THE MAN

Others may disagree, but I think the year 1980 marked the release of some of the greatest films Hollywood ever produced, rivaling the golden year of 1939. For bravado, tenderness, invention, power, and sheer force of will, 1980 stands in my mind as a landmark: *Raging Bull. Ordinary People. The Elephant Man. The Stunt Man. Coal Miner's Daughter. The Big Red One. Kagemusha. Melvin and Howard. My Brilliant Career.* These were films that did not need to strain to be new and different; the people who made them knew that boldness is not an effect but rather an ethos. There were fledgling efforts, like Robert Redford's Oscar-winning debut direction of *Ordinary People* and David Lynch's perversely beautiful meditation, *The Elephant Man*; but there were also culminations in the careers of those who had already bled their share of bile and bravery: Samuel L. Fuller (*The Big Red One*) and Akira Kurosawa (*Kagemusha*). There have been other great years in movies, but few that seemed to provide as much of a sense of hope for the future of film as 1980 did. (Jonathan Demme, director of *Melvin and Howard*, later made *The Silence of the Lambs*; Martin Scorsese's *Raging Bull* paved the way for *The Last Temptation of Christ*, *GoodFellas*, and *Casino*.) The best of the films of the '80s somehow seemed to be inspired by the template of the year that kicked off the decade.

The '80s would also see the rise of technology *as* storytelling. After years of waffling between being presented as a special achievement or a competitive award, the trophy for best visual effects seemed to settle in as a yearly category; for the first time since the '40s (when it was considered part of "special effects" in general), an Oscar for sound effects (called sound effects editing, starting in 1982) became an annual category. Two honorary awards for makeup had been given in the '60s, but it took root in 1981 as a regular category—due in no small part to the increasing use of prosthetics and complex latex concoctions on the faces of (more often than not) transforming monsters or other horribly disfigured humans. (*An American Werewolf in London, Quest for Fire, Mask, The Fly*, and *Beetlejuice* all won the award.) Directors, it seemed, were getting flashy—big explosions, violent action films, and jingoistic (even pro-war) movies dominated the market during the Reagan years.

The '80s was also the era of AIDS, and although it took Hollywood a while to deal with the topic intelligently and honestly, there was a slow evolution in the way sex was portrayed during the latter half of the decade. The free love and ribald sex comedies of the '60s and '70s were replaced with more cautionary parables about sex, including *Fatal Attraction* (1987, picture [n+]) and *The Fly* (1986, makeup [w]). The word "condom" actually made it into a Hollywood film that did *not* contain teenagers fumbling for the word with a druggist. The Academy was slower to acknowledge these changing social conditions than the industry as a whole was; the first film dealing directly with AIDS to receive an Oscar nomination wasn't until 1990.

But the 1980s will not be remembered as a creative and technological renaissance or for its changing portrait of sex so much as for the financial revolution it bred.

Star Wars was still making Fox money when they released *The Empire Strikes Back* in 1980; that was followed three years later by *The Return of the Jedi*. The '80s also introduced us to Indiana Jones, John Rambo, Axel Foley, and a short, wrinkly foreigner named E.T. Those movies—and those responsible for them, and a slew of others—redefined what a hit film was. Budgets skyrocketed, stars' salaries shot up, and the video and foreign markets made ancillary income a factor in the cost of the film up front. Hollywood had gone through growth spurts before, but nothing quite as uncontrollable as this.

The Academy was hesitant to embrace the success of excess; in the '80s, not a single top moneymaker of its year won the best picture Oscar; in the '50s and '70s it happened four times each; in the '60s, twice. Indeed, best picture winners *Ordinary People* (1980), *Gandhi* (1982), *Amadeus* (1984), and *The Last Emperor* (1987) all failed to make the box office top 10 for their years. The most successful director of the '80s (Steven Spielberg) and the most successful producer (George Lucas) failed to win an Oscar between them. Probably no one disputes that 1975's *One Flew Over the Cuckoo's Nest* is a better film than *Jaws*, so despite the backlash over the latter's unprecedented success, the choice for best picture seemed justified. That argument seemed more strained when the popular, roundly praised *E.T.* lost to *Gandhi*. (*E.T.* wasn't itself the best film of 1982, but it was as good as *Gandhi*.) Money has often been seen as its own reward in Hollywood; in the '80s, however, it was somehow seen as a badge of dishonor. (But, as Liberace so cattily observed, the dishonorees cried all the way to the bank.)

Still, although the dollar figure quoted by the pundits changes from year to year, everyone is in agreement that Oscar = money (if not the reverse). A nomination can add box office revenues to a film still in the theaters, and a win can shoot it through the roof. In fact, beginning in the '40s, studios took to rereleasing the past year's hits in theaters (there was no TV or video market) right around Oscar time, both to generate nominations and to capitalize on buzz if they won. The practice tended to dwindle after television, with only occasional efforts being made at rereleases, until the 1990s, when the independent studios used the prestige of insider Hollywood to their advantage.

Quiz: The Dollars

Q. **The magic number: Which best picture nominee was the first to break $100 million in domestic rentals?**
A. *Jaws* (1975).

Q. **What was the first film to make $100 million before winning the best picture Oscar?**
A. Reports on film grosses are often in conflict, depending upon the source and how often it is updated. It appears, though, that *Terms of Endearment* (1983) hit the $100 million mark soon before the ceremonies.

Q. **What was the first film to make $100 million *before* it was *nominated* for (and later won) the best picture Oscar?**
A. *The Silence of the Lambs* (1991) made virtually all of its money ($100 million-plus) before the year was even over. *Jaws* (1975) was the first film to break the $100 million mark in domestic grosses, and it was nominated for best picture, but it didn't win.

Q. **What is the most financially successful film to win the best picture Oscar?**

A. Financial success is a sliding term, of course, depending on cost of film, inflation, etc. But the highest domestic-grossing best picture nominee and winner, by far, is *Titanic* (1997), with ticket sales in excess of $337 million on the day the nominations were announced, and eventual domestic grosses of $601 million by the time it was released on video eight months later.

Q. **What best picture winner, produced by a Broadway showman, sold its tickets like a play: reserved seating, no concessions in the theater, playbills, etc.?**
A. Mike Todd's *Around the World in 80 Days* (1956).

Q. **What was the first film to win best picture that had already been released to home video?**
A. *The Silence of the Lambs* (1991).

🎞 The highest grossing best picture winners

Financial success is rarely indicative of artistic achievement—if that were so, *Home Alone, Three Men and a Baby,* and *Die Hard with a Vengeance* would all have won the best picture Oscar in their given year—but occasionally the number-one films of the year do go on to win the best picture Oscar. (Nothing says success like success: In both the 1950s and 1970s, the four best picture winners were also the top-grossing films of their years.) Naturally, accounting for inflation and the vagaries of audience attendance, what it takes to qualify as the top grosser varies from year to year, but here are some of the most successful best picture winners in reverse chronological order:

YEAR	WINNER	DOMESTIC GROSSES*
1997	*Titanic*	$601,000,000
1994	*Forrest Gump*	$327,000,000
1976	*Rocky*	$54,000,000
1975	*One Flew Over the Cuckoo's Nest*	$56,500,000
1973	*The Sting*	$78,000,000
1972	*The Godfather*	$81,500,000
1965	*The Sound of Music*	$42,500,000
1961	*West Side Story*	$19,000,000
1959	*Ben-Hur*	$38,000,000
1957	*The Bridge on the River Kwai*	$18,000,000
1956	*Around the World in 80 Days*	$22,000,000
1952	*The Greatest Show on Earth*	$12,000,000
1946	*The Best Years of Our Lives*	$11,500,000
1944	*Going My Way*	$6,400,000
1942†	*Mrs. Miniver*	$6,000,000

Quiz: Trivia from the '80s

Q. In what context did Jon Voight make the following comment: "I don't think that there's anyone

---

*Estimated/reported domestic box office grosses from initial release. Release sometimes extends over several years. "Year" is year of film's initial release (and eligibility for best picture Oscar), not necessarily year it achieved quoted grosses.

†Prior to 1942, no accurate records of box office grosses are available. However, *Gone with the Wind* (1939) surely qualifies as the top-grossing film of its year, and one of the all-time champs when rereleases are totaled.

here or watching who doesn't appreciate the amount of love and gratitude represented by this Oscar selection tonight.''

A. He was presenting Katharine Hepburn with her record-breaking fourth acting Oscar. As with Hepburn's three previous wins, she was not present to accept it in person, so Voight accepted it on her behalf.

Q. **Name four of the six men, known primarily as actors, who won their Oscars for directing (and sometimes producing)—three of which wins occurred in consecutive years in the '80s?**

A. Robert Redford (*Ordinary People*, 1980); Warren Beatty (*Reds*, 1981); Richard Attenborough (*Gandhi*, 1982); Kevin Costner (*Dances with Wolves*, 1990); Clint Eastwood (*Unforgiven*, 1992); and Mel Gibson (*Braveheart*, 1995).

Q. **What Oscar winner for best director features the story of the only American buried inside the Kremlin?**

A. *Reds* (1981).

Q. **What performer appeared in the most best picture nominees in the 1980s?**

A. William Hurt appeared in four consecutive best picture nominees: *Kiss of the Spider Woman* (1985), *Children of a Lesser God* (1986), *Broadcast News* (1987), and *The Accidental Tourist* (1988). None of the films won best picture, although Hurt won best actor for the first and was nominated for the next two. Runners-up, with three each, include Dustin Hoffman, Harrison Ford, and Jack Nicholson.

Q. **What two 1983 best picture nominees featured American astronauts?**

A. *The Right Stuff* and winner *Terms of Endearment*.

Q. **Even with the death of the musical in the '70s, what leading performers won Oscars for singing roles (country music, both times) in the 1980s?**
A.   Sissy Spacek (actress, *Coal Miner's Daughter*, 1980) and Robert Duvall (actor, *Tender Mercies*, 1983).

Q. **Although nations submit their own selections for consideration as best foreign language film, what pro-Solidarity film almost had its nomination pulled after martial law was declared in Poland?**
A.   *Man of Iron* (1981). Although the Polish government attempted to withdraw it, the Academy kept it on the list. The award, though, went to Hungary's *Mephisto*.

Q. **What Olympic competition was the setting for 1981's best picture winner, *Chariots of Fire*?**
A.   The 1924 Paris Summer Games.

Q. **What two-time supporting actor winner was married to Helen Gahagan Douglas, who famously lost a contentious 1950 Senate race to Richard Nixon?**
A.   Melvyn Douglas.

Q. **What was the surprise best foreign language film winner in 1980—and why was it a surprise?**
A.   The film was *Moscow Does Not Believe in Tears*, from the U.S.S.R. Political tensions at the time were high (the United States did not even participate in the Moscow Olympic games later that year), and the opportunity for the Academy to reward Truffaut (for *The Last Metro*) or Kurosawa (for *Kagemusha*) seemed to favor those films.

Q. **Who became the first deaf person to win an Oscar?**
A.   Marlee Matlin, best actress honoree for *Children of a Lesser God* (1986). An unusually large

number of movies featuring handicapped or disabled characters dominated the Oscars during the late 1980s (and into the '90s), including wins for Dustin Hoffman (actor, *Rain Man*, 1988; autism) and Daniel Day-Lewis (actor, *My Left Foot*, 1989; cerebral palsy). The number of nominees is even greater.

Q. **What fledgling studio tallied a remarkable four best picture wins in eight years—and then went bankrupt?**
A. Orion.

Q. **Who was the first person to win an acting award after winning for producing?**
A. Michael Douglas, who won for best picture for *One Flew Over the Cuckoo's Nest* (1975) and best actor for *Wall Street* (1987). Laurence Olivier won for acting and producing *Hamlet* (1948) in the same year—though based on order of presentation at the ceremony, technically he won the acting award *before* winning the picture award.

Q. **What was the first Oscar-nominated film to feature a character with AIDS?**
A. Bruce Davison was nominated as best supporting actor in *Longtime Companion* (1990), as a character stricken with the virus.

Q. **Only once have three people—each considered among the greatest film directors of all time—jointly presented the best picture award, in 1985. Name them.**
A. John Huston, Akira Kurosawa, and Billy Wilder.

Q. **What film became the first best picture winner since *Gigi* in 1958 to receive Oscars for every category in which it was nominated?**
A. *The Last Emperor* (1987).

Q. **What best actress winner said during her acceptance speech: "This show has been longer than my career"?**
A. Shirley MacLaine, *Terms of Endearment* (1983).

Q. **What is the only film studio to tally a best picture win in each decade from the 1930s through the 1980s?**
A. Columbia.

Q. **What year was the first time since 1957 that *all* the best picture nominees also received best director nominations?**
A. 1981. The nominated films were *Chariots of Fire, Reds, Raiders of the Lost Ark, On Golden Pond*, and *Atlantic City*. Oddly, also in 1981, and for the first time since 1973 (one of only four times since 1958), the best picture award and the best director award went to different films.

Q. **What picture set the record for the most nominations ever bestowed on a foreign language film? How many was it?**
A. In 1982, *Das Boot* received six nominations, including best picture; it won none. Ironically, it was *not* nominated for best foreign language film, where it might have taken home the prize. The following year, *Fanny and Alexander* also received six nominations, including one for best foreign language film. It fared better, winning four.

Q. **In 1983, James L. Brooks became the third writer-director-producer to win three Oscars for the same film, *Terms of Endearment*. Who were the first two?**
A. Billy Wilder, for *The Apartment* (1960) and Francis Ford Coppola, for *The Godfather Part II* (1974). Marvin Hamlisch won three Oscars in

1973, but for two films: *The Way We Were* and *The Sting*; and James Cameron went on to win three Oscars for the same film in 1997—though he was not even nominated for his screenplay, he also won for film editing on *Titanic*.

Q. What real-life jazz great received an Oscar nomination for his acting debut playing another jazz musician?
A. Dexter Gordon, *'Round Midnight* (1986).

OSCAR HIGHLIGHTS AND LOWLIGHTS OF THE DECADE

The Great Kate Count, part VI. Katharine Hepburn received another Oscar nomination—and win—as best actress, for *On Golden Pond* (1982), breaking her own records: four wins, twelve nominations. (She has yet to receive an honorary award, and was never nominated for supporting actress.)

....

THE WINNERS

1980

Picture—*Ordinary People*
Direction—Robert Redford, *Ordinary People*
Actor—Robert De Niro, *Raging Bull*
Actress—Sissy Spacek, *Coal Miner's Daughter*
Supporting Actor—Timothy Hutton, *Ordinary People*
Supporting Actress—Mary Steenburgen, *Melvin and Howard*

Screenplay Written Directly for the Screen—*Melvin and Howard*
Screenplay Based on Material from Another Medium—*Ordinary People*
Cinematography—*Tess*
Original Score—*Fame*
Original Song—"Fame," *Fame*
Foreign Language Film—*Moscow Does Not Believe in Tears* (U.S.S.R.)
Honorary Award—Henry Fonda

1981

Picture—*Chariots of Fire*
Direction—Warren Beatty, *Reds*
Actor—Henry Fonda, *On Golden Pond*
Actress—Katharine Hepburn, *On Golden Pond*
Supporting Actor—John Gielgud, *Arthur*
Supporting Actress—Maureen Stapleton, *Reds*
Screenplay Written Directly for the Screen—*Chariots of Fire*
Screenplay Based on Material from Another Medium—*On Golden Pond*
Cinematography—*Reds*
Original Score—*Chariots of Fire*
Original Song—"The Best That You Can Do (Arthur's Theme)," *Arthur*
Foreign Language Film—*Mephisto* (Hungary)
Irving G. Thalberg Memorial Award—Albert R. "Cubby" Broccoli
Jean Hersholt Humanitarian Award—Danny Kaye
Honorary Award—Barbara Stanwyck

1982

Picture—*Gandhi*
Direction—Richard Attenborough, *Gandhi*
Actor—Ben Kingsley, *Gandhi*
Actress— Meryl Streep, *Sophie's Choice*

Supporting Actor—Louis Gossett Jr., *An Officer and a Gentleman*
Supporting Actress—Jessica Lange, *Tootsie*
Screenplay Written Directly for the Screen—*Gandhi*
Screenplay Based on Material from Another Medium—*Missing*
Cinematography—*Gandhi*
Original Score—*E.T.—The Extra-Terrestial*
Original Song Score and its Adaptation or Adaptation Score—*Victor/Victoria*
Original Song—"Up Where We Belong," *An Officer and a Gentleman*
Foreign Language Film—*Volver a Empezar (To Begin Again)* (Spain)
Jean Hersholt Humanitarian Award—Walter Mirisch
Honorary Award—Mickey Rooney

1983

Picture—*Terms of Endearment*
Direction—James L. Brooks, *Terms of Endearment*
Actor—Robert Duvall, *Tender Mercies*
Actress—Shirley MacLaine, *Terms of Endearment*
Supporting Actor—Jack Nicholson, *Terms of Endearment*
Supporting Actress—Linda Hunt, *The Year of Living Dangerously*
Screenplay Written Directly for the Screen—*Tender Mercies*
Screenplay Based on Material from Another Medium—*Terms of Endearment*
Cinematography—*Fanny and Alexander*
Original Score—*The Right Stuff*
Original Song Score or Adaptation Score—*Yentl*
Original Song—"Flashdance . . . What a Feeling," *Flashdance*
Foreign Language Film—*Fanny and Alexander* (Sweden)

Jean Hersholt Humanitarian Award—M. J. "Mike" Frankovich

<u>1984</u>

Picture—*Amadeus*
Direction—Milos Forman, *Amadeus*
Actor—F. Murray Abraham, *Amadeus*
Actress—Sally Field, *Places in the Heart*
Supporting Actor—Haing S. Ngor, *The Killing Fields*
Supporting Actress—Peggy Ashcroft, *A Passage to India*
Screenplay Written Directly for the Screen—*Places in the Heart*
Screenplay Based on Material from Another Medium—*Amadeus*
Cinematography—*The Killing Fields*
Original Score—*A Passage to India*
Original Song Score—*Purple Rain*
Original Song—"I Just Called to Say I Love You," *The Woman in Red*
Foreign Language Film—*Dangerous Moves* (Sweden)
Jean Hersholt Humanitarian Award—David L. Wolper

<u>1985</u>

Picture—*Out of Africa*
Direction—Sydney Pollack, *Out of Africa*
Actor—William Hurt, *Kiss of the Spider Woman*
Actress—Geraldine Page, *The Trip to Bountiful*
Supporting Actor—Don Ameche, *Cocoon*
Supporting Actress—Anjelica Huston, *Prizzi's Honor*
Screenplay Written Directly for the Screen—*Witness*
Screenplay Based on Material from Another Medium—*Out of Africa*
Cinematography—*Out of Africa*
Original Score—*Out of Africa*
Original Song—"Say You, Say Me," *White Nights*

Foreign Language Film—*The Official Story* (Argentina)
Jean Hersholt Humanitarian Award—Charles "Buddy" Rogers
Honorary—Paul Newman; Alex North

1986

Picture—*Platoon*
Direction—Oliver Stone, *Platoon*
Actor—Paul Newman, *The Color of Money*
Actress—Marlee Matlin, *Children of a Lesser God*
Supporting Actor—Michael Caine, *Hannah and Her Sisters*
Supporting Actress—Dianne Wiest, *Hannah and Her Sisters*
Screenplay Written Directly for the Screen—*Hannah and Her Sisters*
Screenplay Based on Material from Another Medium—*A Room with a View*
Cinematography—*The Mission*
Original Score—*'Round Midnight*
Original Song—"Take My Breath Away," *Top Gun*
Foreign Language Film—*The Assault* (The Netherlands)
Irving G. Thalberg Memorial Award—Steven Spielberg
Honorary Award—Ralph Bellamy

1987

Picture—*The Last Emperor*
Direction—Bernardo Bertolucci, *The Last Emperor*
Actor—Michael Douglas, *Wall Street*
Actress—Cher, *Moonstruck*
Supporting Actor—Sean Connery, *The Untouchables*
Supporting Actress—Olympia Dukakis, *Moonstruck*
Screenplay Written Directly for the Screen—*Moonstruck*

Screenplay Based on Material from Another Medium—*The Last Emperor*
Cinematography—*The Last Emperor*
Original Score—*The Last Emperor*
Song—"(I've Had) The Time of My Life," *Dirty Dancing*
Foreign Language Film—*Babette's Feast* (Denmark)
Irving G. Thalberg Memorial Award—Billy Wilder

1988

Picture—*Rain Man*
Direction—Barry Levinson, *Rain Man*
Actor—Dustin Hoffman, *Rain Man*
Actress—Jodie Foster, *The Accused*
Supporting Actor—Kevin Kline, *A Fish Called Wanda*
Supporting Actress—Geena Davis, *The Accidental Tourist*
Screenplay Written Directly for the Screen—*Rain Man*
Screenplay Based on Material from Another Medium—*Dangerous Liaisons*
Cinematography—*Mississippi Burning*
Original Score—*The Milagro Beanfield War*
Song—"Let the River Run," *Working Girl*
Foreign Language Film—*Pelle the Conqueror* (Denmark)

1989

Picture—*Driving Miss Daisy*
Direction—Oliver Stone, *Born on the Fourth of July*
Actor—Daniel Day-Lewis, *My Left Foot*
Actress—Jessica Tandy, *Driving Miss Daisy*
Supporting Actor—Denzel Washington, *Glory*
Supporting Actress—Brenda Fricker, *My Left Foot*
Screenplay Written Directly for the Screen—*Dead Poets Society*
Screenplay Based on Material from Another Medium—*Driving Miss Daisy*
Cinematography—*Glory*
Original Score—*The Little Mermaid*
Song—"Under the Sea," *The Little Mermaid*
Foreign Language Film—*Cinema Paradiso* (Italy)
Jean Hersholt Humanitarian Award—Howard W. Koch
Honorary—Akira Kurosawa

Chapter
Thirteen

The '90s: An Independent Spirit

VIVE LA DIFFÉRENCE!

Since their inception, the Oscars have always suffered from a split personality: at once a cheerleader for the Hollywood establishment *and* the peer review committee for what "great" films are, and what films should be. When, in 1996, *Jerry Maguire*, itself a surprising and offbeat film, became the only major studio release to be nominated for best picture, a friend opined that the studios might try to make more "independent-style" films. Of course, that cannot happen—once the hierarchy adopts what is "different" and "unique" about indies, they co-op them and smooth out the rough spots, and they stop being different and unique.

But there's no denying that the single greatest effect the Oscars have is in focusing our critical attention on what the Academy perceives as "the best of the year." When *Driving Miss Daisy* becomes the sleeper hit of the year; when the best actor and actress winners in 1985 are both from independent companies (*Kiss of the Spider Woman* and *The Trip to Bountiful*); when *Blue Velvet* and *The Last Temptation of Christ* manage best director nominations, and *The Prince of Tides* and *Awakenings* do not—this is what focuses attention on the debate about what end the Oscars serve, and there have no doubt been occasions where the backlash (or expected backlash) has guilted the Academy into recognizing films and individuals they might not, on their own, have recognized.

In the 1990s, this guilt trip became the rule, not the exception. It became clear early in the decade—first when Marisa Tomei won the supporting actress award against more highbrow competition, then confirmed later when veteran Lauren Bacall was arguably robbed of the same award by Juliette Binoche's surprise victory—that a new breed of Academy voter had taken over. Perhaps this interest in independent films is the result of an American "new wave" similar to what occurred in postwar France. Film geeks like Quentin Tarantino (*Pulp Fiction*, 1994) and the Coen Brothers (*Fargo*, 1996)—writer-directors steeped in various genres of film, and having both a keen sense for dialogue and a willingness to push movies to their extremes—raised the quality of the indie picture. The fall of the studio system, the predominance of film festivals, and clamor for "art" films with popular appeal put to the test tired notions of what the public would pay to see. Maybe audiences have become inured to the "low budget" look of independent films; maybe Generation X'ers—among them the richest crop of potential filmmakers since the heyday in the '60s and '70s of the film school grad—have begun to appreciate the kind of movies they believe themselves capable of making; or maybe the quality of independent films has just increased manifold as the result of the new economics of Hollywood: Video, cable, and festivals all have provided new outlets for artistic (and not-so-artistic) efforts. The big studio picture will never completely disappear—the year after *Fargo, Shine, Secrets & Lies*, and *The English Patient* were all in contention, the "big" film of the year was the biggest yet, *Titanic*—but there seems to be an uneasy truce, bordering on alliance, forming. The indie production looks to be here to stay.

🎥 A casting guide: how to score an Oscar

Are you an aspiring actor or actress desperate to break through with an Oscar win? It might not be as difficult as you think. Over the past 20 years, certain types of roles win Oscars and nominations more often than others. Merely choose the category you want to win, and ask your agent to get you a part meeting these criteria—it's that easy! (Note: Because it is possible to be more than one of these—indeed, it's often preferable—numbers do not necessarily add up to 100%.)

Approximate percentage of nominees playing . . .

MALE ROLES	ACTOR	SUPPORTING ACTOR
Musician	8%	--
Athlete	2%	6%*
Soldier or veteran	8%	10%
Cop or detective	2%	4%
Lawyer/politician or royal	11%	7%
Gangster, killer, or con man	12%	16%
Writer/poet/journalist	7%	4%
Pilot or astronaut	1%	3%
Farmer	1%	6%
Teacher	7%	2%
Artist	--	2%
Prisoner or ex-con	5%	5%
Disabled or mentally ill	15%	4%
Alcoholic or addict	8%	3%
Actor/dancer/singer	7%	4%
Millionaire or socialite	4%	3%

*Supporting actors almost never portray athletes, but coaches.

	2%	--
Cleric or saint	2%	--
Servant	5%	2%
Bum	4%	2%
Sleazeball	2%	3%
Doctor/psychiatrist	2%	2%
Devoted father/son	7%	6%
Tycoon/mogul/busi-nessman	7%	4%

FEMALE ROLES	ACTRESS	SUPPORTING ACTRESS
Lawyer/politi-cian or royal	2%	2%
Farmer/rancher	6%	2%
Disabled or mentally ill	9%	1%
Writer/journalist	2%	1%
Alcoholic or ad-dict	3%	2%
Actress/dancer/singer	14%	8%
Independent/ca-reer woman	15%	4%
Activist	6%	3%
Long-suffering wife/girlfriend/mom/moll	37%	44%
Best friend	--	12%
Caretaker	1%	3%
Doctor	1%	2%
Bitch	8%	15%
Bimbo	7%	14%
Socialite	7%	5%
Cleric or saint	3%	1%
Servant	2%	1%

Quiz: Trivia from the '90s

Q. **Tom Hanks's teary acceptance speech for** *Philadelphia* **(1993) inspired the plot for what other Oscar-nominated film?**

A. *In & Out* (Joan Cusack, supporting actress, 1997 [n]). Hanks accidentally "outed" a closeted gay man in his speech, which triggered this hilarious Paul Rudnick comedy about a small-town teacher outed by a former student at the Oscars.

Q. **Although Leonardo DiCaprio plays an artist preoccupied drawing Kate Winslet nude, whose hands are seen on screen doing the actual sketching in** *Titanic* **(1997)?**

A. James Cameron's, the film's director.

Q. **What 1977 Oscar nominee for best picture became, for a while, the top-grossing film of all time . . . in 1997?**

A. *Star Wars*. It was rereleased for a twentieth-anniversary edition, complete with remastered effects and new scenes. It surpassed *E.T.* as the number-one film of all time, until it was itself surpassed by *Titanic*.

Q. **What film about a talking pig won the visual effects award in 1995?**

A. *Babe*.

Q. **What performer appeared in the most best picture nominees during the 1990s?**

A. Emma Thompson, in four films: *Howards End* (1992), *The Remains of the Day*, *In the Name of the Father* (both 1993), and *Sense and Sensibility* (1995). She also received acting nominations for each of the nominated films. None won for best picture. Runners-up, with three apiece, include Anthony Hopkins, Hugh Grant, and Ralph Fiennes.

Q. **In what country—and among what people—is *The Piano* (1993) set?**
A. New Zealand. The locals are the Maori.

Q. **The British comedy troupe Beyond the Fringe was made up of four performers: Dudley Moore, Peter Cook, Jonathan Miller, and Alan Bennett. Two of these have been Oscar-nominated—one is Moore, for *Arthur* (1981). Name the other, and the film for which he was cited.**
A. Bennett, who received a screenplay nomination for *The Madness of King George* (1994), adapted from his play.

Q. **How long did best supporting actress winner Anna Paquin (*The Piano*, 1993) stand glassy-eyed after the processional music ceased before trying to speak?**
A. She stood still for a full 20 seconds (and stammered for a few more) while the audience chuckled in delight at the honesty of the moment.

Q. **To what film was its best actress award–winner referring when she said it spent more than three years "in a bank vault in New York City" after the studio that made it, Orion, went bankrupt?**
A. *Blue Sky* (1994). Jessica Lange's delay in winning between when her performance was delivered is probably the longest ever.

Q. **A bad omen? In what director's films had the four losing 1997 best actress nominees all appeared in the past, and for whom the sole winner (Helen Hunt) never worked?**
A. Kenneth Branagh. Dame Judi Dench, nominated for *Mrs. Brown*, appeared in *Henry V*; Helena

Bonham-Carter (*The Wings of the Dove*) appeared in *Mary Shelley's Frankenstein;* and Kate Winslet (*Titanic*) and Julie Christie (*Afterglow*) both appeared in *Hamlet*.

Q. Helen Hunt is one of five American-born performers to defeat four foreign-born competitors. Name at least two of the other four.
A. Marisa Tomei, supporting actress in *My Cousin Vinny* (1991); Robert Duvall, actor in *Tender Mercies* (1983); Jason Robards, supporting actor in *Julia* (1977); and Jane Fonda, actress in *Klute* (1971). Elizabeth Taylor won best actress for *Who's Afraid of Virginia Woolf?* (1966), but Taylor, although an American citizen, was born in England. Elizabeth Hartman, best actress nominee in *A Patch of Blue* (1965), was the only American nominated, but she lost to Julie Christie.

Q. Name the former best actress winner who went on to win the award for adapted screenplay.
A. Emma Thompson, for *Sense and Sensibility* (1996).

Q. What biopic of Tina Turner netted Oscar nominations for stars Angela Basset and Laurence Fishburne, and in what other previous Oscar-nominated film did Basset and Fishburne play a divorced couple?
A. *What's Love Got to Do with It* (1993) was the Ike and Tina Turner story; they also starred in *Boyz N the Hood* (1991; nominated for best director and original screenplay).

Q. For what two films did Robert Altman achieve some kind of dubious distinction for receiving consecutive best director Oscar nominations— but whose films did not receive concomitant best picture nominations?
A. *The Player* (1992) and *Short Cuts* (1993).

Q. **A party game centering around Kevin Bacon was inspired by what play—later an Oscar-nominated film—written by John Guare?**
A. *Six Degrees of Separation* (1993).

Q. **Who was the first star of a currently running sitcom to receive a leading acting Oscar?**
A. Helen Hunt, *As Good As It Gets* (1997). Before her, the only recurring performer in a sitcom to win an Oscar in the same year she played on TV was Cloris Leachman: She played the daffy Phyllis Lindstrom on *The Mary Tyler Moore Show* from 1970 to 1975, and won her best supporting actress Oscar in 1971 for *The Last Picture Show*. (The same calendar year that Glenda Jackson won her first best actress Oscar for *Women in Love*, she also appeared in the *Masterpiece Theatre* miniseries *Elizabeth R*, although the TV show aired after the Oscar was won and *Masterpiece Theatre* could not be considered, in general, a sitcom.)

Q. **Within a three-month period, three best supporting actor winners—George Burns, Martin Balsam, and Dr. Haing S. Ngor—all died. What was the year?**
A. 1996.

Q. **Who said upon accepting the best foreign language film award: "I would like to believe in God so that I could thank him, but I just believe in Billy Wilder, so thank you, Billy Wilder."**
A. Fernando Trueba, director of *Belle Epoque* (1993).

Q. **What two actor-comedians from the cable fund-raising charity Comic Relief have won supporting Oscars, and what third Comic Relief staple has been left out?**
A. Whoopi Goldberg (*Ghost*, 1990) and Robin Williams (*Good Will Hunting*, 1997) have bested

friend and frequent Oscar host Billy Crystal, who has yet to receive even a nomination.

Q. **What honorary Oscar recipient—a director known for his musicals—sang and danced "Cheek to Cheek" as his acceptance speech in 1997?**
A. Stanley Donen.

Q. **What was the only time in Oscar history that a mother and daughter were simultaneous acting nominees?**
A. In 1991, when Laura Dern and Diane Ladd were both nominated for *Rambling Rose*.

Q. **What was the first film from the recently formed Czech Republic to win the foreign language film Oscar?**
A. *Kolya* (1996).

Q. **What film about a group of unemployed men who become male strippers was a surprise best picture nominee?**
A. *The Full Monty* (1997). It lost the best picture to *Titanic*, but won best original score for a comedy.

Q. **What then-25-year-old stage musical won the best song Oscar for an original composition composed specifically for the movie?**
A. *Evita*, with the song "You Must Love Me" (1996). The win was composer Andrew Lloyd Webber's first, although his librettist, Tim Rice, had won twice before for Disney musicals.

Q. **The Genie is the Canadian equivalent of the Oscar. Name a Genie award winner for best picture also to be nominated for a best picture Oscar.**
A. The answer is none. No Genie award winner has ever won an Oscar nomination for best picture.

In fact, the only Genie award winner in any of the major categories (picture, director, actor, or actress) to receive *any* Oscar nominations is *The Sweet Hereafter* (1997), which netted writer-director Atom Egoyan two nominations from the Academy, but no wins.

Q. Name a major César Award winner (France's Oscar) to be nominated for an Academy Award.
A. More successfully than Canada, France's César has produced several Oscar nominees, including Gerard Depardieu (best actor for *Cyrano de Bergerac*, 1990) Isabelle Adjani (best actress for *Camille Claudel*, 1989) and Catherine Deneuve (best actress for *Indochine*, 1992). Best film César winner *Au Revoir, Les Enfants* (1987) was nominated for best original screenplay.

Q. Whose acceptance speech for best supporting actor in 1996 joined Sally Field's for sheer naked goofiness?
A.   Cuba Gooding Jr.'s. Gooding didn't get a standing ovation when he walked up to accept his award for *Jerry Maguire*, but he did by the end: After continuing to shout over the exit music for a good 30 seconds, thanking everyone while jumping around as he did in the touchdown celebration scene in the movie, even his competition was on their feet applauding.

Q. Who is Keyser Soze?
A. You're crazy if you think I'm going to give that one away!

OSCAR HIGHLIGHTS AND LOWLIGHTS OF THE DECADE

- **Flubs with a flourish.** There's probably no better Oscar presenter than Sharon Stone, whose enthusiasm, preparation, and appeal alone can carry some of the less high-profile awards. When she and copresenter Quincy Jones could not find the envelopes, she ad-libbed the following: "I don't have the envelope, so I'd like us all to have a psychic moment. Let's just concentrate, it's coming to me. . . . Oh, you can do better than that."

- **How's it feel?** "I have friends who have won this before but—and I swear—I have never held one before; this is the first time I've ever had one of these in my hands."—*Schindler's List*'s notoriously overlooked director Steven Spielberg, accepting his award in 1993.

- **Sweet revenge.** In best picture nominee *L.A. Confidential* (1997), James Cromwell gets to kill Kevin Spacey—a nice bit of revenge for Cromwell (Farmer Hoggett from *Babe*), who lost the supporting actor Oscar to Spacey (*The Usual Suspects*) in 1995.

- **The Great Kate Count, final chapter**. Hepburn made her only film appearance of the '90s in the tepidly received *Love Affair*, and so had to be content with 12 leading actress nominations, four wins—and *no* honorary awards.

THE WINNERS

1990

Picture—*Dances with Wolves*
Direction—Kevin Costner, *Dances with Wolves*
Actor—Jeremy Irons, *Reversal of Fortune*

Actress—Kathy Bates, *Misery*
Supporting Actor—Joe Pesci, *GoodFellas*
Supporting Actress—Whoopi Goldberg, *Ghost*
Screenplay Written Directly for the Screen—*Ghost*
Screenplay Based on Material from Another Medium—*Dances with Wolves*
Cinematography—*Dances with Wolves*
Score—*Dances with Wolves*
Song—"Sooner or Later," *Dick Tracy*
Foreign Language Film—*Journey of Hope* (Switzerland)
Irving G. Thalberg Memorial Award—Richard D. Zanuck and David Brown
Honorary—Sophia Loren; Myrna Loy

1991

Picture—*The Silence of the Lambs*
Direction—Jonathan Demme, *The Silence of the Lambs*
Actor—Anthony Hopkins, *The Silence of the Lambs*
Actress—Jodie Foster, *The Silence of the Lambs*
Supporting Actor—Jack Palance, *City Slickers*
Supporting Actress—Mercedes Ruehl, *The Fisher King*
Screenplay Written Directly for the Screen—*Thelma & Louise*
Screenplay Based on Material from Another Medium—*The Silence of the Lambs*
Cinematography—*JFK*
Original Score—*Beauty and the Beast*
Song—"Beauty and the Beast," *Beauty and the Beast*
Foreign Language Film—*Mediterraneo* (Italy)
Irving G. Thalberg Memorial Award—George Lucas

1992

Picture—*Unforgiven*
Direction—Clint Eastwood, *Unforgiven*
Actor—Al Pacino, *Scent of a Woman*

Actress—Emma Thompson, *Howards End*
Supporting Actor—Gene Hackman, *Unforgiven*
Supporting Actress—Marisa Tomei, *My Cousin Vinny*
Screenplay Written Directly for the Screen—*The Crying Game*
Screenplay Based on Material from Another Medium—*Howards End*
Cinematography—*A River Runs Through It*
Score—*Aladdin*
Song—"A Whole New World," *Aladdin*
Foreign Language Film—*Indochine* (France)
Jean Hersholt Humanitarian Award—Audrey Hepburn; Elizabeth Taylor
Honorary—Federico Fellini

1993

Picture—*Schindler's List*
Direction—Steven Spielberg, *Schindler's List*
Actor—Tom Hanks, *Philadelphia*
Actress—Holly Hunter, *The Piano*
Supporting Actor—Tommy Lee Jones, *The Fugitive*
Supporting Actress—Anna Paquin, *The Piano*
Screenplay Written Directly for the Screen—*The Piano*
Screenplay Based on Material from Another Medium—*Schindler's List*
Cinematography—*Schindler's List*
Score—*Schindler's List*
Song—"Streets of Philadelphia," *Philadelphia*
Foreign Language Film—*Belle Epoche* (Spain)
Jean Hersholt Humanitarian Award—Paul Newman
Honorary—Deborah Kerr

1994

Picture—*Forrest Gump*
Direction—Robert Zemeckis, *Forrest Gump*
Actor—Tom Hanks, *Forrest Gump*
Actress—Jessica Lange, *Blue Sky*

Supporting Actor—Martin Landau, *Ed Wood*
Supporting Actress—Dianne Wiest, *Bullets Over Broadway*
Screenplay Written Directly for the Screen—*Pulp Fiction*
Screenplay Based on Material from Another Medium—*Forrest Gump*
Cinematography—*Legends of the Fall*
Score—*The Lion King*
Song—"Can You Feel the Love Tonight," *The Lion King*
Foreign Language Film—*Burnt by the Sun* (Russia)
Irving G. Thalberg Memorial Award—Clint Eastwood
Jean Hersholt Humanitarian Award—Quincy Jones
Honorary—Michelangelo Antonioni

1995

Picture—*Braveheart*
Direction—Mel Gibson, *Braveheart*
Actor Nicolas Cage, *Leaving Las Vegas*
Actress—Susan Sarandon, *Dead Man Walking*
Supporting Actor—Kevin Spacey, *The Usual Suspects*
Supporting Actress—Mira Sorvino, *Mighty Aphrodite*
Screenplay Written Directly for the Screen—*The Usual Suspects*
Screenplay Based on Material from Another Medium—*Sense and Sensibility*
Cinematography—*Braveheart*
Dramatic Score—*Il Postino*
Comedy Score—*Pocahontas*
Song—"The Colors of the Wind," *Pocahontas*
Foreign Language Film—*Antonia's Line* (The Netherlands)

1996

Picture—*The English Patient*
Direction—Anthony Minghella, *The English Patient*
Actor—Geoffrey Rush, *Shine*

Actress—Frances McDormand, *Fargo*
Supporting Actor—Cuba Gooding Jr., *Jerry Maguire*
Supporting Actress—Juliette Binoche, *The English Patient*
Screenplay Written Directly for the Screen—*Fargo*
Screenplay Based on Material from Another Medium—*Sling Blade*
Cinematography—*The English Patient*
Dramatic Score—*The English Patient*
Comedy Score—*Emma*
Song—"You Must Love Me," *Evita*
Foreign Language Film—*Kolya* (Czech Republic)
Irving G. Thalberg Memorial Award—Saul Zaentz
Honorary—*Toy Story*

1997

Picture—*Titanic*
Direction—James Cameron, *Titanic*
Actor—Jack Nicholson, *As Good As It Gets*
Actress—Helen Hunt, *As Good As It Gets*
Supporting Actor—Robin Williams, *Good Will Hunting*
Supporting Actress—Kim Basinger, *L.A. Confidential*
Screenplay Written Directly for the Screen—*Good Will Hunting*
Screenplay Based on Material from Another Medium—*L.A. Confidential*
Cinematography—*Titanic*
Dramatic Score—*Titanic*
Comedy Score—*The Full Monty*
Song—"My Heart Will Go On," *Titanic*
Foreign Language Film—*Character* (The Netherlands)
Honorary—Stanley Donen

Part IV
Trivia by Category

Production And Scenario:
Picture, Director, Foreign Language Film,
Original and Adapted Screenplay

TAKE ONE

Ever since *Cahiers du Cinéma*, the revered French film
journal of the '50s, propounded the "*auteur* policy"—
the philosophy that the director is the "author" of his
films, putting his individual stamp on all his movies—
there's been a distinct emphasis on the superstar director. The truth is, superstar directors have been around
almost since film itself, beginning with D. W. Griffith
and Cecil B. DeMille and continuing on through the '30s
(Frank Capra, John Ford), '40s (Alfred Hitchcock, Orson
Welles), and into the '80s and '90s (Steven Spielberg,
Oliver Stone). Each of these directors made their own
personalities known on virtually every film they made,
whether in subject matter, theme, or style. The critics for
Cahiers later confessed that the policy was entirely a
gimmick designed to pave the way for their own creative
control when they started making movies themselves,
but the effect had already taken root: The rise of film
schools made the sexy allure of the director's chair ir-
resistible.

In many instances, the great directors were also the
producer and frequently the writers of their films. (Most
writers-turned-directors state they moved into directing

so that they could exert greater control over their own written product.) Remarkably, though, some of the best-remembered directors made brief Oscar-notable forays outside their chosen field, and the work of some—William Wyler, George Cukor, and Michael Curtiz come quickly to mind—seemed at odds with the idea of being the *auteur* of their films; they were instead the master craftsman, often better known for their careful handling of actors and dramatic structure than for their singular, identifiable camerawork or editing or thematic consistency.

The directors listed below all received at least five Oscar nominations for directing only; it would take up too much space to list all the nominations for writing and producing (and also documentary, acting, film editing, even special effects) many of them also received, but recipients of honorary awards like the Irving G. Thalberg Memorial Award are noted.

William Wyler—12

Dodsworth (1937)
Wuthering Heights (1939)
The Letter (1940)
The Little Foxes (1941)
Mrs. Miniver (1942) [w]
The Best Years of Our Lives (1946) [w]
The Heiress (1949)
Detective Story (1951)
Roman Holiday (1953)
Friendly Persuasion (1957)
Ben-Hur (1959) [w]
The Collector (1965)

• Thalberg

Billy Wilder—8

Double Indemnity (1944)
The Lost Weekend (1945) [w]

Sunset Boulevard (1950)
Stalag 17 (1953)
Sabrina (1954)
Witness for the Prosecution (1957)
Some Like It Hot (1959)
The Apartment (1960) [w]

• Thalberg

Fred Zinnemann—7

The Search (1948)
High Noon (1952)
From Here to Eternity (1953) [w]
The Nun's Story (1959)
The Sundowners (1960)
A Man for All Seasons (1966)
Julia (1977)

David Lean—6

Brief Encounter (1946)
Great Expectations (1947)
Summertime (1955)
The Bridge on the River Kwai (1957) [w]
Lawrence of Arabia (1962) [w]
A Passage to India (1984)

Frank Capra —6

Lady for a Day (1932/33)
It Happened One Night (1934) [w]
Mr. Deeds Goes to Town (1936) [w]
You Can't Take It with You (1938) [w]
Mr. Smith Goes to Washington (1939)
It's a Wonderful Life (1946)

Woody Allen—6

Annie Hall (1976) [w]
Interiors (1978)
Broadway Danny Rose (1984)
Hannah and Her Sisters (1986)
Crimes and Misdemeanors (1989)
Bullets Over Broadway (1994)

Clarence Brown—6*

Anna Christie (1929/30)
Romance (1929/30)
A Free Soul (1930/31)
The Human Comedy (1943)
National Velvet (1944)
The Yearling (1946)

Elia Kazan—5

Gentleman's Agreement (1947) [w]
A Streetcar Named Desire (1951)
On the Waterfront (1954) [w]
East of Eden (1955)
America, America (1963)

George Stevens—5

The More the Merrier (1943)
A Place in the Sun (1951) [w]
Shane (1953)
Giant (1956) [w]
The Diary of Anne Frank (1959)

• Thalberg

---

*The most director nominations without a single win.

John Ford—5

The Informer (1935) [w]
Stagecoach (1939)
The Grapes of Wrath (1940) [w]
How Green Was My Valley (1941) [w]
The Quiet Man (1952) [w]

George Cukor—5

Little Women (1932/33)
The Philadelphia Story (1940)
A Double Life (1947)
Born Yesterday (1950)
My Fair Lady (1964) [w]

Frank Lloyd—5

The Divine Lady (1928/29) [w]
Drag (1928/29)
Weary River (1928/29)
Cavalcade (1932/33) [w]
Mutiny on the Bounty (1935)

King Vidor—5

The Crowd (1927/28)
Hellelujah! (1929/30)
The Champ (1931/32)
The Citadel (1938)
War and Peace (1956)

• Honorary

John Huston—5

The Treasure of the Sierra Madre (1948) [w]
The Asphalt Jungle (1950)
The African Queen (1951)
Moulin Rouge (1953)
Prizzi's Honor (1985)

Alfred Hitchcock—5

Rebecca (1940)
Lifeboat (1944)
Spellbound (1945)
Rear Window (1954)
Psycho (1960)

- Thalberg

📽 The remarkable Oscar career of Woody Allen

Woody Allen is best known to the public for performing in movies, but his achievements, as far as the Academy is concerned have been more noteworthy in the areas of writing and directing. He's received a grand total of 20 Oscar nominations, only one for acting (making him the person to receive the most total nominations ever received by someone who has also been nominated in an acting category). His Oscar resume:

- Actor, *Annie Hall* (1976)
- Original screenplay, *Annie Hall* (1976) [w]
- Director, *Annie Hall* (1976) [w]
- Original screenplay, *Interiors* (1978)
- Director, *Interiors* (1978)
- Original screenplay, *Manhattan* (1979)
- Original screenplay, *Broadway Danny Rose* (1984)
- Director, *Broadway Danny Rose* (1984)
- Original screenplay, *The Purple Rose of Cairo* (1985)

- Original screenplay, *Hannah and Her Sisters* (1986) [w]

- Director, *Hannah and Her Sisters* (1986)

- Original screenplay, *Radio Days* (1987)

- Original screenplay, *Crimes and Misdemeanors* (1989)

- Director, *Crimes and Misdemeanors* (1989)

- Original screenplay, *Alice* (1990)

- Original screenplay, *Husbands and Wives* (1992)

- Original screenplay, *Bullets Over Broadway* (1994)

- Director, *Bullets Over Broadway* (1994)

- Original screenplay, *Mighty Aphrodite* (1995)

- Original screenplay, *Deconstructing Harry* (1997)

FADE IN

In the modern era, the two screenwriting awards that the Academy presents have been for best original screenplay (that is, one written directly for the screen) and best adapted screenplay (that is, a screenplay that adapts a preexisting story to screenplay form—from a book, play, sometimes a magazine article).[5] There's a natural, unforced obviousness to these category divisions; assuming that you are not going to inquire into touchy areas like "best dialogue," "best plot twist," or (perish the thought) "best devised chase scene," the division makes

[5]The technical name for the "original screenplay" award is "Writing: Screenplay Written Directly for the Screen"; and the formal name for "adapted screenplay" is "Writing: Screenplay Based on Material Previously Published or Produced." The categories have kept essentially these same names since 1957, with some variations.

sense—the kind an average moviegoer might automatically have invented himself. There's one especially convenient, ancillary effect: By definition, every screenplay is *either* original or not original, which doubles the number of slots available to the writers' branch.

But despite the apparent logic and usefulness of the categories, there have been some occasions where the line between "original" and "adapted" is not so clearly drawn. In 1995, Amy Heckerling's amusing script for *Clueless* was not eligible in the "original" screenplay category because Heckerling admitted that her inspiration was Jane Austen's eighteenth-century comedy of manners, *Emma*. *Emma* was set in England during the Regency period, and Austen's dialogue, delightful and insightful as it can be, bears little resemblance to the Valleyspeak of the SoCal teens that populate Heckerling's movie. In fact, other than the use of one common name and a plot that follows the general outline of *Emma*, *Clueless* was as "original" as any movie nominated for best original screenplay that year. This problem is symptomatic of a more puzzling definition of "original" in general. *Apocalypse Now* (1979), for instance, a fairly faithful interpretation of Conrad's *Heart of Darkness* (significant in that the location was moved from the Congo to Vietnam), was nominated for its adapted screenplay, while *Broken Lance* (1954) won the motion picture story award despite basically being a rip-off of *House of Strangers*, an earlier film, both written by Phillip Yorgan. *The Court-Martial of Billy Mitchell* (1955), based upon the true story of a military commander who protested the army's use of airpower, received a nomination as original screenplay despite its real-life roots. The hypocrisy, or at least inconsistency, seemed to reach its pinnacle in 1980, when one of the entries for screenplay based on material "previously produced," *The Elephant Man*, was based on the true story of John Merrick (but *not* the Broadway play), while *original* screenplay winner *Melvin and Howard* was also based on actual people—millionaire Howard Hughes and a pretender to his fortune, Melvin Dummar. Go figure.

From 1940 through 1956, there were three writing awards: "original story" (also called "motion picture story" and "original motion picture story"), "screenplay" (which was essentially an adapted screenplay category), and "original screenplay" (also called "story and screenplay"). I frankly have never understood the distinction between the "original story" and the "original screenplay"; on occasion, it appears that the Academy hasn't either, and films have sometimes won (or at least been nominated) in both, notably in years such as 1947, when *Miracle on 34th Street* won two separate awards, for its story and screenplay, attributable to two different people, or when the motion picture story to *Love Me or Leave Me* (1955) won the Oscar, but the screenplay itself did not. In 1978, by comparison, the original screenplay winners for *Coming Home* were divided between Waldo Salt and Robert C. Jones for the actual screenplay, and Nancy Dowd for the original story. (Actually, Dowd wrote the original draft of the screenplay on which the final version was based, not a separate novel or short story as the credit suggests.) Since 1957, only two writing awards have been bestowed.

Quiz

Q. **Many film critics have taken a stab at writing, but only nine well-known critics have ever been nominated for their screenplays. How many can you name?**

A. The only film critic/Oscar-nominated screenwriters are: Graham Greene (*The Fallen Idol*, 1948 [n]); James Agee (*The African Queen*, 1951 [n]); Francois Truffaut (*The 400 Blows*, 1959 [n+]); Pe-

nelope Gilliat (*Sunday, Bloody Sunday*, 1971 [n]);
Peter Bogdanovich (*The Last Picture Show*, 1971
[n]); Paul Schrader (*Taxi Driver*, 1975 [n]); Jay
Cocks (*The Age of Innocence*, 1993 [n]); Paul At-
tanasio (*Quiz Show*, 1994 [n+]). It appears that the
only former film critic ever to win a writing Oscar—although he was not a critic of any note—was
Norman Krasna, who won the original screenplay
award for *Princess O'Rourke* (1943).

Q. **Who received more nominations for producing
than anyone else?**
A. Hal B. Wallis, with 19. Remarkably, he won
only once, for *Casablanca* (1943).

Q. **What country has won the most foreign language film awards? What director has been responsible for the most foreign language wins?**
A. Italy and France have both nine competitive
foreign language film Oscars. From 1948 through
1955, however, the Academy's Board of Governors
bestowed an honorary award for best foreign language film of the year. France won two of those,
Italy one, and Italy and France coproduced another
honoree. But the wins are virtually tied: In 1947,
Shoeshine received an honorary award that did not
refer to it as the best foreign language film, but in
effect bestowed that accolade on it, and indeed the
success of *Shoeshine* led to the establishment of
the foreign award. As for directors, if you include
the honorary awards, both Federico Fellini and Vit-
torio De Sica directed four best foreign language
winners each (all for Italy). Ingmar Bergman (all
for Sweden) and Akira Kurosawa (two for his native Japan, one for the Soviet Union) directed three
of the winners. Ironically, because the two Japanese
films Kurosawa directed received honorary awards,
he has thus never directed a Japanese-made foreign
language film competitive winner.

Q. **Who won the most producing Oscars?**
A. Darryl Zanuck and Sam Spiegel, with three apiece.

Q. **Sometimes it takes toiling away at one career before achieving success in another. People like Sydney Pollack were actors before finding their niche as Oscar-winning directors, but some people reversed the process: They won their Oscars in surprising categories, and went on to (or returned to) less-lauded careers elsewhere. Match the writing, producing, or directing personality (identified by some of their most noteworthy achievements) with the functions they performed that won them an Oscar.**

a. **Irwin Allen (disaster-movie producer of *The Towering Inferno*, *The Poseidon Adventure*)**

i. **Winner, best director, *Ordinary People* (1981) [w+].**

b. **Hal Ashby (director of *Being There* and *Harold and Maude*)**

ii. **Winner, best original story, *The Invaders* (1942).**

c. **John Farrow (director, *Wake Island*)**

iii. **Winner, best writing adaptation, *Boys Town* (1937).**

d. **Emeric Pressburger (producer-director, with Michael Powell, of *The Red Shoes* and *Black Narcissus*)**

iv. **Winner, best writing adaptation, *Around the World in 80 Days* (1956).**

e. **Robert Redford**
    (star of *The Sting,*
    Butch Cassidy and
    the Sundance Kid,
    and *All the*
    President's Men)

v. **Winner, best**
    original
    screenplay, *The*
    Bachelor and
    the Bobby-
    Soxer (1947).

f. **Dore Schary**
    (studio head and
    producer)

vi. **Winner, best**
    film editing, *In*
    the Heat of the
    Night (1968).

g. **Sidney Sheldon**
    (romance novelist;
    creator of the TV
    show *I Dream of*
    Jeannie)

vii. **Winner, best**
    documentary,
    The Sea
    Around Us
    (1952).

A. a.-vii.; b.-vi.; c.-iv.; d.-ii.; e.-i.; f.-iii.; g.-v.

Q. Who was the first writer-director to win both awards for a single film?
A. Leo McCarey, for *Going My Way* (1945). He also won for directing *The Awful Truth* (1958).

Q. Who received the most nominations for directing without a single win?
A. Clarence Brown. Brown also never received any kind of honorary award, making him among the most overlooked directors in Oscar history.

Q. What two films received the most nominations without a single win?
A. *The Turning Point* (1977) and *The Color Purple* (1985). Interestingly enough, the number of nominations received is the same as the most won by the most honored films, *Ben-Hur* (1959) and *Titanic* (1997): 11.

Q. Who directed more performers to Oscar wins than any other director?
A. The record rests with William Wyler, who helmed 13 parts to Oscar wins: Walter Brennan in

Come and Get It (1936) and *The Westerner* (1940);
Bette Davis in *Jezebel* (1938); Greer Garson and
Teresa Wright in *Mrs. Miniver* (1942); Fredric
March and Harold Russell in *The Best Years of Our
Lives* (1946); Olivia de Havilland in *The Heiress*
(1949); Audrey Hepburn in *Roman Holiday* (1953);
Burl Ives in *The Big Country* (1958); Charleton
Heston and Hugh Griffith in *Ben-Hur* (1959); and
Barbra Streisand in *Funny Girl* (1968). The closest
runner-up: Elia Kazan, with nine (James Dunn in
A Tree Grows in Brooklyn, 1945; Celeste Holm in
Gentleman's Agreement, 1947; Vivien Leigh, Kim
Hunter, and Karl Malden in *A Streetcar Named Desire*,
1951; Anthony Quinn in *Viva Zapata!*, 1952;
Marlon Brando and Eva Marie Saint in *On the Waterfront*,
1954; and Jo Van Fleet in *East of Eden*,
1955).

Q. **Who is the only director to direct himself to an acting Oscar?**
A. Laurence Olivier in *Hamlet* (1948). He lost the
directing award to John Huston for *The Treasure
of the Sierra Madre*. No director has ever won a
directing and acting award for the same film. Other
directors to be nominated for directing and acting
in the same film: Orson Welles in *Citizen Kane*
(1941), Woody Allen in *Annie Hall* (1977), Warren
Beatty in *Heaven Can Wait* (1978) and *Reds*
(1981), Kenneth Branagh in *Henry V* (1989), Kevin
Costner in *Dances with Wolves* (1990), and Clint
Eastwood in *Unforgiven* (1992). Branagh is the
only one who didn't direct a film nominated for
best picture.

Q. **What film has received the most Oscar wins
without receiving even a best picture nomination?**
A. *The Bad and the Beautiful* (1952), with five
wins, mostly in craft categories.

Q. Who are the only three performers to win two Oscars in different films directed by the same director?

A. Jack Nicholson, whose leading win in *As Good As It Gets* (1997) followed a supporting win for *Terms of Endearment* (1983), both from James L. Brooks; Dianne Wiest, who won Oscars for *Hannah and Her Sisters* (1986) and *Bullets Over Broadway* (1994), both under the guidance of Woody Allen; and Walter Brennan, who won two of his three supporting Oscars (*Come and Get It*, 1936; *The Westerner*, 1938) in William Wyler films.

Q. What Oscar-nominated screenplay had the most writers officially attached to it?

A. *Toy Story* (1995), with four people credited as screenplay authors and four as story writers, for a total of eight. It lost to the single-attributed *The Usual Suspects*.

Q. What is the only dog to receive an Oscar nomination?

A. No, not Lassie or Rin Tin Tin; this one didn't even *earn* it. The nominee was for adapted screenplay in 1984 for *Greystoke: The Legend of Tarzan, Lord of the Apes*. The nominee was "P. H. Vazak"—the pet pooch of the real screenwriter (Robert Towne) who was so disappointed by the rewrites he wanted his name removed from the final credits.

Q. What screenwriter has received the most nominations?

A. Woody Allen with 13, followed closely by Billy Wilder with 12. (Allen directed all of his nominated screenplays; Wilder wrote some for others.)

Q. In what year did the best picture award first go to the individual producer of the film rather than the head of the studio?
A. 1951.

Q. Who directed two versions of the Lillian Hellman play *The Children's Hour*, first as *These Three* (1936), later under its original title (1962)?
A. William Wyler. In both cases, each film received an Oscar nomination for best supporting actress, although for different characters.

Q. Robert C. Jones, best screenplay award cowinner for *Coming Home* (1978), failed to win on his three other nominations: for *It's a Mad, Mad, Mad, Mad World* (1963), *Guess Who's Coming to Dinner* (1967), and *Bound for Glory* (1976). In which category was he nominated in those times?
A. Film editing. *Coming Home*'s director was former Oscar-winning editor Hal Ashby, who enlisted pal Jones's help in retooling the script.

Q. Who is the only person to direct both his parent and his child to Oscar victories?
A. John Huston, who directed his father (Walter, *The Treasure of the Sierra Madre*, 1948) and daughter (Anjelica, *Prizzi's Honor*, 1985) to supporting acting wins.

Q. What is notable about the best story and screenplay nominees in both 1961 and 1962?
A. Each time, three of the nominees were foreign language films.

Q. What well-known American schlock king was the U.S. distributor for best picture and foreign language film nominee *Cries and Whispers* (1973), an art-house hit from Sweden by Ingmar Bergman?

A. Roger Corman, through his New World Pictures company.

Q. **The two times that Steven Spielberg has directed a best picture nominee without receiving a corresponding best director nomination, he was trumped by foreign language directors. Who were they?**
A. Federico Fellini for *Amarcord* shut him out for *Jaws* (1975) and Akira Kurasawa's *Ran* was chosen over *The Color Purple* (1985).

Q. **Who is the only person to win the Pulitzer Prize and the Oscar for adapting his own work?**
A. Alfred Uhry, whose play *Driving Miss Daisy* won the Pulitzer for drama, and his adaptation won best adapted screenplay (1989).

Q. **In 1950, each writing category has a husband and wife team nominated. Name at least one team, and the movie for which they were nominated.**
A. Frances Goodrich and Albert Hackett were nominated for best screenplay for *Father of the Bride*, Ruth Gordon and Garson Kanin for best story and screenplay for *Adam's Rib*, and the only team to win: Edna and Edward Anhalt for best motion picture story for *Panic in the Streets*.

Q. **What was the first best foreign language film winner elected following the requirement that voting members see all five nominees?**
A. *Black and White in Color* (1976).

Q. **In what year was every best director nominee foreign-born?**
A. 1987.

Q. **What is the only remake of a best picture winner also to receive a nomination as best picture?**

A. *Mutiny on the Bounty*—a winner in 1935, a loser in 1962. Probably the most egregious instance of a remake *not* receiving a best picture nomination is Kenneth Branagh's *Hamlet* (1996), a stunning pageant that runs the entire four-hour-plus length of the play. (Olivier's Oscar winner from 1948 ran a mere two and a half hours.)

DID YOU KNOW . . .

- A big stink is made most years when one (occasionally two) of the best picture nominees do not receive a best director nomination. (The controversy seems foolish to me—if there wasn't a difference between best picture and best director, why have two categories?) But if it seems bad during the '80s and '90s, imagine what it was like in 1963 and 1966, when *three* of the best picture nominees did not have like directors. (Those years are also considered among the weakest ever in Hollywood history.)

- The problematic issues regarding origin of the "foreign language film" is highlighted by *Z*, which was *about* Greece, starred a Frenchman, was directed by a man born on Cyprus, and submitted by Algeria.

- The Writers Guild often arbitrates screen credits, giving those who had the most input attribution on screen, even though others helped out with dialogue, plotting, scenes, etc. On the screen, writing teams are identified by an ampersand ("&"), whereas those writers acting independently are credited with an "and." Thus, on certain occasions, the winning team may never have met before (such as happened on *Father Goose*) and in some instances, even after they won their awards (*Patton*).

- Warner Brothers's success at winning Oscars for best picture seems accidental, at best. With the exception of *My Fair Lady* (1965), none of the Warners films to win best picture were considered favorites from the outset: *Emile Zola* (1937) was made on a shoestring budget, *Casablanca* (1943) was besieged by production problems and was written on the fly, *Chariots of Fire* (1981) was the sleeper winner of its year, and *Driving Miss Daisy* (1989) became the first film since *Grand Hotel* (1933) to win best picture without also being nominated for best director.

- All three versions of both *A Star Is Born* (1937; 1954; 1976) and *Little Women* (1932/33; 1949; 1994) received at least one Oscar nomination.

Performance:
Actor, Actress, Supporting Actor, Supporting Actress

THEY LIKE YOU, THEY REALLY LIKE YOU!

The Academy sometimes can't get enough of a good thing: In the history of the awards, about 1,300 acting nominations have been handed out. (The number isn't exact because of the confusion about who was a "nominee" and how nominations were calculated during the early days of Academy rule-making.) Of those 1,300 nominations, 150—well over 10 percent—are held by only 18 people, all listed below. On a number of occasions, the Academy could not even content itself to confine their nominations to the acting categories, frequently bestowing honorary awards and nominations in nonperforming areas of expertise. Every female nominee receiving six or more nominations in an acting category, and every man receiving seven or more, is listed below, with a [w] indicating a win. Also mentioned are other categories in which the performer met with Academy approval.

Actresses

KATHARINE HEPBURN—12*

Actress, *Morning Glory* (1932/33) [w]
Actress, *Alice Adams* (1935)
Actress, *Woman of the Year* (1942)
Actress, *The African Queen* (1951)
Actress, *Summertime* (1955)
Actress, *The Rainmaker* (1956)
Actress, *Suddenly Last Summer* (1959)
Actress, *Long Day's Journey into Night* (1962)
Actress, *Guess Who's Coming to Dinner* (1967) [w]
Actress, *The Lion in Winter* (1968) [w]
Actress, *On Golden Pond* (1982) [w]

BETTE DAVIS—11

Actress, *Of Human Bondage* (1934)†
Actress, *Dangerous* (1935) [w]
Actress, *Jezebel* (1938) [w]
Actress, *Dark Victory* (1939)
Actress, *The Letter* (1940)
Actress, *The Little Foxes* (1941)
Actress, *Now, Voyager* (1942)
Actress, *Mr. Skeffington* (1944)
Actress, *All About Eve* (1950)
Actress, *The Star* (1952)
Actress, *What Ever Happened to Baby Jane?* (1962)

MERYL STREEP—10

Supporting actress, *The Deer Hunter* (1978)
Supporting actress, *Kramer vs. Kramer* (1979) [w]
Actress, *The French Lieutenant's Woman* (1981)

---

*The most acting nominations—all leading—and the most wins in Oscar history.
†Although not officially a nominee this year, she finished as one of the top three vote-getters after a write-in campaign. The Academy now lists her as a nominee in its records.

Actress, *Sophie's Choice* (1982) [w]
Actress, *Silkwood* (1983)
Actress, *Out of Africa* (1985)
Actress, *Ironweed* (1987)
Actress, *A Cry in the Dark* (1988)
Actress, *Postcards from the Edge* (1990)
Actress, *The Bridges of Madison County* (1995)

GERALDINE PAGE—8*

Supporting actress, *Hondo* (1953)
Actress, *Summer and Smoke* (1961)
Actress, *Sweet Bird of Youth* (1962)
Supporting actress, *You're a Big Boy Now* (1966)
Supporting actress, *Pete 'N' Tillie* (1972)
Actress, *Interiors* (1978)
Supporting actress, *The Pope of Greenwich Village* (1984)
Actress, *The Trip to Bountiful* (1985) [w]

GREER GARSON 7

Actress, *Goodbye, Mr. Chips* (1939)
Actress, *Blossoms in the Dust* (1941)
Actress, *Mrs. Miniver* (1942) [w]
Actress, *Madame Curie* (1943)
Actress, *Mrs. Parkington* (1944)
Actress, *The Valley of Decision* (1944)
Actress, *Sunrise at Campobello* (1960)

JANE FONDA—7

Actress, *They Shoot Horses, Don't They?* (1969)
Actress, *Klute* (1971) [w]
Actress, *Julia* (1977)
Actress, *Coming Home* (1978) [w]
Actress, *The China Syndrome* (1979)

*Although Richard Burton and Peter O'Toole tied the record for most nominations without a win, Page set the same record for a woman—which she held for a single year.

Supporting actress, *On Golden Pond* (1981)
Actress, *The Morning After* (1986)

INGRID BERGMAN—7

Actress, *For Whom the Bell Tolls* (1943)
Actress, *Gaslight* (1944) [w]
Actress, *The Bells of St. Mary's* (1945)
Actress, *Joan of Arc* (1948)
Actress, *Anastasia* (1956) [w]
Supporting actress, *Murder on the Orient Express* (1974) [w]
Actress, *Autumn Sonata* (1978)

DEBORAH KERR—6*

Actress, *Edward, My Son* (1949)
Actress, *From Here to Eternity* (1953)
Actress, *The King and I* (1956)
Actress, *Heaven Knows, Mr. Allison* (1957)
Actress, *Separate Tables* (1958)
Actress, *The Sundowners* (1960)

• Honorary (1993)

THELMA RITTER—6†

Supporting actress, *All About Eve* (1950)
Supporting actress, *The Mating Season* (1951)
Supporting actress, *With a Song in My Heart* (1952)
Supporting actress, *Pickup on South Street* (1953)
Supporting actress, *Pillow Talk* (1959)
Supporting actress, *Bird Man of Alcatraz* (1962)

---

*Kerr holds the record for nominations for best actress without ever winning a competitive award.

†Ritter received more supporting nominations than anyone without a win. Having never received even an honorary award, she holds the distinction of being Oscar's most overlooked actress.

Actors

JACK NICHOLSON—11

Supporting actor, *Easy Rider* (1969)
Actor, *Five Easy Pieces* (1970)
Actor, *The Last Detail* (1973)
Actor, *Chinatown* (1974)
Actor, *One Flew Over the Cuckoo's Nest* (1975) [w]
Supporting actor, *Reds* (1981)
Supporting actor, *Terms of Endearment* (1983) [w]
Actor, *Prizzi's Honor* (1985)
Actor, *Ironweed* (1987)
Supporting actor, *A Few Good Men* (1992)
Actor, *As Good As It Gets* (1997) [w]

LAURENCE OLIVIER—10†

Actor, *Wuthering Heights* (1939)
Actor, *Rebecca* (1939)
Actor, *Henry V* (1946)
Actor, *Hamlet* (1948) [w]
Actor, *Richard III* (1956)
Actor, *The Entertainer* (1960)
Actor, *Othello* (1965)
Actor, *Sleuth* (1972)
Supporting actor, *Marathon Man* (1976)
Actor, *The Boys from Brazil* (1979)

* Honorary (1946) [w]
* Honorary (1979) [w]
* Director, *Hamlet* (1948)
* Producer, *Hamlet* (1948) [w]

SPENCER TRACY—9†

Actor, *San Francisco* (1936)
Actor, *Captains Courageous* (1937) [w]

---

†Olivier and Tracy received more *leading* actor nominations than any other actor.

Actor, *Boys Town* (1938) [w]
Actor, *Father of the Bride* (1950)
Actor, *Bad Day at Black Rock* (1955)
Actor, *The Old Man and the Sea* (1958)
Actor, *Inherit the Wind* (1960)
Actor, *Judgment at Nuremberg* (1961)
Actor, *Guess Who's Coming to Dinner* (1967)

PAUL NEWMAN—8

Actor, *Cat on a Hot Tin Roof* (1958)
Actor, *The Hustler* (1961)
Actor, *Hud* (1963)
Actor, *Cool Hand Luke* (1967)
Actor, *Absence of Malice* (1981)
Actor, *The Verdict* (1982)
Actor, *The Color of Money* (1987) [w]
Actor, *Nobody's Fool* (1994)

* Producer, *Rachel, Rachel* (1968)

* Honorary (1982) [w]

* Jean Hersholt Humanitarian Award (1993) [w]

MARLON BRANDO—8

Actor, *A Streetcar Named Desire* (1951)
Actor, *Viva Zapata!* (1952)
Actor, *Julius Caesar* (1953)
Actor, *On the Waterfront* (1954) [w]
Actor, *Sayonara* (1957)
Actor, *The Godfather* (1972) [w]
Actor, *Last Tango in Paris* (1973)
Supporting actor, *A Dry White Season* (1989)

JACK LEMMON—8

Supporting actor, *Mister Roberts* (1955) [w]
Actor, *Some Like It Hot* (1959)
Actor, *The Apartment* (1960)
Actor, *Days of Wine and Roses* (1962)
Actor, *Save the Tiger* (1973) [w]

Actor, *The China Syndrome* (1979)
Actor, *Tribute* (1980)
Actor, *Missing* (1982)

AL PACINO—8

Supporting actor, *The Godfather* (1972)
Actor, *Serpico* (1973)
Actor, *The Godfather Part II* (1974)
Actor, *Dog Day Afternoon* (1974)
Actor, *. . . And Justice for All* (1979)
Supporting actor, *Dick Tracy* (1991)
Supporting actor, *Glengarry Glen Ross* (1992)
Actor, *Scent of a Woman* (1992) [w]

PETER O'TOOLE—7†

Actor, *Lawrence of Arabia* (1962)
Actor, *Becket* (1964)
Actor, *The Lion in Winter* (1968)
Actor, *Goodbye, Mr. Chips* (1969)
Actor, *The Ruling Class* (1972)
Actor, *The Stunt Man* (1980)
Actor, *My Favorite Year* (1982)

RICHARD BURTON—7†

Supporting actor, *My Cousin Rachel* (1952)
Actor, *The Robe* (1953)
Actor, *Becket* (1964)
Actor, *The Spy Who Came in From the Cold* (1965)
Actor, *Who's Afraid of Virginia Woolf?* (1966)
Actor, *Anne of the Thousand Days* (1969)
Actor, *Equus* (1977)

---

†Tied overall for the most acting nominations without a win or an honorary award; O'Toole received the most unsuccessful leading nominations. The two costarred in, and each received an Oscar nomination for, *Becket*.

Quiz: Inauspicious Beginnings, Inconspicuous Endings

For everyone who was taught to believe "there are no small parts, only small actors," the following information might prove comforting: No matter how humbly you start out, you can still surprise everyone and win an Oscar one day.

Q. **He had only small parts in movies (*Scarface* and others) and the humiliating role of a leotard-clad piece of fruit in Fruit of the Loom underwear commercials in the 1970s. Name the best actor winner, and the film he won for.**
A. F. Murray Abraham, *Amadeus* (1984).

Q. **Name the slasher quickie that marks two-time Oscar winner Tom Hanks's first film appearance.**
A. *He Knows You're Alone*.

Q. **What future one-time Oscar winner and multiple nominee got his start in the comedy *Carbon Copy*, a flat variation of the plot to the brilliant *Secrets & Lies* about a black child and his white parent?**
A. Denzel Washington.

Q. **What octogenarian supporting actor winner got his start on the stage in vaudeville?**
A. George Burns, who in 1975's *The Sunshine Boys* became at age 80 the oldest male actor ever to win.

Q. **The Roger Corman film *Piranha II: The Spawning* marked the directorial debut of what infamously over-spending director?**
A. James Cameron (*Titanic*, 1997). The water dangers presented in each film were quite different.

But for all the comfort you take in knowing that from tiny acorns—like Fruit of the Loom ads—mighty oaks do grow, you might want to keep your feet firmly planted on the ground. An Oscar victory is no guarantee of a charmed career. (Neither is it a security on a luxurious lifestyle: Screenwriter John Osborne eventually had to auction off his Oscar for his *Tom Jones* screenplay to buy food and pay bills.) Now, certain stars are well enough entrenched that they can appear in schlock without seriously diminishing their star power: After all, Bette Davis gave us Margo Channing and Baby Jane Hudson, so isn't she allowed to *also* appear in *Wicked Stepmother* and *The Nanny*? Less established winners often find they still have to sing for their supper. So, if it isn't where you start but where you finish, be appropriately respectful of how Oscar-winning status doesn't necessarily give you your choice of the best parts in the world, and learn by these cautionary examples of people who have gone from winner to wiener.

Q. **What memorable Oscar-winning actress has turned up most recently in *Best of the Best, Flowers in the Attic, Two Moon Junction*, and other schlock, usually in cameo roles?**
A.   Louise Fletcher, whose much-deserved win as Nurse Ratched in *One Flew Over the Cuckoo's Nest* (1975) early in her career was also its high point (despite delivering good performances since then).

Q. **Louis Gossett Jr. made his film debut in *A Raisin in the Sun*, later appearing in no less than *three* *Iron Eagle* movies and sidekick roles to the likes of Jim Belushi (*The Principal*) and Chuck Norris (*Firewalker*). For what film did he win his only Oscar?**
A.   He was the supporting actor winner for *An Officer and a Gentleman* (1982), but the quality of his roles petered out quickly.

Q. **Gig Young was one of Hollywood's top second bananas until a revealing, Oscar-winning performance in** *They Shoot Horses, Don't They?* **(1969). He only made five more films before dying on October 19, 1978, less than 10 years later. How did he die?**

A. Sadly, Young murdered his young bride and then committed suicide.

Q. **For what movie did TV's "Hazel" win an Oscar in her film debut, and what was the actress's name?**

A. Shirley Booth, best actress winner for *Come Back, Little Sheba* (1952).

Q. **What foreign-born best actor winner, frustrated by Hollywood, returned to his homeland soon after his win?**

A. Emil Jannings. After 1930, he never appeared in an American-made film again, although his role in *The Blue Angel*, made in Germany, is still considered one of his best. He was hamstrung by the Nazi regime, and ceased acting while still a popular box office attraction.

Leading performances relegated to supporting awards; supporting performances elevated to leading status

The supporting categories for acting were instigated largely in order to give Oscar access to memorable performers in smaller parts, such as Frank Morgan's widely praised turn in *The Affairs of Cellini,* which couldn't compete with Clark Gable in *It Happened One Night.* But despite the best of intentions, the categories have been subjectively applied throughout the years. The following are examples of performers given leading status (usually as a result of star power) for supporting performances, and supporting nominees and winners who carried their films.

• **Spencer Tracy**, actor [n], *San Francisco*; **Stuart Erwin**, supporting actor [n], *Pigskin Parade* (both 1936). No better place to start than the first year of the supporting division, in which the Academy set the stage for the politicking that was to follow: second-lead Tracy getting leading status for a prestige picture, while Erwin, the lead in a B-movie football comedy, got his shot in the lesser category.

• **Greer Garson**, actress [n], *Goodbye, Mr. Chips* (1939). The British film queen got her start in a comparatively small (but pivotal) role in *Chips*, and managed a leading nomination—despite the fact she had less screen time that year than supporting actress nominee Olivia de Havilland in *Gone with the Wind*.

• **Walter Huston**, actor [n], *All That Money Can Buy* (1941). Huston plays the devil, Edward Arnold is Daniel Webster, but the protagonist is really James Craig as the American Faust whose soul is at stake.

• **Barry Fitzgerald**, actor [n], supporting actor [w], *Going My Way* (1944). In one of the Academy's most notorious examples of arbitrariness, Fitzgerald is nominated for leading *and* supporting the same year, winning only for the latter.

• **Don Murray**, supporting actor [n], *Bus Stop* (1956). Murray is the male lead (opposite Marilyn Monroe), but he was a newcomer relegated to the supporting category in order to increase his chances. It didn't work.

• **Frank Finlay**, supporting actor [n], *Othello* (1965). Finlay plays what is actually the larger part, Iago, but there's no doubting that this is Olivier's movie, so Finlay was removed from competition with him.

• **Walter Matthau**, supporting actor [w], *The Fortune Cookie* (1966). Arguably the first person to win a supporting award for a leading performance, co-star Jack Lemmon was the nominal lead. It's instructive to know that the British title of the film is *Meet Whiplash Willie*; Matthau plays Willie.

• **Gene Wilder**, supporting actor [n], *The Producers* (1968). The film is a comic blend of the equally balanced interplay between Zero Mostel and Wilder, but Wilder was placed in the secondary position.

• **Marlon Brando**, actor [w] and **Al Pacino**, supporting actor [n], *The Godfather* (1972). Paramount made it clear to Academy voters that Brando was the only "leading" performer in the film and everyone else was supporting, even though Pacino carries the narrative forward. Brando is brilliant, but the role, memorable as it is, is smallish compared to Pacino's.

• **Tatum O'Neal**, supporting actress [w], *Paper Moon* (1973). Maybe you have to put a nine-year-old in a supporting category, even if she does occupy almost every frame of the film, if only because she seems to physically support all the adults towering over her.

• **Louise Fletcher**, actress [w], *One Flew Over the Cuckoo's Nest* (1975). Fletcher's win in the leading category has been attributed to what was generally considered a weak year for female parts.

• **Peter Finch**, actor [w], *Network* (1976). Finch

reportedly balked at the suggestion that Howard Beale was a "supporting character," although his flashy performance, in the context of the film, is essentially that.

• **Timothy Hutton**, supporting actor [w], *Ordinary People* (1980). Along with O'Neal, there is probably no plainer example of a patently leading role being put in the supporting department. Hutton's beautiful performance could probably not have defeated De Niro in *Raging Bull*, however; it's just a shame he defeated a truly great supporting performance in doing it—Judd Hirsch's understanding therapist in the same movie.

• **Anthony Hopkins**, actor [w], *The Silence of the Lambs* (1991). In what is probably the briefest amount of screen time to win the best actor trophy, Hopkins's charismatic villainy elevated a supporting performance to legendary—and ultimately leading—Oscar status.

• **John Travolta**, actor [n], and **Samuel L. Jackson**, supporting actor [n], *Pulp Fiction* (1994). Some argued placing the black actor in a supporting category and the white in leading as the covert racism of the Academy, although the divisions are, for the most part, justified, if only to increase the film's chances of winning in two categories.

A note on billing. Occasionally the most interesting aspect of leading/supporting divisions is how it conflicts with star billing in the movies. On at least two occasions—*Working Girl* (1988) and *The English Patient* (1996)—the supporting actress nominees (Sigourney Weaver and Juliette Binoche) actually had billing higher than that of the leading actress nominees from the same films

(Melanie Griffith and Kristin Scott Thomas). Alphabetical listings also have an impact, as when Glenn Close was the top-listed woman in *The Big Chill* (1983) but was nominated as supporting actress. And when more than one performer of the same sex vies for an Oscar, the results can also be interesting. William Hurt and Albert Brooks shared billing over their novice co-star Holly Hunter in *Broadcast News* (1987), but Brooks was cast as a supporting actor, while Hunter leapfrogged him to leading status, alongside Hurt. And in *Good Will Hunting* (1997), Robin Williams received top billing over relative newcomer Matt Damon, but Damon was put in the leading category, Williams in supporting.

Quiz: Performance in General

Q. **What two Pulitzer Prize–*winning* playwrights are Academy Award–*losing* supporting actors? Name their films (and, for extra credit, their *plays*).**
A. Sam Shepard (Pulitzer: *Buried Child*, 1979; Oscar: *The Right Stuff*, 1983) and Jason Miller (Pulitzer: *That Championship Season*, 1973; Oscar: *The Exorcist*, 1973).

Q. **Both of Gena Rowlands's best actress nominations (*A Woman Under the Influence*, 1974; *Gloria*, 1988) came in roles directed by the same man. Name him.**
A. The director was husband John Cassavetes.

Q. **Who was probably the heaviest person to be nominated for an Oscar?**

A. It would appear to be Jocelyn Lagarde, the 400-pound Hawaiian who appeared in, not surprisingly, *Hawaii* (1966). As far as I can tell, the nonprofessional never appeared in another movie.

Q. **In addition to Lagarde, what other supporting actress nominee made only one film appearance?**
A. Leslie Browne, a ballet dancer who made her debut in *The Turning Point* (1977) and then ceased making film appearances.

Q. **In what year (for the first and apparently only time) were all 10 leading acting nominees (actor and actress) American-born?**
A. 1985.

Q. **What is the longest performance (in terms of screen time) to win a supporting acting nomination?**
A. The winner would probably be Alec Guinness, who appeared in both parts of *Little Dorrit* (1988), which ran in excess of six hours. As a percentage of screen time, however, the winner would probably be Tatum O'Neal for *Paper Moon* (1973), in which she appears in all but a few minutes of the film. Timothy Hutton in *Ordinary People* (1980) and Tommy Lee Jones in *The Fugitive* (1993) are probably the two supporting actor winners whose roles could have easily been characterized as leading.

Q. **Who are the only two performers to receive two Oscars before turning 30?**
A. Luise Rainer and Jodie Foster.

Q. **The name "Jane Hudson" can bring *some* luck—it was the name of the character played by two actresses in Oscar-nominated (but not-winning) roles. What were the movies?**
A. Both Katharine Hepburn in *Summertime* (1955) and Bette Davis in *What Ever Happened to Baby Jane?* (1962) were named Jane Hudson.

Quiz: Time Heals All Wounds

Q. Even if you discount such flaws as megalomania (Broderick Crawford, *All the King's Men*), low self-esteem (Olivia de Havilland, *The Heiress*), out-and-out stupidity (Peter Ustinov, *Topkapi*), and proboscosis (José Ferrer, *Cyrano de Bergerac*), there's still an extensive catalogue of award-generating performances owing to the actors' portrayal of the physically or mentally disadvantaged. Match the disability or disease with the role that won each performer an Oscar:

a. Deafness *and* muteness (2)

b. Mental illness* (4)

c. AIDS

d. Cerebral palsy

e. Muteness

f. Amnesia

g. Multiple personality disorder

h. Blindness *and* deafness

i. Tom Hanks, *Philadelphia*

ii. Holly Hunter, *The Piano*

iii. Dustin Hoffman, *Rain Man*

iv. Jane Wyman, *Johnny Belinda*

v. Jon Voight, *Coming Home*

vi. Vivien Leigh, *A Streetcar Named Desire*

vii. Al Pacino, *Scent of a Woman*

viii. Marlee Matlin, *Children of a Lesser God*

---

*A good case could be made for any number of other winners portraying people suffering from mental illness, from Shelley Winters in *A Patch of Blue* to Laurence Olivier in *Hamlet*; this list is intended to represent characters diagnosed as such, or who are clearly insane within the context of the film, and not just suffering from depression or a severe case of the nasties.

i. **Paraplegia (legs)**

j. **Paraplegia (hands)**

k. **Blindness**

l. **Alcoholism (2)†**

m. **Autism**

n. **Mental retardation**

ix. **Patty Duke,** *The Miracle Worker*

x. **Daniel Day-Lewis,** *My Left Foot*

xi. **Peter Finch,** *Network*

xii. **Joanne Woodward,** *The Three Faces of Eve*

xiii. **Jack Nicholson,** *One Flew Over the Cuckoo's Nest*

xiv. **Ingrid Bergman,** *Anastasia*

xv. **Nicolas Cage,** *Leaving Las Vegas*

xvi. **Geoffrey Rush,** *Shine*

xvii. **Ray Milland,** *The Lost Weekend*

xviii. **Harold Russell,** *The Best Years of Our Lives*

xviv. **Cliff Robertson,** *Charly*

---

†It would be almost impossible to create an exhaustive list of all the performers who have won Oscars for portraying alcoholics in the space above (and even less possible to list the nominees); they include Claire Trevor, *Key Largo*; Thomas Mitchell, *Stagecoach*; Van Heflin, *Johnny Eager*; Humphrey Bogart, *The African Queen*; Dorothy Malone, *Written on the Wind*; and Elizabeth Taylor, *Who's Afraid of Virginia Woolf?* This list is limited to the two persons whose sole purpose during the movie was to remain constantly drunk. Curiously, no one has won outright playing a drug addict—with the possible exception of Dianne Wiest in *Hannah and Her Sisters*, but her addiction was played more for laughs and so doesn't (or shouldn't) count.

A. a.-iv. and viii.; b.-vi., xi., xiii., and xvi.; c.-i.;
d.-x.; e.-ii.; f.-xiv.; g.-xii.; h.-ix.; i.-v.; j.-xviii.; k.-
vii.; l.-xv. and xvii.; m.-iii.; n.-xviv.

Quiz: It was a very good year

Q. Occasionally, an actor or a director will just hit
his or her stride one year, and everything seems
to click. Everyone named below starred in (or
directed) *two* best picture nominees in one year;
sometimes they were recognized themselves,
sometimes not. Name the two best picture nominees from the given year with which each is associated.

* **Robert De Niro, 1993**
A. Starred in nominees *Awakenings* and *Good-
Fellas*; nominated as best actor for *Awakenings*.

* **Herbert Ross, 1977**
A. Directed nominees *The Turning Point* and *The
Goodbye Girl*; nominated as best director for *The
Turning Point*.

* **Francis Ford Coppola, 1974**
A. Wrote and directed nominee *The Conversation*
and winner *The Godfather Part II*; nominated for
writing both; nominated for producing and directing *The Godfather Part II* (he won three for *The
Godfather Part II*).

* **Sidney Poitier, 1967**
A. Starred in nominee *Guess Who's Coming to
Dinner* and winner *In the Heat of the Night*; Poitier
himself did not receive a nomination for either, or
for his third film that year, *To Sir, with Love*.

- **Julie Christie, 1965**
A. Starred in nominees *Doctor Zhivago* and *Darling*; won the best actress Oscar for the latter.

- **Yul Brynner, 1956**
A. Starred in nominees *The Ten Commandments* and *The King and I*; won best actor for the latter.

- **Ingrid Bergman, 1945**
A. Starred in nominees *The Bells of St. Mary's* and *Spellbound*; was Oscar-nominated for the former.

- **Alfred Hitchcock, 1940**
A. His best picture winner *Rebecca* had to compete with nominee *Foreign Correspondent*, which he also directed; he was nominated for directing *Rebecca*.

- **John Ford, 1940**
A. His best director award beat out Hitchcock with *The Grapes of Wrath*, but *The Long Voyage Home* was also a nominee that year.

And another notable achievement. Natalie Wood appeared in both screenplay award winners in 1961, as she starred in *Splendor in the Grass* (original screenplay) and *West Side Story* (adapted screenplay). Wood was nominated as best actress in *Splendor*, but lost to Sophia Loren.

Quiz: Never Had a Dinner

Being popular, being prominent, being talented, and being an Oscar nominee—or Oscar winner—have little, if any, relationship. *None* of the following well-known, even beloved performers ever won an Oscar—and 30 were *never even nominated* for a competitive award.

Q. Can you select which are the bridesmaids—and which never even got invited to the church?

Jane Alexander
Judith Anderson
Dana Andrews
Alan Arkin
Jean Arthur
Fred Astaire
Lew Ayres
Lauren Bacall
Lucille Ball
Bridget Bardot
John Barrymore
Jacqueline Bisset
Dirk Bogarde
Charles Boyer
Richard Burton
John Cassavetes
Montgomery Clift
Joseph Cotten
Doris Day
James Dean
Catherine Deneuve
Marlene Dietrich
Kirk Douglas
Irene Dunne
Mia Farrow
W.C. Fields
Albert Finney
Errol Flynn

Glenn Ford
Harrison Ford
Greta Garbo
Ava Gardner
Judy Garland
James Garner
Elliott Gould
Cary Grant
Sydney Greenstreet
Jean Harlow
Richard Harris
Laurence Harvey
Rita Hayworth
Leslie Howard
Trevor Howard
Rock Hudson
James Earl Jones
Louis Jourdan
Boris Karloff
Gene Kelly
Deborah Kerr
Alan Ladd
Angela Lansbury
Janet Leigh
Peter Lorre
Myrna Loy
Ida Lupino
Roddy MacDowell
Fred MacMurray

Dean Martin
James Mason
Marsha Mason
Joel McCrea
Malcolm McDowell
Steve McQueen
Burgess Meredith
Bette Midler
Robert Mitchum
Marilyn Monroe
Robert Montgomery
Agnes Moorehead
Merle Oberon
Peter O'Toole
Sean Penn
Anthony Perkins
Tyrone Power
Vincent Price
Claude Rains
Ronald Reagan
Ralph Richardson
Thelma Ritter
Edward G. Robinson
Mickey Rooney
Gena Rowlands
Rosalind Russell

George Segal	Barbara Stanwyck	Lana Turner
Peter Sellers	Donald Suther-	Clifton Webb
Robert Shaw	land	Natalie Wood
Jean Simmons	Shirley Temple	Robert Young

A. The omission of the following talents numbers among the great black marks in Oscar history: Andrews (sincere star of *The Ox-Bow Incident* and *The Best Years of Our Lives*); Ball (a TV doyenne but perpetual Oscar wannabe); Bardot (a popular sex kitten, who showed herself capable of genuine acting in such films as *Contempt*); Barrymore (his stage success did not translate as successfully to the screen as those of siblings Ethel and Lionel); Bisset (gifted, beautiful international star); Bogarde (the respected British character actor); Cotten (*Citizen Kane, The Magnificent Ambersons, Shadow of a Doubt*); Farrow (*Rosemary's Baby, Broadway Danny Rose*); Fields (instantly identifiable comedy star); Flynn (flamboyant action star); Glenn Ford (*3:10 to Yuma, The Blackboard Jungle*—one of the most popular actors of the late '50s); Harlow (troubled but popular platinum blonde comedienne); Hayworth (*Gilda, The Lady from Shanghai*—known as the sex goddess); Jourdan (suave French leading man in *Gigi* and *Letter from an Unknown Woman*); Karloff (spooky, tall star of horror films); Ladd (short, forceful action star: *Shane, This Gun for Hire*); Lorre (creepy personality from *M* to *The Maltese Falcon*); Loy (sardonic, sophisticated star of *The Thin Man* films); Lupino (respected character actress, later a director); Roddy MacDowall (child star of vehicles like *How Green Was My Valley* to varied adult roles in *Cleopatra* and *Fright Night*); Fred MacMurray (*Double Indemnity*); McCrea (buoyant, likable star of the '30s and '40s); Malcolm McDowell (distinctive British star of *A*

Clockwork Orange and *Time After Time*); Dean Martin (singer-comedian who expanded into strong dramatic roles); Monroe (sex goddess from several '50s vehicles); Power (moody, intelligent star of the '40s); Price (deliciously wicked character actor, often in horror roles); Reagan (B-movie star with some good moments—*Kings Row*; his political career outshone his Hollywood tenure); Robinson (intense, unexpectedly thoughtful star from *Little Caesar* to *The Stranger*); Sutherland (offbeat star of *M*A*S*H*, *Don't Look Now*, and *Ordinary People*); Temple (adorable child star, and youngest-ever honorary award recipient); Young (*H.M. Pulham, Esq.*, later popular on TV).

These people *were* nominated, without ever winning the Oscar: Alexander (*The Great White Hope*, 1970 [+]); Anderson (*Rebecca*, 1940); Arkin (*The Russians Are Coming! The Russians Are Coming!*, 1966); Arthur (*The More the Merrier*, 1943); Astaire (*The Towering Inferno*, 1974); Ayres (*Johnny Belinda*, 1948); Bacall (*The Mirror Has Two Faces*, 1996); Boyer (*Algiers*, 1938 [+]); Burton (*My Cousin Rachel*, 1952 [+]); Cassavetes (*The Dirty Dozen*, 1967 [+]); Clift (*The Search*, 1948 [+]); Day (*Pillow Talk*, 1959); Dean (*East of Eden*, 1955); Deneuve (*Indochine*, 1992); Dietrich (*Morocco*, 1930/31); Douglas (*Champion*, 1949 [+]); Dunne (*Theodora Goes Wild*, 1936 [+]); Finney (*Tom Jones*, 1963 [+]); Ford (*Witness*, 1985); Garbo (*Anna Christie*, 1929/30 [+]); Gardner (*Mogambo*, 1953); Garland (*A Star Is Born*, 1954 [+]); Garner (*Murphy's Romance*, 1984); Gould (*Bob & Carol & Ted & Alice*, 1969); Grant (*Penny Serenade*, 1941 [+]); Greenstreet (*The Maltese Falcon*, 1941); Harris (*This Sporting Life*, 1963); Harvey (*Room at the Top*, 1959); Leslie Howard (*Pygmalion*, 1938); Trevor Howard (*Sons and Lovers*,

1960); Hudson (*Giant*, 1956); Jones (*The Great White Hope*, 1970); Kelly (*Anchors Aweigh*, 1945); Kerr (*Edward My Son*, 1949 [+]); Lansbury (*Gaslight*, 1944 [+]); Leigh (*Psycho*, 1960); McQueen (*The Sand Pebbles*, 1966); James Mason (*A Star Is Born*, 1954 [+]); Marsha Mason (*Cinderella Liberty*, 1973 [+]); Meredith (*The Day of the Locust*, 1975 [+]); Midler (*The Rose*, 1979 [+]); Mitchum (*The Story of G.I. Joe*, 1945); Montgomery (*Night Must Fall*, 1938 [+]); Moorehead (*The Magnificent Ambersons*, 1942 [+]); Oberon (*Wuthering Heights*, 1939); O'Toole (*Lawrence of Arabia*, 1962 [+]); Penn (*Dead Man Walking*, 1995); Perkins (*Friendly Persuasion*, 1956); Rains (*Mr. Smith Goes to Washington*, 1939 [+]); Richardson (*The Heiress*, 1948 [+]); Ritter (*All About Eve*, 1950 [+]); Rooney (*Babes in Arms*, 1939 [+]); Rowlands (*A Woman Under the Influence*, 1974 [+]); Russell (*My Sister Eileen*, 1942 [+]); Segal (*Who's Afraid of Virginia Woolf?*, 1966); Sellers (*Dr. Strangelove*, 1964 [+]); Shaw (*A Man for All Seasons*, 1966 [+]); Simmons (*Hamlet*, 1948 [+]); Stanwyck (*Stella Dallas*, 1937 [+]); Turner (*Peyton Place*, 1957); Webb (*Laura*, 1944 [+]); Wood (*Rebel Without a Cause*, 1955 [+]).

🎬 Lucky to be there

It occurred to me once that no matter what happens, for all time, *Love Story* will be able to claim the distinction of being (1) an Oscar winner; and (2) a Oscar nominee for best picture. Yet you'd be hard-pressed to find a dopier romance if you tried. On the other hand, a terrific little film like *Brassed Off* can't even claim the slight solace of an Oscar nomination in any category. What follows is a list of what must qualify as the most forgettable and unqualified winning films in Oscar history—movies that, but for their Oscar win (which, occasionally, might even be deserved), would have fallen into obscurity—and with good reason.

• *The Alamo* (1960; sound). This loud, long, dreary film, directed by John Wayne, was a tremendous financial and critical flop that somehow managed a best picture nomination at the expense of *Psycho*.

• *The Bachelor and the Bobby-Soxer* (1947; original screenplay). Only the charm and appeal of Cary Grant could come close to explaining this oddball entry in the *writing* category (beating out, among others, *Shoeshine* and *Body and Soul*). Sidney Sheldon, of all people, won the award.

• *The Big Broadcast of 1938* (1938; song). This was the fourth in a series of "Broadcast" movies Paramount trotted out in the '30s, all pretty much like one another—except this one contained Bob Hope, and featured his signature song, "Thanks for the Memory."

• *Butterfield 8* (1960; actress). A sordid little potboiler, it won Elizabeth Taylor her first Oscar (the second was actually *deserved*), and was widely seen as a sympathy vote for the seriously ill actress. She recovered, but the Academy's dignity didn't.

• *Captain Carey, U.S.A.* (1950; song). If I voted for the single most obscure Oscar winner, it would be this wholly forgettable Alan Ladd film . . . wholly forgettable except for the Nat King Cole song "Mona Lisa."

• *Harry and the Hendersons* (1987; makeup). Despite a syndicated series bearing its name, this goofy family comedy qualifies as one of the quickest films to drop from memory in Academy history.

• *A Little Night Music* (1977; adaptation score). What possessed the Academy to feel compelled to hand out an unnecessary Oscar to a stifling, off-key stage hit like this (dreadfully transferred to screen) is incomprehensible.

• *Logan's Run* (1976; special visual effects). The honorary award bestowed on this giant turkey seems today like a colossal joke—even by '50s standards, it's garishly overdecorated and blindingly overproduced.

• *Neptune's Daughter* (1949; song). As is often the case, a memorable song (this time, ''Baby, It's Cold Outside'') can sometimes spell the difference between everlasting obscurity and legendary Oscar status.

• *Thank God It's Friday* (1978; song). The name alone says it all. Only one more word: *Disco!*

• *Yesterday, Today and Tomorrow* (1964; foreign language film). Something of a surprise winner, and one of the least memorable (and slightest) of all foreign films to take the prize.

• *You Light Up My Life* (1977; song). Even on its release, this was a known dud, but the song was the most successful of the '70s. Most people have probably already forgotten there ever *was* a movie.

Special Mention. Rather predictably, the most notably non-notable Oscar winners are *The Fair Co-ed, Telling the World*, and *Laugh, Clown, Laugh*, three rather ordinary silent films that jointly won the most obscure of Oscars, eligible only for silent films: best title writing.

Quiz: The Luckiest Stiffs in the World

Whereas some giants of cinema have gone winless or even nomination-less, others seem to have greatness thrust upon them—sometimes almost unfairly, as evidenced by some of the populist, if questionably artistic, selections below. Some of the 15 people named here, many of whom have endured their share of critical scoffs, have actually *won* an Oscar in at least some category (the others have never even been nominated).

Q. Can you pick out which of the performers below have actually won an Oscar?

Tallulah Bank-head	Art Carney	Jerry Lewis
Pat Boone	Carrie Fisher	Steve Martin
Mel Brooks	Annette Funi-cello	Elvis Presley
Red Buttons	Taylor Hack-ford	Tony Randall
Irene Cara	John Lennon	Roy Rogers

A. Brooks received a screenplay Oscar for his first film, *The Producers* (1968); Buttons won for his performance in *Sayonara* (1957); *The Honeymooners*' Carney got a best actor award for *Harry and Tonto* (1974); director Hackford won a live action short award (1977); Lennon, as one of the Beatles, won original score for *Let It Be* (1970); Cara cowrote best song winner from *Flashdance* (1983). None of the others were, as far as the records show, ever close to the gold.

KEEP 'EM COMING

At the end of *The Candidate*, the dark horse liberal stuns his backers and the pundits by surging ahead in the polls and claiming victory over his popular opponent—even though everyone was planning on him losing. "What do we do now?" he asks his campaign manager. It's a familiar refrain: Where do you go from up? Sean Connery has said that Hollywood permits three flops for every hit, but does the same hold true for Oscar? Observe the following list of Oscar winners, whose follow-up films were almost as good as their honored roles—or at least brought them sizable acclaim or box office clout.

- **Charles Laughton**. After winning an Oscar for *The Private Life of King Henry VIII* (1932/33), he followed it up with an equally impressive *Barretts of Wimpole Street* (1934).

- **Luise Rainer**. Rainer won two Oscars for her first three film roles. Her back-to-back Oscars are both among the least deserved in history, especially her overwrought turn in *The Good Earth* (1937). But two victories in a row is nothing to sneeze at.

- **Spencer Tracy**. Unlike Rainer's, Tracy's consecutive wins (*Captains Courageous* in 1937, *Boys Town* in 1938) are both warranted.

- **Gary Cooper**. Coop seemed to be able to do no wrong with this impressive string of films: *Meet John Doe* (1941), *Sergeant York* (1941; best actor), *Ball of Fire* (1942), *The Pride of the Yankees* (1942; nomination), *For Whom the Bell Tolls* (1943; nomination).

- **Ingrid Bergman**. The exquisite Bergman's performance in *Gaslight* (1944) won her an Oscar; she had to settle for great reviews for Hitchcock's

Oscar-nominated *Spellbound* (1945).

- **Joan Crawford**. Her late-coming (and not exactly deserved) Oscar for *Mildred Pierce* (1945) came, unfortunately, before her best weepy ever, *Humoresque* (1946).

- **Olivia de Havilland**. Her best actress award, for 1946's *To Each His Own*, is one of the oddities of the Oscar voters; it was probably more deserved for *The Dark Mirror* the same year, and definitely more deserved for her big 1947 film, *The Snake Pit*.

- **Broderick Crawford**. Crawford's only two really noteworthy leading roles were in consecutive years: as the corrupt politician in *All the King's Men* (1949, best actor) and the mobster in *Born Yesterday* (1950).

- **Audrey Hepburn**. Her leading debut in *Roman Holiday* (1953) won her the best actress trophy; the Academy knew they made a good decision when her next film turned out to be *Sabrina* (1954).

- **William Holden**. Three years after *deserving* the Oscar (for *Sunset Boulevard*), he won it for *Stalag 17* (1953)—also well-deserved. The same year, he showed his gift for comedy in *The Moon Is Blue* and *Sabrina* (1954), and his power in the riveting boardroom drama, *Executive Suite* (1954).

- **Yul Brynner**. Aside from a hirsute role in 1949, Brynner's career got rolling (bald-headed) in 1956 with a trio of stellar movies: *Anastasia, The Ten Commandments*, and *The King and I* (which won him the best actor trophy); his next film was almost as good: *The Brothers Karamazov* (1958).

- **Anne Bancroft**. Bancroft's screen career was the epitome of ordinary until she re-created her Tony-winning performance in *The Miracle Worker*

(1962) for Oscar gold. Her next film was *The Pumpkin Eater* (1964), which won her another nomination.

- **Julie Andrews**. Maybe the best first two years in Oscar history: Julie won her best actress trophy for *Mary Poppins* (1964), then proceeded to get a second nomination for one of the most popular films of all time, *The Sound of Music* (1965).

- **Katharine Hepburn**. Her Oscar in 1967 for *Guess Who's Coming to Dinner* was seen largely as a valentine to Spencer; her win in 1968 (in a tie with Streisand) was for just plain killer acting, as the arch Eleanor of Aquitaine in *The Lion in Winter*.

- **Diane Keaton**. *Annie Hall*, her best actress win, was one of her two high-profile films of 1977 (the other was *Looking for Mr. Goodbar*) that landed her on the cover of *Time* magazine. Over the course of the next four years, she appeared in *Interiors* (1978), *Manhattan* (1979), and *Reds* (1981)—an impressive hat trick.

- **Dustin Hoffman**. It was three years after *Kramer vs. Kramer* (1979) before Hoffman released another film—understandable, when you consider the all-around quality of *Tootsie* (1982), which received ten Oscar nominations, including one for Hoffman and a win for costar Jessica Lange.

- **Jodie Foster**. There's a reason Foster has been lauded as one of the best actresses of her generation: Her three-year wait after winning best actress honors for *The Accused* (1988) led to a second win for *The Silence of the Lambs* (1991).

- **Nicolas Cage**. After the grim art-house hit *Leaving Las Vegas* (1995) won him the best actor award, Cage decided to lighten up by doing an action picture, *The Rock*. Although the movie itself was merely adequate, Cage and his talented costars (Sean Connery and Ed Harris) raised the level of the proceedings, and Cage reinvigorated his career, going from reliable indie king to buff box office champ.

- **James Dean**. He died young, and with only three starring roles to his name: as the troubled teen in *Rebel without a Cause* (the only film released before his death on September 30, 1955), *East of Eden* (both 1955; the latter an Oscar nomination), and *Giant* (1956; nomination). He never won. He's the only actor to be nominated twice posthumously.

THE SOPHOMORE SLUMP

Unlike the stars above, who parlayed an Academy Award into a one-two punch, these Oscar winners made the kind of boneheaded career choices after they'd won that make the voters wonder whether they had made a mistake awarding them the Oscar in the first place.

- **Elizabeth Taylor**. Her victory for *Butterfield 8* (1960) is widely regarded as one of the Academy's less well-informed consolation prizes, but when *Cleopatra* (1963) followed it, she entered a unique and frightening realm where kitsch, bad acting, big budgets, and cheesy melodrama magically become one.

- **Rod Steiger**. *In the Heat of the Night* (1967) may have been sensitive to racial issues, but *The Sergeant* offended another American culture in its lurid and insulting depiction of a gay serviceman lusting after a straight colleague.

- **Barbra Streisand**. You can't blame her for taking the choice role of Dolly Levi in *Hello, Dolly!* (1969) the year after her win for *Funny Girl* (1968), but you can't say she was right for the part, either.

- **Liza Minnelli**. The *Cabaret* (1972) star steered clear of acting for a while (she did a voice-over for *Journey Back to Oz* and "hosted" a segment of *That's Entertainment*), but the wait was hardly worth it: *Lucky Lady* nearly destroyed her career almost from its inception, and she never really recovered.

- **Jack Lemmon**. His only best actor award, for *Save the Tiger* (1973), was succeeded by a strained remake of *The Front Page*.

- **Ellen Burstyn**. Her Oscar for *Alice Doesn't Live Here Anymore* (1974) didn't improve her judgment: Her next film was the erratic, annoying "art" film, *Providence*, and it took her three years to make it.

- **Art Carney**. Carney's surprise victory for *Harry and Tonto* (1974) must have caught him off-guard: He appeared the following year in the cheesy comedy *W.W. and the Dixie Dance Kings*.

- **Faye Dunaway**. The speckled career of the screen's ice princess was confirmed when *Network* (1976) was followed up with the supernatural (non)thriller, *The Eyes of Laura Mars*.

- **Vanessa Redgrave**. After taking home the best supporting actress trophy for *Julia* (1977), she took a leading role *Agatha*, a slow and boring fictional biography of Agatha Christie.

- **Richard Dreyfuss**. 1977 was a good year for him, with *Close Encounters of the Third Kind* and *The Goodbye Girl* (best actor) both doing big box office, but 1978's *The Big Fix* was a charmless and lackluster successor.

- **Jon Voight**. His paraplegic veteran in *Coming Home* (1978) brought him the gold, but his punch-drunk fighter in *The Champ* was the kind of revoltingly syrupy picture that can almost single-handedly turn a viewer diabetic.

- **Sally Field**. Maybe the Academy didn't ''like her, really like her'' because she responded to their best actress award for *Norma Rae* (1979) with a small part in Burt Reynolds's mindless tripe, *Smokey and the Bandit II*.

- **Anthony Hopkins**. His career is now firmly established after a checkered period in the '70s and '80s, but he was still insecure enough after 1991's *The Silence of the Lambs* (which brought him the best actor award) to appear in the dreadful action film *Freejack*.

- **Henry Fonda** and **Peter Finch**. They didn't have to worry about not living up to expectations: Each won their Oscar for their final film.

Quiz: All in the Family

An ex-lover of Warren Beatty once observed that he had a peculiar tendency to date women who had just won, or just been nominated for, Academy Awards. (His eventual wife, Annette Bening, was nominated as best supporting actress for *The Grifters* two years before they met on the set of *Bugsy*.) Could it be that Beatty thought Oscars were bestowed by association? Are the stars themselves as obsessed with Oscar as entertainment reporters portray the general public to be? Beatty finally got his own Oscar—as director of *Reds* (1981)—but aside from his Oscar-nominated wife, Beatty can also boast a similarly laureled sister: Shirley MacLaine, who after five best actress nominations finally took home the prize for *Terms of Endearment* (1983). Now there's enough gold in the family to keep everyone happy.

The popular romance of entertainment dynasties—the Barrymores, the Redgraves, etc.—has been an allure for centuries, but the movies have made it an easier fantasy to indulge. Family members frequently make films together as much for the Valentine effect as for the showmanship: Was Jane Fonda, nominated as best supporting actress for *On Golden Pond*, really that good, or did her colleagues simply respond to the power, the *honesty*, of seeing her bare her resentments and her love to her real-life father Henry? *On Golden Pond* is a sappy if effective film, but the casting of two Fondas transcended gimmickry, and the Academy rewarded them each appropriately (Jane with a nomination, Hank with his only win).

Q. **Spouses, siblings, children and parents have frequently scored a nomination or a win, sometimes appearing with each other, sometimes merely by following in each others' footsteps. Did you realize how many kinfolk actually managed some form of Academy notoriety? (And this list isn't even exhaustive!) Given the last name of the dynasty, list all the family members who were nominated or won, and at least one of their nominated films.**

- Fonda
  A. Father Henry (*On Golden Pond*, actor [w+], 1981), daughter Jane (*Klute*, actress [w+], 1971), and son Peter (*Ulee's Gold*, actor [n+], 1997). Bridget could easily come through with a third-generation nod.

- Huston
  A. Father Walter (*The Treasure of the Sierra Madre*, supporting actor [w+], 1948), son John (*The Treasure of the Sierra Madre*, director [w+]), and granddaughter Anjelica (*Prizzi's Honor*, supporting actress [w+], 1985) all turned up winners—the only such hat trick in Oscar history. Grandson Tony also got a nod for *The Dead* (adapted screenplay [n], 1987), starring Anjelica and directed by John.

- Dern
  A. Father/husband Bruce (*Coming Home*, supporting actor [n], 1978), wife/mother Diane Ladd (*Alice Doesn't Live Here Anymore*, supporting actress [n+], 1974), daughter Laura (*Rambling Rose*, actress [n], 1991)—the foil for the Huston legacy—none has ever won.

- Minnelli
  A. Father/husband Vincente (*An American in Paris*, director [w+], 1951), wife/mother Judy Garland (*A Star Is Born*, actress [n+], 1954), daughter Liza (*Cabaret* 1972, actress [w+]).

- Fontaine/deHavilland
  A. The feud between sisters Joan Fontaine (*Suspicion*, actress [w+], 1941) and Olivia de Havilland (*The Heiress*, actress [w+], 1949) is almost as well-known as their Oscar-winning movies.

- Coppola
  A. Writer-director Francis (*The Godather Part II*, director [w+], 1974) and his sister Talia Shire (*Rocky*, actress [n+], 1976) aren't the only family members to have achieved some Oscar recognition: Father Carmine (*The Godfather Part II*, score [w]), Talia's (now ex) husband David Shire (*The Milagro Beanfield War*, score [n+], 1987), and nephew Nicolas Cage (*Leaving Las Vegas*, actor [w], 1995) have all racked up some notice. Sofia Coppola never should have been cast in *The Godfather Part III*.

- Barrymore
  A. Sister Ethel (*None But the Lonely Heart*, supporting actress [w+], 1944) and brother Lionel (*A Free Soul*, actor [w+], 1930/3) each won, but their even-more-famous sibling, John, was never even nominated. Granddaughter/niece Drew is still out there plugging away.

- Redgrave
  A. Father Michael (*Mourning Becomes Electra*, actor [n], 1947) sired two Oscar-recognized daughters: Lynn (*Georgy Girl*, actress [n], 1966) and Vanessa (*Julia*, supporting actress [w+], 1977); son Corin, also an actor, turned up short.

- Powell
  A. The brilliant English director/producer Michael Powell (*The Red Shoes*, producer [n+], 1948) never won, but his widow, Scorsese perennial film editor Thelma Schoonmaker (*Raging Bull*, film editing [w+], 1980) carries on the family's proud tradition.

- Newman (music)
  A. Probably the greatest family tradition in Oscar history belongs to some behind-the-scenes types—four composers: Alfred (*Alexander's*

Ragtime Band, score [w+], 1938), brother Lionel (*Camelot*, scoring [w+], 1967), and nephews Randy (*The Natural*, song [n+], 1984) and Thomas (*Unstrung Heroes*, score [n+], 1995).

• Anhalt
A. The husband and wife writing team of Edward and Edna (*Panic in the Streets*, screenplay [w+], 1950) netted one victory and several nominations.

• Brooks/Bancroft
A. Wife Anne Bancroft (*The Miracle Worker*, actress [w+], 1962) won while she was still just engaged to husband Mel Brooks (*The Producers*, original screenplay [w+], 1968), but they both went on to multiple nominations during their 30-plus year marriage.

• Lunt and Fontanne
A. Renowned stage acting team Alfred Lunt and Lynne Fontanne both received acting nominations early in the history of talkies, for their joint appearance in *The Guardsman* (1931), but neither won. Overall, their screen careers were unremarkable.

• Olivier
A. Laurence (*Hamlet*, actor [w+], 1958) and his then-wife Vivien Leigh (*Gone with the Wind*, actress [w+], 1939) and later widow Joan Plowright (*Enchanted April*, supporting actress [n], 1992), all met with varying degrees of film-award success.

• Curtis/Leigh
A. Neither husband Tony (*The Defiant Ones*, actor [n], 1958) nor wife Janet Leigh (*Psycho*, supporting actress [n], 1960) ever won, but to-date-unnominated daughter Jamie Lee Curtis still has a promising career ahead of her.

- Newman/Woodward
  A. One of Hollywood's darling couples, each has won an acting Oscar, he for *The Color of Money* (actor, 1986), she for *The Three Faces of Eve* (actress, 1957), in addition to multiple nominations.

- Powell/Lombard/Gable
  A. This interesting triangle produced a total of seven nominations: three for Gable (*It Happened One Night*, actor [w+], 1934), three for Powell (*The Thin Man*, actor [n+], 1934), and one for Lombard (*My Man Godfrey*, actress [n], 1936). What's especially interesting about it all is this: Gable defeated Powell for best actor in 1934, at which time Powell was married to Lombard; Powell and Lombard then divorced, and Lombard married Gable, but she got her only Oscar nomination appearing opposite fellow nominee—and ex-husband—Powell. They both lost.

Quiz: Kids These Days

Q. Do parents really want life for their children to be better than it was for them? Maybe. It might be luck, it might be skill, but sometimes the adulation of the Oscars skips a generation. Given the name of the Oscar winner, see if you can identify the film for which he or she won, as well as the name of the as-well-known parents who never won a competitive Oscar.

- Mira Sorvino
  A. Best supporting actress, *Mighty Aphrodite* (1995); daughter of respected character actor Paul Sorvino.

- Michael Douglas
  A. Best actor, *Wall Street* (1987) and best picture producer, *One Flew Over the Cuckoo's Nest*

(1975); son of tough-guy icon Kirk Douglas (who after four nominations finally received an honorary award in 1996).

- Timothy Hutton
  A. Best supporting actor, *Ordinary People* (1980); son of lightweight-but-enjoyable comedic actor Jim Hutton.

- Keith Carradine
  A. Best song, *Nashville* (1975); the only nomination ever for the Carradine bunch trumps an award-free career by father John (despite appearances in more than 100 movies, including *The Grapes of Wrath*).

- Tatum O'Neal
  A. Best supporting actress, *Paper Moon* (1973); her father is Ryan O'Neal.

Quiz: Oscar winners who played real-life or historical figures

Q. Below are Oscar-winning performers. Identify the films for which they won an Oscar for portraying as real-life or historical figures.
- George Arliss
  A. *Disraeli* (1929/30) (title role)

- Charles Laughton
  A. *The Private Life of Henry VIII* (1932/33) (title role)

- Paul Muni
  A. *The Story of Louis Pasteur* (1936) (title role)

- Spencer Tracy
  A. *Boys Town* (1938) (as Father Flanagan)

- Gary Cooper
  A. *Sergeant York* (1941) (title role)

- James Cagney
  A. *Yankee Doodle Dandy* (1942) (as showman George M. Cohan)

- Yul Brynner
  A. *The King and I* (1956) (as the King of Siam)

- Paul Scofield
  A. *A Man for All Seasons* (1966) (as Sir Thomas More)

- Robert De Niro
  A. *Raging Bull* (1980) (as boxer Jake LaMotta)

- Ben Kingsley
  A. *Gandhi* (1981) (title role)

- F. Murray Abraham
  A. *Amadeus* (1984) (as composer Antonio Salieri)

- Daniel Day-Lewis
  A. *My Left Foot* (1989) (as artist Christy Brown)

- Jeremy Irons
  A. *Reversal of Fortune* (1990) (as socialite Claus von Bulow)

- Geoffrey Rush
  A. *Shine* (1996) (as pianist David Helfgott)

- Luise Rainer
  A. *The Great Ziegfeld* (1936) (as Flo Ziegfeld's wife, Anna Held)

- Jennifer Jones
  A. *The Song of Bernadette* (1943) (as Bernadette of Lourdes)

- Susan Hayward
  A. *I Want to Live!* (1958) (as convicted murderess Barbara Graham)

- Anne Bancroft
  A. *The Miracle Worker* (1962) (as Helen Keller's teacher, Annie Sullivan)

- Katharine Hepburn
  A. *The Lion in Winter* (1968) (as Eleanor of Aquitaine)

- Barbra Streisand
  A. *Funny Girl* (1968) (as comedienne Fanny Brice)

- Sissy Spacek
  A. *Coal Miner's Daughter* (1980) (as singer Loretta Lynn)

- Susan Sarandon
  A. *Dead Man Walking* (1995) (as Sister Helen Prejean)

- Joseph Schildkraut
  A. *The Life of Emile Zola* (1937) (as Captain Dreyfus)

- Edmund Gwenn
  A. *Miracle on 34th Street* (1947) (as Santa Claus) (Come on!)

- Anthony Quinn
  A. *Lust for Life* (1956) (as Paul Gauguin)

- Jason Robards
  A. *All the President's Men* (1976) (as *Washington Post* editor Ben Bradlee); and *Julia* (1977) (as Dashiell Hammett)[6]

- Dr. Haing S. Ngor
  A. *The Killing Fields* (1984) (as journalist Dith Pran)

---

[6]Robards was also nominated for portraying Howard Hughes, and Ben Kingsley was nominated for portraying Meyer Lansky, making them the only multiple-nominees and winners to receive all their nominations for portraying real-life people.

- Martin Landau
  A.   *Ed Wood* (1994) (as Bela Lugosi)

- Alice Brady
  A.   *In Old Chicago* (1937) (as Mrs. O'Leary)

- Shelley Winters
  A.   *The Diary of Anne Frank* (1959) (as hideaway Mrs. Van Daan)

- Patty Duke
  A.   *The Miracle Worker* (1962) (as Helen Keller)

- Vanessa Redgrave
  A.   *Julia* (1977) (title role)

- Maureen Stapleton
  A.   *Reds* (1981) (as journalist Emma Goldman)

Special mention. Estelle Parsons, *Bonnie and Clyde* (1967), and Brenda Fricker, *My Left Foot* (1989), played real-life, but marginal and not especially historical, figures.

ISN'T IT ROMANTIC?

It's one thing to lose to your best friends or former roommates (as Rosalind Russell lost to Loretta Young, Henry Fonda lost to James Stewart, and Gene Hackman lost to Dustin Hoffman); it's quite another to lose the same year your spouse wins. That doesn't always happen (sometimes you both get treated equally), but the following married (or soon-to-be-married) couples were all nominated in the same year.

- **1939.** Laurence Olivier, best actor nominee for *Wuthering Heights,* got only a nomination; new wife Vivien Leigh wound up the best actress winner for *Gone with the Wind.*

- **1943**. Writer Frank Ross's screenplay seemed tailor-made for wife Jean Arthur—and both were nominated for *The More the Merrier*.

- **1948**. The great husband and wife writing team of Garson Kanin and Ruth Gordon were not victorious with their nominated screenplay for *A Double Life* or for *Adam's Rib* in 1950 or *Pat and Mike* in 1952—but Ruth did win a supporting actress award many years later—without any of Garson's help, thank you.

- **1953**. Although their marriage was apparently already on the rocks, Ava Gardner (*Mogambo*) and Frank Sinatra (*From Here to Eternity*) figured in this year's awards, with only Sinatra coming out on top.

- **1957**. Charles Laughton had the lead as the lawyer, his wife Elsa Lancaster the showy supporting role as his doting nurse, but both were nominated for *Witness for the Prosecution*.

- **1960**. Best actress nominee Melina Mercouri and her fiancé, writer-director-costar Jules Dassin, were in contention together for *Never on Sunday*.

- **1962**. The debut film of Oscar-nominated director Frank Perry, *David and Lisa*, was written by his nominated wife, Eleanor Perry.

- **1963**. Best actor nominee Rex Harrison (*Cleopatra*) does not share screen time with his wife Rachel Roberts, but she was nominated for best actress in her own film (*This Sporting Life*). They both walked home empty-handed.

- **1964**. Julie Andrews was married to Tony Walton, the costume designer on *Mary Poppins*, at the time both were nominated.

- **1966**. Richard Burton and Elizabeth Taylor, *Who's Afraid of Virginia Woolf?* She won for best actress, he lost the best actor award to Paul Scofield in *A Man for All Seasons*.

- **1969**. *Rachel, Rachel*: Paul Newman produced and directed (and got a best picture nod), wife Joanne Woodward starred (and walked away with a best actress nomination).

- **1973**. The songwriting team of Marilyn and Alan Bergman hit Oscar gold with *The Way We Were*, and repeated their success for *Yentl* in 1983, racking up several more nominations along the way.

- **1974**. Gena Rowlands frequently starred in director-husband John Cassavetes's screenplays, and they each vied for an award this year for *A Woman Under the Influence*. Neither won.

- **1978**. George Lucas got two nominations this year (for writing and directing *Star Wars*) but only his wife, Marcia Lucas, emerged victorious, for her editing of the same film. (They were also similarly teamed, though unsuccessfully, in 1973 for *American Graffiti*.)

- **1978**. Three of Neil Simon's screenplays have led to best actress nominations for wife Marsha Mason, although the only time they were both in contention was for *The Goodbye Girl*.

- **1982**. The husband and wife team of actress Julie Andrews and writer-director Blake Edwards made them both unsuccessful contenders for *Victor/Victoria*.

- **1993**. Best actress winner Holly Hunter (*The Piano*) fared slightly better than future hubbie Janusz Kaminski (cinematography, *Schindler's List*)— she was also nominated for best supporting actress the same year for *The Firm*.

And some other notable relationships in particular years:

- **1952**. Best supporting actor winner Anthony Quinn (*Viva Zapata!*) was the son-in-law of best picture honoree Cecil B. DeMille (*The Greatest Show on Earth*).

- **1966**. Although Vanessa and Lynn Redgrave have not always seen eye-to-eye, there were no hard feelings this year, when both were nominated: for *Morgan* and *Georgy Girl*, respectively; they both lost to Elizabeth Taylor.

- **1969**. Peter Fonda and Jane Fonda were both hot properties this year, Peter for his screenplay for *Easy Rider*, Jane for her performance in *They Shoot Horses, Don't They?*

DID YOU KNOW . . .

- In 1975, two best actor nominees—James Whitmore in *Give 'Em Hell, Harry!* and Maximilian Schell in *The Man in the Glass Booth*—appeared in filmed plays. Other examples of nominated performances that were essentially stage transfers include Laurence Olivier, Frank Finlay, Maggie Smith, and Joyce Redman in *Othello* (1965) and Glenda Jackson in *Hedda* (1975).

- Walter Matthau received one of his two best actor nominations in *Kotch* (1971), directed by his frequent costar, Jack Lemmon.

- In what must have been a fun irony, Steven Spielberg cast Richard Attenborough, the man responsible for defeating Spielberg's *E.T.* as best picture and best director (1982), in the monster hit *Jurassic Park*—in the same year that Spielberg cast Gandhi himself, Ben Kingsley, in *Schindler's List* (1993), which won Spielberg the elusive award.

Design and Look:
Cinematography, Film Editing, Art Direction, Costume Design, Visual Effects, and Makeup

YOU GOT THE LOOK

Critics and industry insiders refer to these awards as the "craft" or "technical" categories; the man on the street is less kind, calling them "the minor awards." However you choose to characterize them, these are essential elements to the filmmaking process; indeed, film theorists will tell you there are no more fundamental concepts to the art of cinema than the photography and editing—they are the elements that set film apart from other art forms. It's rather remarkable, then, to think that film editing wasn't an original award, while interior decoration (later renamed art direction) was. (Maybe not so remarkable: Cedric Gibbons, who helped found the Academy, was a designer.) Costumers were a little slower to make an impression on the Academy: They didn't receive an award until 1948.

Although the craft categories are not as well-known to the public, there have been some popularly recognized individuals (or movies) that even the man on the street would have known about at the time; Edith Head, costume designer extraordinaire, was so well-known that once she even appeared as herself on the TV show *Col-*

umbo. Fans of creature makeup no doubt can recite the credits of Rob Bottin and Rick Baker, while the more effects-minded can point out Stan Winston's touches. Anyone who sat gape-mouthed at the scenery in *Lawrence of Arabia* or *Gone with the Wind* has some appreciation for cinematography. Anyone who can remember the ominous buzzing sign of the Bates Motel and the mansion looming on the hill can claim some familiarity with the Oscar-nominated art direction in *Psycho*; and fans of movies like *Bullitt* and *The French Connection* probably appreciate film editing more than they realize (*French Connection* director William Friedkin claims the film was "made" in the editing room, and that the famed chase was one of the easiest scenes to do).

Quiz

Q. **What was the first year in which awards were given for the following categories: cinematography; film editing; art direction; costume design; visual effects; and makeup, and what film was the winner?**

A. Cinematography: *Sunrise*, 1927/28 (the first year of the awards). Film editing: *Eskimo*, 1934. Art direction (under the name interior decoration): *The Dove* and *Tempest* (cowinners), 1927/28. Set decorators were given an award as well beginning in 1947, for *Great Expectations* (b&w) and *Black Narcissus* (color). Costume design: *Hamlet* (b&w); *Joan of Arc* (color), 1948. Visual effects: An award for "engineering effects" was given to *Wings* in 1927/28; the first category for "special effects," however, was presented in 1939 for both audible and photographic effects, and the category was converted to "special visual effects" in 1963, when *Cleopatra* won. Make-up: *An American Werewolf in London*, 1981.

Q. **What film received the first-ever award for makeup?**

A. If you guessed *An American Werewolf in London* (1981), you'd be right if the question applied only to competitive Oscars. The first makeup award was honorary (not a regular category), going to *The 7 Faces of Dr. Lao* in 1964. In 1968, *Planet of the Apes* received an honorary award as well—the only two times they were handed out for makeup.

Q. **Who received the most Oscar nominations for cinematography? How many was it? Who won the most?**

A. It's a tie between Charles Lang and Leon Shamroy, who were each nominated 18 times. Shamroy faired better than Lang overall, however, also holding the record for wins (four, along with Joseph Ruttenberg), while Lang won only once.

Q. **What well-known film received a cinematography nomination despite being confined to a single room for all but one shot?**

A. *Rear Window* (1954). In this classic from Alfred Hitchcock, James Stewart spends his screen time confined to a chair in a plaster cast, observing everything from his window. Despite this constraint, the film is enormously entertaining, and never confining or claustrophobic (except as it heightens the tension of Stewart's confinement). Hitchcock was not afraid to attempt such daring efforts, and in fact made two other closed-set films: *Rope*, which is virtually one long shot; and *Lifeboat* (1944), also a cinematography nominee, set in the somewhat less confining set of the Atlantic Ocean.

Q. **Who is Oscar-winning actress Anne Baxter's grandfather?**

A. Architect Frank Lloyd Wright. It is said Wright visited the set of one of his granddaughter's movies, *The Magnificent Ambersons* (1942), and was appalled by the cluttered mustiness of the "old money" look. The film went on to receive an art direction nomination anyway.

Q. What was the first (and only) film shot in Cinerama to be nominated for best picture?

A. *How the West Was Won* (1963). Cinerama was a revolutionary three-projector process that was a fad of "specialty" (i.e., non-narrative) films in the '50s. It required an incredibly wide, curved screen on which three separate images were shot in synchronized time. *How the West Was Won,* however, was a traditional Western that was well-received; because Cinerama was short-lived and complex to show it is no longer possible to view it in its original format.

Q. What actor twice appeared in films nominated for makeup—*Edward Scissorhands* and winner *Ed Wood*—each time playing the title character named Ed?

A. Johnny Depp.

Q. How did Daniel Mandell fix the problem of having hopelessly right-handed Gary Cooper play world-famous southpaw Lou Gehrig in *The Pride of the Yankees* (1942)?

A. Since Gehrig had retired only three years before the film's release, no audience member would have accepted a right-handed actor playing the left-handed hitter—especially when it was discovered he couldn't even fake batting left-handed, he did it so poorly. The solution was to have Cooper hit right-handed, run from home to third base, and to have everyone wear numbers reversed on their jerseys. Mandell, the film's editor, them flip-flopped the film, making it appear everything was as it should be. Indeed, the film's only Oscar win was for its film editing.

Q. **What film was nominated for its costumes and art direction in 1982, even though it had not been released theatrically?**
A. *La Traviata*. Photographs of the designs were submitted for consideration.

Q. **The Oscar-nominated costume designer known simply as "Irene" was the sister-in-law of what famed production designer?**
A. Cedric Gibbons.

Q. **Edith Head won two of her costuming Oscars largely for dressing that most elegant of screen stars, Audrey Hepburn. What were the films?**
A. *Roman Holiday* (1953) and *Sabrina* (1954). Ironically, Hepburn usually wore clothes from her own designer, Hubert de Givenchy, who himself received only one costuming nomination—for *Funny Face* (1957), which starred Hepburn.

Q. **In what category and for what film did the great producer-writer-director Stanley Kubrick win his only Oscar . . . out of 13 nominations?**
A. Remarkably, he won for designing the special effects for *2001: A Space Odyssey* (1968). Kubrick was nominated in three categories in four consecutive films: *Dr. Strangelove* (1964; writing, directing, producing), *2001* (1968; writing, directing, special effects), *A Clockwork Orange* (1971; writing, directing, producing) and *Barry Lyndon* (1975; writing, directing, producing). He was also nominated for adapted screenplay for *Full Metal Jacket* (1987).

Q. **When Leon Shamroy won the Oscar in 1963, he asked the presenter, "Which one did I win for?" (He did the cinematography on two nominated films that year.) Which film *had* he won for?**
A. *The Cardinal*.

Q. The art directors on the period picture *Barton
    Fink* (1991) defeated themselves—with their art
    direction on the period picture *Bugsy*. In what
    city were both films principally set?
A. Both films were set in, and were largely about,
    Hollywood.

Q. What Oscar-winning art director on *Batman*
    (1989), committed suicide a year after winning
    by jumping off a building?
A. Anton Furst.

Q. Nowhere has the Academy vacillated more in
    whether to present an honorary or competitive
    award than it has with visual effects, which un-
    der different names had been routinely pre-
    sented since the '30s until 1972. What is the chief
    factor in whether to give it as honorary or com-
    petitive honor?
A. The decision hinges on the number of eligible
    (or deserving) potential nominees screened by the
    Academy.

Q. One of the most respected of the "new breed" of
    cinematographers, Gordon Willis—responsible
    for the chiaroscuro look of the *Godfather* films—
    received his first nomination for his remarkable
    work on *Zelig* for Woody Allen, in which he
    seamlessly inserted Allen and others into old doc-
    umentary footage. How did Willis and Allen re-
    portedly manage to get the film to look so old?
A. The two are said to have put the exposed cel-
    luloid itself on the floor and walked over it with
    their shoes until it was sufficiently trashed.

Q. Three-time cinematography winner Freddie Young
    won each of his Oscars shooting a film by that
    master of mixing intimate stories with sweeping
    landscapes, David Lean. Name the films.

A. *Doctor Zhivago* (1965), *Lawrence of Arabia* (1967), and *Ryan's Daughter* (1970).

Q. **Thelma Schoonmacher won her only Oscar for editing what Martin Scorsese picture?**
A. *Raging Bull* (1980). Ironically, Schoomacher's late husband, Michael Powell, was renowned for his use of color in films such as *Black Narcissus* and *The Red Shoes*; *Raging Bull* was shot entirely in black-and-white.

Q. *The Four Musketeers* **(1975) was a sequel shot at the same time as its predecessor,** *The Three Musketeers***. Despite being filmed simultaneously, only the sequel received a nomination. What was the category?**
A. Costume design.

Q. **What was the first NC-17 film to receive an Oscar nomination, and what was the category?**
A. *Henry & June* (1990), which lost the cinematography award.

Q. **What film won an Oscar for art direction largely by recreating the city room of the** *Washington Post***?**
A. *All the President's Men*, 1976.

Q. **Costumer Paul Zastupnevich received three Oscar nominations for dressing Irwin Allen films. Name two.**
A. *The Poseidon Adventure* (1972), *The Swarm* (1977), and *When Time Ran Out* (1980). On each occasion, he lost to Anthony Powell.

Q. **Stanley Kubrick and his Oscar-winning cinematographer, John Alcott, used special lenses designed by NASA to photograph in low, natural light—including a scene lit entirely with candles—in what film?**
A. *Barry Lyndon* (1975).

Noise:
Score, Song, Sound,
and Sound Effects Editing

AURAL EXAM

It was pretty much just a coincidence that the Academy
was formed at about the same time that synchronized
recorded sound took over the movies. In fact, the very
first Oscar ceremony forbade competition from sound
films in the two major "best picture" categories—best
production and artistic quality of production. (*The Jazz
Singer*, the first film to use synchronized sound exten-
sively, was given a special award in 1927/28.) It didn't
take long for sound and music to take a firm hold on
the market, however. From the third year of the Oscars
there was a category for sound recording, and score and
song arrived in the seventh year, 1934.

The days of nominations for "scoring" (versus
"score") became numbered as musicals dwindled in
popularity; "score of a musical picture [original or ad-
aptation]" was last presented in 1969, and included, as
a nominee, *They Shoot Horses, Don't They?*—hardly a
"musical" of the Busby Berkeley style from years past.
The name would change in the '70s (to "Original song
score," "Scoring: adaptation or original song score"
and "scores" of others), the number of eligible nominees would dip from a solid five to a desperate three,

and by 1980, the extra category would be abandoned altogether. The Academy still occasionally trots out a third music category when the number of nominees demands it, usually by drawing a distinction between scores written for ''comedy'' and ''dramatic'' motion pictures.

A TUNE YOU CAN DANCE TO

We all remember our favorite lines from movies (''Frankly, my dear, I don't give a damn,'' ''Louis, this could be the beginning of a beautiful friendship,'' etc.), and there are images that linger with us long after the celluloid has stopped flickering by (the explosion of the Death Star, Bonnie and Clyde being slowly riddled with bullets), but I would wager that, overall, few aspects of the movies are more memorable than the music we hear when we're watching them. Sure, this is especially the case for Westerns and action films, but it can be equally true of dramas (*The Piano*) and comedies (*Driving Miss Daisy*). Below are some memorable songs and musical scores from movies. What you might find most interesting is comparing which songs were in direct competition with one another . . . and which ones ended up on top. (You might want to ask yourself this as well: Did you even *know* each of these was a movie song?)

Quiz: Nominated and Winning Songs

Q. Match the Oscar-winning song (first column) with the movie it was from (second column).

 a. **''Lullaby of   i. *State Fair*
      Broadway''
      (1935), music by
      Harry Warren,
      lyrics by Al
      Dubin**

b. "The Way You Look Tonight" (1935), music by Jerome Kern, lyrics by Dorothy Fields

ii. *Gold Diggers of 1935*

c. "Thanks for the Memory" (1938), music by Ralph Rainger, lyrics by Leo Robin

iii. *A Star Is Born*

d. "Over the Rainbow" (1939), music by Harold Arlen, lyrics by E. Y. Harburg

iv. *The Sandpiper*

e. "When You Wish Upon a Star" (1940), music by Leigh Harline, lyrics by Ned Washington

v. *The Man Who Knew Too Much*

f. "It Might As Well Be Spring" (1945), music by Richard Rodgers, lyrics by Oscar Hammerstein II

vi. *Top Gun*

g. "Zip-A-Dee-Doo-Dah" (1947), music by Allie Wrubel, lyrics by Ray Gilbert

vii. *The Big Broadcast of 1938*

h. "Baby, It's Cold Outside" (1949), music and lyrics by Frank Loesser

viii. *Dirty Dancing*

i. "Do Not Forsake Me, Oh My Darlin' " (1952), music by Dimitri Tiomkin, lyrics by Ned Washington

ix. *Swing Time*

j. "(Whatever Will Be, Will Be) (Que Será Será)" (1955), music and lyrics by Jay Livingston and Ray Evans

x. *Butch Cassidy and the Sundance Kid*

k. "High Hopes" (1959), music by Jimmy Van Heusen, lyrics by Sammy Cahn

xi. *Working Girl*

l. "Moon River" (1961), music by Henry Mancini, lyrics by Johnny Mercer

xii. *Pinocchio*

m. "The Shadow of Your Smile" (1965), music by Johnny Mandel, lyrics by Paul Francis Webster

xiii. *An Officer and a Gentleman*

n. "Talk to the Animals" (1967), music and lyrics by Leslie Bricusse

xiv. *Neptune's Daughter*

o. "Raindrops Keep Fallin' on My Head" (1969), music by Burt Bacharach, lyrics by Hal David

xv. *The Woman in Red*

p. "Evergreen" (1976), music by Barbra Streisand, lyrics by Paul Williams

xvi. *Song of the South*

q. "The Best That You Can Do" (1981), music and lyrics by Burt Bachrach, Carol Bayer Sager, Peter Allen, and Christopher Cross

xvii. *The Wizard of Oz*

r. "Up Where We Belong" (1982), music by Jack Nitzsche and Buffy Sainte-Marie, lyrics by Will Jennings

xviii. *Breakfast at Tiffany's*

s. "I Just Called to Say I Love You" (1984), music and lyrics by Stevie Wonder

xix. *High Noon*

t. "Take My Breath Away" (1986), music by Giorgio Moroder, lyrics by Tom Whitlock

xx. *A Hole in the Head*

u. "(I've Had) The   xxi. *Doctor Doolittle*
Time of My
Life" (1987),
music by Franke
Previte, John
DeNicola, and
Donald
Markowitz, lyrics
by Previte

v. "Let the River   xxii. *Arthur*
Run" (1988),
music and lyrics
by Carly Simon

A. a.-ii.; b.-ix.; c.-vii.; d.-xvii.; e.-xii.; f.-i.;
g.-xvi.; h.-xiv.; i.-xix.; j.-v.; k.-xx.; l.-xviii.; m.-iv.;
n.-xxi.; o.-x.; p.-iii.; q.-xxii.; r.-xiii.; s.-xv.;
t.-vi.; u.-viii.; v.-xi.

Q. **Match the Oscar-nominated song (first column)
with the movie it was from (second column).**

a. "Cheek to   i. *Buck Privates*
Check" (1935),
music and lyrics
by Irving Berlin

b. "I've Got You   ii. *An American Tail*
Under My Skin"
(1936), music and
lyrics by Cole
Porter

c. "They Can't   iii. *The Muppet*
Take That Away   *Movie*
from Me"
(1937), music by
George
Gershwin, lyrics
by Ira Gershwin

d. "Boogie Woogie Bugle Boy of Company B" (1941), music by Hugh Prince, lyrics by Don Raye

iv. *Wet Blanket Policy* (cartoon)

e. "Chattanooga Choo Choo" (1941), music by Harry Warren, lyrics by Mack Gordon

v. *Star Spangled Rhythm*

f. "That Old Black Magic" (1943), music by Harold Arlen, lyrics by Johnny Mercer

vi. *Top Hat*

g. "Accentuate the Positive" (1945), music by Harold Arlen, lyrics by Johnny Mercer

vii. *The Jungle Book*

h. "The Woody Woodpecker Song" (1948), music and lyrics by Ramey Idriss and George Tibbles

viii. *The Umbrellas of Cherbourg*

i. "The Man That Got Away" (1954), music by Harold Arlen, lyrics by Ira Gershwin

ix. *Honeysuckle Rose*

j. "Unchained Melody" (1955), music by Alex North, lyrics by Hy Zaret

x. *Tammy and the Bachelor*

k. "Tammy" (1957), music and lyrics by Ray Evans and Jay Livingston

xi. *The Spy Who Loved Me*

l. "I Will Wait for You" (1965), music by Michel Legrand, lyrics by Jacques Demy

xii. *Mahogany*

m. "The Bare Necessities" (1967), music and lyrics by Terry Gilkyson

xiii. *Rocky III*

n. "The Look of Love" (1967), music by Burt Bacharach, lyrics by Hal David

xiv. *Born to Dance*

o. "Do You Know Where You're Going To" (1975), music by Michael Masser, lyrics by Gerry Goffin

xv. *Poetic Justice*

p. "Gonna Fly Now" (1976), music by Bill Conti, lyrics by Carol Connors and Ayn Robbins

xvi. *Sun Valley Serenade*

q. "Nobody Does It   xvii. *Unchained*
Better" (1977),
music by Marvin
Hamlisch, lyrics
by Carole Bayer
Sager

r. "The Rainbow   xviii. *Shall We Dance*
Connection"
(1978), music and
lyrics by Paul
Williams and
Kenny Ascher

s. "On the Road   xix. *A Star Is Born*
Again" (1980),
music and lyrics
by Willie Nelson

t. "Eye of the   xx. *Casino Royale*
Tiger" (1982),
music and lyrics
by Jim Peterik
and Frankie
Sullivan III

u. "Somewhere Out   xxi. *Rocky*
There" (1986),
music by James
Horner and
Barry Mann,
lyrics by Cynthia
Weil

v. "Again" (1993),   xxii. *Here Come the*
music and lyrics   *Waves*
by Janet
Jackson, James
Harris III, and
Terry Lewis

A. a.-vi.; b.-xiv.; c.-xviii.; d.-i.; e.-xvi.; f.-v.;
g.-xxii.; h.-iv.; i.-xix.; j.-xvii.; k.-x.; l.-viii.; m.-vii.;

n.-xx.; o.-xii.; p.-xxi.; q.-xi.; r.-iii.; s.-ix.; t.-xiii.;
u.-ii.; v.-xv.

Q. **It's no big surprise to learn the names of the movies each of these songs originated from. But which ones were winners, and which had to suffice with only a nomination?**

- "Pennies from Heaven" from *Pennies from Heaven* (1935), music by Arthur Johnson, lyrics by Johnny Burke

- "White Christmas" from *White Christmas* (1942), music and lyrics by Irving Berlin

- "Love Is a Many-Splendored Thing" from *Love Is a Many-Splendored Thing* (1955), music by Sammy Fain, lyrics by Paul Francis Webster

- "Never on Sunday" from *Never on Sunday* (1960), music and lyrics by Manos Hadjidakis

- "What's New Pussycat?" from *What's New Pussycat?* (1965), music by Burt Bacharach, lyrics by Hal David

- "(What's It All About) Alfie" from *Alfie* (1966), music by Burt Bacharach, lyrics by Hal David

- "Georgy Girl" from *Georgy Girl* (1966), music by Tom Springfield, lyrics by Jim Dale

- "Born Free" from *Born Free* (1966), music by John Barry, lyrics by Don Black

- "Chitty Chitty Bang Bang" from *Chitty Chitty Bang Bang* (1968), music and lyrics by Richard M. Sherman and Robert B. Sherman

- "The Theme from *Shaft*" from *Shaft* (1971), music and lyrics by Isaac Hayes

- "Live and Let Die" from *Live and Let Die* (1973), music and lyrics by Paul and Linda McCartney

- "The Way We Were" from *The Way We Were* (1973), music by Marvin Hamlisch, lyrics by Alan and Marilyn Bergman

- "You Light Up My Life" from *You Light Up My Life* (1977), music and lyrics by Joseph Brooks

- "9 to 5" from *9 to 5* (1980), music and lyrics by Dolly Parton

- "Endless Love" from *Endless Love* (1980), music and lyrics by Lionel Ritchie

- "For Your Eyes Only" from *For Your Eyes Only* (1981), music by Bill Conti, lyrics by Mick Leeson

A. "White Christmas," "Love Is a Many-Splendored Thing," "Never on Sunday," "Born Free," "The Theme from *Shaft*," "The Way We Were," and "You Light Up My Life" all won; the rest were also-rans.

. . . and a few surprise omissions

Despite enduring popularity and quality—not to mention good old-fashioned hum-ability—the following Oscar-eligible scores and songs walked away mentionless, without so much as a nomination:

- "Hooray for Hollywood" from *Hollywood Hotel* (1937)

- "Let's Call the Whole Thing Off" from *Shall We Dance* (1937)

- "Someday My Prince Will Come" and "Whistle

While You Work" from *Snow White and the Seven Dwarfs* (1937)

- "See What the Boys in the Back Room Will Have" from *Destry Rides Again* (1940)
- "Is You Is Or Is You Ain't My Baby" from *Follow the Boys* (1944)
- "Have Yourself a Merry Little Christmas" from *Meet Me in St. Louis* (1944)
- "Put the Blame on Mame" from *Gilda* (1945)
- "You Make Me Feel So Young" from *Three Little Girls in Blue* (1945)
- "Silver Bells" from *The Lemon Drop Kid* (1951)
- "Make 'Em Laugh" from *Singin' in the Rain* (1952)
- "Love Me Tender" from *Love Me Tender* (1956)
- "I Remember It Well" and "Thank Heaven for Little Girls" from *Gigi* (1958)
- *Anatomy of a Murder* (score by Duke Ellington) (1959)
- "Can't Buy Me Love" from *A Hard Day's Night* (1964)
- "Help!" and "Ticket to Ride" from *Help!* (1965)
- "To Sir, with Love" from *To Sir, with Love* (1967)
- "Love Theme from *The Valley of the Dolls*" (1967)
- "Suicide Is Painless" from *M*A*S*H* (1970)
- "The Long and Winding Road" and "Let It Be" from *Let It Be* (1970)
- "Staying Alive," "How Deep Is Your Love," "If I Can't Have You," "More Than a Woman," and "Night Fever" from *Saturday Night Fever* (1977)

- "New York, New York" from *New York, New York* (1977)
- "When Doves Cry," "Purple Rain," and "Let's Go Crazy" from *Purple Rain* (1984)—although the film won collectively for all of them by the award of "best original song score"
- *Driving Miss Daisy* (score) (1989)
- "Tears in Heaven" from *Rush* (1990)
- *The Piano* (score) (1993)

ROCK 'N' ROLL IS HERE TO STAY

There have often been popular songwriters who composed for the movies, but the 1980s started a real trend when well-known singer-songwriters began to rack up Oscar nominations. Consider some of the following Oscar contenders for best song (except as noted):

- Pete Townshend (song score), *Tommy* (1975) [n]
- Willie Nelson, "On the Road Again," *Honeysuckle Rose* (1980) [n]
- Dolly Parton, "9 to 5," *9 to 5* (1980) [n]
- Tom Waits (song score), *One from the Heart* (1982)
- Stevie Wonder, "I Just Called to Say I Love You," *The Woman in Red* (1984) [w]
- Kenny Loggins, "Footloose," *Footloose* (1984) [n]
- Prince (song score), *Purple Rain* (1984) [w]
- Lionel Ritchie, "Say You, Say Me," *White Nights* (1985) [w+]
- Huey Lewis, "Power of Love," *Back to the Future* (1985) [n]
- Peter Cetera, "Glory of Love," *The Karate Kid Part II* (1986) [n]

- David Byrne (score), *The Last Emperor* (1987) [w]

- Bob Seger, "Shakedown," *Beverly Hills Cop II* (1987) [n]

- Carly Simon, "Let the River Run," *Working Girl* (1988) [w]

- Phil Collins, "Two Hearts," *Buster* (1988) [n+]

- Jon Bon Jovi, "Blaze of Glory," *Young Guns II* (1990) [n]

- Bryan Adams, "(Everything I Do) I Do It for You," *Robin Hood: Prince of Thieves* (1991) [n+]

- Bruce Springsteen, "Streets of Philadelphia," *Philadelphia* (1993) [w+]

- Neil Young, "Philadelphia," *Philadelphia* (1993) [n]

- Janet Jackson, "Again," *Poetic Justice* (1993) [n]

- Elton John, "Can You Feel the Love Tonight," *The Lion King* (1994) [w+]

Quiz

Q. **What was the first musical to win the best picture Oscar?**
A. *The Broadway Melody* in 1928/29—only the second year of the Oscars, and only the second year of sound films overall.

Q. **What was the first film to win a sound award?**
A. *The Big House* (1929/30).

Q. **What original song won the first Oscar in that category? What film was it from?**
A. "The Continental" from *The Gay Divorcée* (1934).

Q. In what year was the award for sound effects editing inaugurated? What film won?

A. 1982 was the first time "sound effects editing" was presented as a regular competitive category, largely due to the rise in splashy, loud special effects movies. But in 1939, a category began named simply "special effects," which was awarded to an individual film, but which divided recognition between "photographic" and "sound" effects.

Q. What composer has won the most original score Oscars?

A. Alfred Newman unfairly holds the record of most scoring wins (he was head of the Fox music department), but of his record-setting nine wins, most were for "scoring of a musical"—basically, arranging music composed by others. John Williams, John Barry and Alan Menken have all won four *original* score Oscars—that is, music they themselves wrote—and each has a few additions as well: Williams for "scoring" *Fiddler on the Roof*, and Barry and Menken are also the recipients of five song Academy Awards between them.

Q. What songwriter (or songwriting team) has won the most song Oscars?

A. Sammy Cahn and Jimmy Van Heusen (as a team), Johnny Mercer, and Alan Menken (in various teams) each won four.

Q. What is unique about all three best song nominees cowritten by Ira Gershwin?

A. They all contain the word "away" in the title: "They Can't Take That Away from Me" from *Shall We Dance* (1937), "Long Ago and Far Away" from *Cover Girl* (1944), and "The Man Who Got Away" from *A Star Is Born* (1954). Despite being responsible for some of the greatest songs in American film history, he never won an Oscar.

Q. **What was the first year in which all the best song nominees were number-one hits on the pop charts?**

A. 1984. The winner was "I Just Called to Say I Love You" from *The Woman in Red;* the other nominees were "Let's Hear It for the Boy" and "Footloose" from *Footloose*, "Take a Look at Me Now" from *Against All Odds*, and the eponymous theme from *Ghostbusters*.

Q. **What was the name for the revolutionary sound system of the '70s that was used in a few disaster films?**

A. Sensurround. Only a few films ever used it, including the disaster epics *Earthquake* (1974), *Midway* (1976), and *Rollercoaster* (1978); *Earthquake* won the sound Oscar in its year. Sensurround sound was so loud and realistic that theater owners claimed it was causing structural cracks in their buildings.

Q. **What MGM sound department head was the brother-in-law of MGM studio head Irving Thalberg?**

A. Douglas Shearer. His sister was Norma Shearer, the queen of the MGM lot in the '30s and Thalberg's wife.

Q. **How many Oscars did Irving Berlin win? How about Cole Porter?**

A. Berlin won only one Oscar, for his song "White Christmas." Porter *never* won.

Q. **What was the first film to have three best song nominees?**

A. *Beauty and the Beast*. The winner was "Be Our Guest."

Q. *Captain Kidd* won the best score award in the final year that studios could submit their nominees for best score to the Academy, rather than having nominators choose them. What was the year?

A.   1945.

Q. Who was the Oscar-nominated songwriter who composed the nominee "Be Honest with Me" from *Ridin' on a Rainbow* in 1941?

A.   Believe it or not, singing cowboy Gene Autry penned the tune.

Q. The record for most people ever to share a single Oscar nomination is 12; the category is score. Name the film.

A.   *The Color Purple* (1985).

Q. What was the first time since 1937 that only one score Oscar was given?

A.   1980. Thereafter, and continuing through the '90s, it was rare for more than one scoring award to be given.

Q. *The 5000 Fingers of Dr. T*, which received a scoring nomination, was based on a story by which famed children's writer?

A.   Dr. Seuss.

Q. *Of Mice and Men* (1939) and *Our Town* (1940) earned their composer two nominations in both score categories in consecutive years, the only composer ever to do so. Who was it?

A.   Aaron Copland. In 1941, the Academy changed the rules so that the vague differences between "score" and "original score" were clarified.

Q. What was the first film from MGM in which the audience got to hear the now-famous roar of Leo the lion?

A. *White Shadows in the South Seas* (1928/29), which was nominated for its cinematography.

Q. **Two very different poets have each received songwriting nominations: for "I'm Checkin' Out" for *Postcards from the Edge* (1990) and "Jean" for *The Prime of Miss Jean Brodie* (1969). Name at least one.**
A. Shel Silverstein and Rod McKuen, respectively.

Q. **Charlie Chaplin's only competitive Oscar win was for cowriting the score to *Limelight*. In what year was the award given?**
A. Remarkably, the film, made in 1952, was not released in the United States until 1972, and so the winning "original" music was actually 20 years old when it won the award.

Q. **Who holds the record for overall nominations in the scoring categories?**
A. Alfred Newman received 45 nominations; John Williams has received 35. While Newman has the technical record for winning score and song Oscars, these are probably not all justified—he was head of the music department of Fox, and under old rules was often awarded the trophy even if he did not personally compose the music.

Q. **Who sang the most Oscar-winning songs?**
A. Bing Crosby, who lent his voice to four prize-winners: "Sweet Leilani" from *Waikiki Wedding* (1938), "White Christmas" from *Holiday Inn* (1943), "Swinging on a Star" from *Going My Way* (1944), and "In the Cool, Cool, Cool of the Evening" from *Here Comes the Groom* (1951). Interestingly, Crosby sang the song as part of the plot in each of the films, personally appearing in them. The singer responsible for singing the most Oscar

winners who never appeared in the films she graced is Jennifer Warnes, whose three performances on "It Goes Like It Goes" from *Norma Rae* (1980), "Up Where We Belong" from *An Officer and Gentleman* (1982), and "(I've Had) The Time of My Life" from *Dirty Dancing* (1987) (not to mention a nomination for "One More Hour" from *Ragtime*) make her the faceless record-holder.

Q. **Who holds the record for most music-writing wins?**
A. Alan Menken, whose eight wins (four for song, four for score) is an impressive individual achievement.

Q. **Who dubbed the singing voices for Deborah Kerr in *The King and I* (1956), Natalie Wood in *West Side Story* (1961), and Audrey Hepburn in *My Fair Lady* (1965)?**
A. Marni Nixon. Only Kerr received an Oscar nomination.

Honorary and Specialized Awards:
Irving G. Thalberg Memorial and
Jean Hersholt Humanitarian Awards,
Documentary Feature,
Documentary Short, Live Action Short,
and Animated Short

TIME FOR A BATHROOM BREAK

That's the unfortunate reaction most people have when
the endless parade of no-names begin to win awards during the Oscar ceremony each March—and usually, unlike with even score and costume awards, no one at
home has even heard of the films and individuals nominated. But when the Academy announced a few years
ago that they would be discontinuing the short film
awards, the outcry was sufficient enough to keep them
around a while longer. The upshot, however, has been
that numerous short film nominations have been given
to "celebrity" filmmakers. Did you realize that Christine Lahti's only win was for live action short, or that
she beat out Jeff Goldblum in the same category for
what was his only Oscar nomination? Sometimes the
stories about the short films are more interesting than
the majors. *Dear Diary* (1995) became the first Academy Award nomination—and win—for the new
DreamWorks SKG studio. DreamWorks, though, lucked

out, at the expense of ABC-TV: The film was originally commissioned as a television pilot, the network didn't like it, and it went on to win its makers an Oscar.

The honorary awards, especially the Irving G. Thalberg Award and the Jean Hersholt Humanitarian Award, also have their appeal to audiences because they often reward people the Academy might otherwise have missed. For example, Steven Spielberg's first Oscar was a Thalberg, and the Thalberg represents George Lucas, Alfred Hitchcock, and Ingmar Bergman's only Oscar wins ever. The general honorary awards are also an excellent opportunity for the Academy to make amends to actors and others for past slights. Cary Grant, Lillian Gish, Edward G. Robinson, and Greta Garbo received their only Oscars in honorary form, and the fact they were presented for a body of work—as opposed to a single performance, where the vagaries of voting and politics play a part—imbue them with a kind of special appeal.

Quiz

Q. What was the first documentary to be nominated for a general competitive award?

A. If you're thinking it occurred late in the game, you couldn't be more wrong. *Chang*, a documentary about peasants in Thailand, got a nomination for artistic quality of production (which at the time was considered equivalent to best picture) during the first year of the awards. (The category was never awarded again.) Although they have not been frequently included in the general lists, other documentaries (and documentary-like films) nominated in general competitive categories include: *With Byrd at the South Pole* (1929/30, cinematography [w]; the first documentary to win any award), *Eskimo* (1934, film editing [w]; the first-ever winner of the editing award), *The Fight for Life* (1940, original score [n]), *Victory Through Air Power* (1943, scoring [n])*, *The Bolshoi Ballet* (1958, scoring of a musical [n]), *Mondo Cane* (1963, song [n]), *Birds Do It, Bees Do It* (1975, score [n]), *Hoop Dreams* (1994, film editing [n]). *This Is Cinerama* (1953, scoring [n]), while not exactly a documentary, is nonetheless a nonnarrative film, being designed to expose the audience to the new technology of "Cinerama."

Q. **What was the first short film to be nominated in a general competitive category?**
A. *Saludos Amigos* (1943), for sound and scoring. *The Three Caballeros* (1945) got the same nominations two years later soon followed by *Wet Blanket Policy* for "The Woody Woodpecker Song" (1948). *The Red Balloon* was the first (and so far only) short film to *win* a general competitive category—for best screenplay (1956).

Q. **Who is the first person to receive both the Thalberg and the Hersholt awards?**
A. Samuel Goldwyn.

Q. **What is the only short film to win *two* Oscars?**
A. *Sentinels of Silence*, a documentary about pre-Columbia Mexican monuments, won both the live action short *and* the documentary short in 1971.

Q. **Who was the first woman to win the Hersholt award?**
A. Martha Raye.

---

*Disney produced this documentary about the importance of air power in the war effort—an unpopular position even after the trial of Billy Mitchell and the attack on Pearl Harbor—but covered up its drier aspects with animation sequences.

Q. **What famous Oscar-winning animated short about an ambitious geometric shape ends with the punny moral: "To the vector belong the spoils"?**
A.   *The Dot and the Line* (1965).

Q. **What seminal twentieth-century tragedy was the focus of both documentary winners in 1995?**
A.   The Holocaust. The documentary short subject *One Survivor Remembers* and documentary feature *Anne Frank Remembered* both dealt with it. (Two years before, the best picture winner was *Schindler's List*, also about the Holocaust.)

Q. **Who presented the Thalberg award to Lawrence Weingarten in 1973?**
A.   Katharine Hepburn—notable primarily because it was the record-setter's only appearance at an Oscar ceremony.

Q. **Whose acceptance speech included the following observation: "What a thrill. You know you've entered new territory when you realize that your outfit cost more than your film. . . . You think I'm joking."**
A.   Jessica Yu, documentary short film winner, *Breathing Lessons* (1996).

Q. **What is the only year in which the Jean Hersholt Humanitarian Award was presented to two separate recipients? Who were they?**
A.   1992, when AIDS activist Elizabeth Taylor and the late UNICEF ambassador Audrey Hepburn were honored.

Q. **Who was the first producer to win two Thalberg awards? Who was the first (and so far only) person to win *three*? What is the only producing team to win a Thalberg?**
A.   Hal B. Wallis won two; Darryl F. Zanuck is

the three-time recipient. Richard D. Zanuck and David Brown (1990) are the producing team.

Q. Who is the only posthumous winner of the Hersholt award?
A.   Audrey Hepburn (1992).

Q. Who became the first actor-producer to win the Irving Thalberg Award?
A.   Clint Eastwood.

Q. Match the following short film or documentary film nominees or winners, all well-known for other endeavors, with the films for which they were nominated or won.

a. **Taylor Hackford** (producer-director of *An Officer and a Gentleman* and *Dolores Claiborne*)	i. Winner, documentary short subject, *Number Our Days* (1976)
b. **Dyan Cannon** (Oscar nominee for *Bob & Carol & Ted & Alice* and *Heaven Can Wait*)	ii. Winner, documentary feature, *He Makes Me Feel Like Dancin'* (1983)
c. **Emile Ardolino** (director of *Dirty Dancing, Sister Act,* and *Three Men and a Little Lady*)	iii. Winner, live action short, *Teenage Father* (1978)
d. **Peter Weller** (star of *RoboCop*)	iv. Winner, live action short, *Lieberman in Love* (1995)

e. **Lynne Littman**
(director of
Testament)

v. **Winner, live
action short,** *The
Chicken (Le
Poulet)* (1965)

f. **John Astin (star**
of *The Addams
Family* on TV)

vi. **Winner, short
subject (one-reel),**
*Amphibious
Fighters* (1943)

g. **Sean Astin (star**
of *Toy Soldiers*
and *Goonies*, son
of John Astin)

vii. **Nominee, live
action short,**
Duke of Groove
(1995)

h. **Jeff Goldblum**
(*The Fly, Jurassic
Park*, and *Inde-
pendence Day*)

viii. **Nominee, live
action short,**
Prelude (1968)

i. **Claude Berri**
(producer-
director of *Jean
de Florette* and
*Manon des
Sources*)

ix. **Nominee, live
action short,**
Partners (1993)

j. **Christine Lahti**
(Oscar-
nominated
performer for
Swing Shift)

x. **Nominee, live
action short,**
Little Surprises
(1995)

k. **Shirley MacLaine**
(Oscar-winning
actress for *Terms
of Endearment*)

xi. **Nominee, live
action short,**
Swan Song
(1992)

l. **Grantland Rice**
(sportswriter who
coined the phrase
"It's not whether
you win or lose
but how you play
the game")

xii. **Nominee,
documentary
feature,** *The
Other Half of the
Sky: A China
Memoir* (1975)

m. **John G. Avildsen** (winner for directing *Rocky*)

xiii. Nominee, live action short, *Kangaroo Court* (1994)

n. **Kenneth Branagh** (nominee for *Henry V* and *Hamlet*)

xiv. Nominee, documentary short subject, *Traveling Hopefully* (1982)

o. **Griffin Dunne** (star and producer of *After Hours*)

xv. Nominee, live action short, *Number One* (1976)

p. **Spike Lee** (director of *Do the Right Thing* and *Malcolm X*)

xvi. Nominee, feature documentary, *Four Little Girls* (1997)

A. a.-iii.; b.-xv.; c.-ii.; d.-ix.; e.-i.; f.-viii.; g.-xiii.; h.-x.; i.-v.; j.-iv.; k.-xii.; l.-vi.; m.-xiv.; n.-xi.; o.-vii; p.-xvi.

Q. **Although an award for "dance direction" was given for a few years in the '30s, only four people have ever received Oscars recognizing their contributions to choreography. Who were they?**
A. Jerome Robbins for *West Side Story* (1961), Onna White for *Oliver!* (1968), and choreographer-dancers whose awards were not directed at a specific film: Gene Kelly (1951) and Michael Kidd (1996).

Q. **Who is the only Oscar-winning performer also to direct a documentary feature (*Marlene*, 1984 [n+]) and a best foreign language film entry (*The Pedestrian*, 1973 [n]) nominated for Oscars?**
A. Best actor winner Maximilian Schell (*Judgment at Nuremberg*, 1962).

Q. **For what film did Walt Disney win his final Oscar?**
A. *Winnie the Pooh and the Blustery Day* (1968), which he won two years after his death.

Q. **Only three films have won two special awards without taking any other Oscars. Name two.**
A. *Fantasia, The Hindenburg*, and *The Little Kidnappers,* for which two child actors were corecipients of the honorary "best juvenile performance" award.

Q. **What individual is credited with 26 Oscar wins and a staggering 64 nominations?**
A. Walt Disney. Because his studio was named for himself, he was often recorded as having at least nominal credit, even though he was not necessarily personally responsible.

Q. **What film received a special award in 1942, a year before it was eligible in other categories (the only non-foreign language film to be so honored)?**
A. *In Which We Serve*.

Q. **What category (and in what year) had the most ever cowinners *and* the most ever nominees?**
A. In 1942, the best documentary category had four cowinners and 25 nominees.

Q. **What deadpan stand-up comedian won the 1988 live action short award for *The Appointment of Dennis Jennings*?**
A. Steven Wright.

DID YOU KNOW . . .

- Foreign language film entry *A Place in the World* (1992) was withdrawn from the final balloting due to the Academy's screwy rules about foreign language submissions. The film was submitted by the nation of Uruguay even though it was Argentine-made, because Argentina refused to sponsor it. The question of national sponsorship is a shady one at best, leading to the exclusion of many viable films—and meaning that especially prolific nations such as Italy and France get only one nominee each year, the same number as less productive countries.

- Probably the film with the least pronounceable title (to Americans, anyway) ever to receive an Oscar nomination would be *Qivitoq*, a Danish picture nominated as best foreign language film in 1956.

- O.J. Simpson was the copresenter of the short film awards in 1975.

ARNOLD WAYNE JONES was born in Georgia and attended the University of Virginia, where he received his bachelor's and law degrees. He moved to Dallas in 1990, where he has served as film critic for *The Dallas Observer, The Met*, and KDFW-TV. His writing has also appeared in *Entertainment Weekly, The San Antonio Current, The L.A. New Times*, and other publications. He lives with his cocker spaniel, Reginald, and can be reached online at *AWJonesJr@aol.com*.